# The Future of Religion
# in American Politics

# THE FUTURE OF RELIGION
# IN AMERICAN POLITICS

*Edited by Charles W. Dunn*

THE UNIVERSITY PRESS OF KENTUCKY

Scholarly publisher for the Commonwealth,
serving Bellarmine University, Berea College, Centre College of Kentucky,
Eastern Kentucky University, The Filson Historical Society, Georgetown
College, Kentucky Historical Society, Kentucky State University, Morehead
State University, Murray State University, Northern Kentucky University,
Transylvania University, University of Kentucky, University of Louisville,
and Western Kentucky University.
All rights reserved.

*Editorial and Sales Offices:* The University Press of Kentucky
663 South Limestone Street, Lexington, Kentucky 40508-4008
www.kentuckypress.com

13 12 11 10 09   5 4 3 2 1

Library of Congress Cataloging-in-Publication Data

The future of religion in American politics / edited by Charles W. Dunn.
    p. cm.
 Includes bibliographical references and index.
 ISBN 978-0-8131-2516-9 (hardcover : alk. paper)
 1. Church and state—United States. 2. Christianity and politics—United
States. 3. United States—Church history. I. Dunn, Charles W.
 BR516.F88 2009
  322'.10973—dc22                                        2008039269

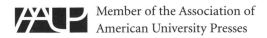 Member of the Association of
American University Presses

# Contents

Introduction: The Dynamic Complexity of Religion
and Politics in America    1
*Charles W. Dunn*

Religion in the Public Square    39
*Jean Bethke Elshtain*

On That "Superintending Principle" That Was There
before the Laws    47
*Hadley Arkes*

Is America a Christian Nation?    61
*Hugh Heclo*

George Washington on Religion's Place in Public Life    97
*Daniel L. Dreisbach*

Virginia and the Origins of Religious Liberty    115
*Michael Novak*

Evangelical Political Models: James Fenimore Cooper
or William Wilberforce?    121
*Marvin Olasky*

Left Turn? Evangelicals and the Future of the Religious Right    129
*D. G. Hart*

The Declining Role of Religion in Politics?    153
*Michael Barone*

Red God, Blue God: Is There a God Gap between the Parties?    159
*Michael Cromartie*

Religion, Civic Engagement, and Political Participation    173
*Corwin E. Smidt*

Faith-Based Politics in American Presidential Elections:
Trends and Possibilities   209
    *John C. Green*

Emerging Trends in Religion, Society, and Politics   229
    *Allen D. Hertzke*

List of Contributors   257
Index   261

# INTRODUCTION

## The Dynamic Complexity of Religion and Politics in America

### *Charles W. Dunn*

> If the intention is to create a pluralistic society, America's church-state divide has the same advantage as democracy under Winston Churchill's definition: it is the worst way for a modern society to deal with religion, "except for all those other forms that have been tried from time to time."
>
> —*The Economist*

From the courthouse to the White House, religion looms large on the landscape of legal controversy and campaign rhetoric, posing heatedly debated and often seemingly insoluble questions:

- What roles should religious leaders, such as Jesse Jackson and James Dobson, play in politics?
- Should politicians use religious appeals in their campaigns, as Senators Hillary Rodham Clinton and Barack Obama did in their quest for the Democratic Party's presidential nomination, and as many Republicans have likewise done in their party, including Ronald Reagan, George W. Bush, and Mike Huckabee?
- What financial aid, if any, should the Salvation Army, Catholic Charities, and other religious organizations receive from the government?
- Should parents receive vouchers to send their children to religious schools?

- What limits, if any, should the government place on abortion?
- Should the government prohibit human cloning?
- To what extent, if at all, should public schools allow religious meetings and practices such as Bible clubs and prayers before athletic events and at commencement and baccalaureate services?
- Should public schools teach both creation and evolution?
- Should religious organizations have the freedom to determine their own standards for employees, including the right to prohibit the employment of homosexuals?
- Should Muslims have the same opportunity to participate in American politics as non-Muslims?
- How should the United States handle the problem of illegal immigration?
- Should nativity scenes, the Ten Commandments, and other religious statements and traditions appear on public property?

The competing groups contesting these and many other religious and political issues on the center stage of America's political theater often divide into two camps, called by various names, including conservative and liberal, religious Right and religious Left, traditionalists and secular progressives, and orthodox and relativists. Stanley Rothman and Amy Black offer two more dimensions, (1) "rugged laissez-faire individualists" and "collectivist liberals" and (2) "traditional Puritans" and "expressive individualists," which they place in helpful historical perspective:

> The first dimension . . . collectivist (or welfare state) liberalism emerged from the Depression Era. Often seen as the major source of contemporary American ideology, this concept rests on the belief that the government should ameliorate the economic inequalities of the capitalist system. Standing in opposition to this view is the traditional "rugged individualist" perspective that economic well being stems from individual effort and personal achievement.
>
> The second dimension places traditional Puritanism on one end and "expressive individualism" on the other. . . . The Protestant ethic stressed sobriety over playfulness, restraint

over expression, and self-restraint over emotion. Expressive individualism tends to reverse that emphasis.[1]

People and groups in the various categories and dimensions usually fall out on differing sides of a variety of questions,[2] including the following:

- Is America a Christian nation, at least in origin, as some conservatives frequently argue, or a secular state, as many liberals often contend?
- Is secular humanism a myth conjured up by the religious Right or a form of theology that significantly influences public policy?
- Have conservatives from Ronald Reagan through George W. Bush enjoyed undue success in influencing public policy?
- Is the National Council of Churches a legitimate representative of American churches, or does it misrepresent the people it claims to represent?
- Have the Christian Coalition, spawned by television evangelist Pat Robertson, and the Moral Majority, created by Baptist preacher Jerry Falwell, made a positive impact on American politics and society?
- Should Jews trust conservatives or liberals more with respect to supporting Israel on Middle East issues?
- Who is a more legitimate representative of Roman Catholic thought in politics, Senator Ted Kennedy or U.S. Supreme Court justice Antonin Scalia?

Religion and politics are uncomfortable subjects for many, and like oil and water, they do not mix in the minds of others. Meanwhile, like "old man river," who just keeps rolling along, they indelibly mark the political landscape. Rhetorical radiation from verbal bombs dropped in heated combat between groups like MoveOn.org on the left and Focus on the Family on the right poses perplexing problems for American democracy. Both sides speak fervently with absolute assurance that their view of American democracy is the correct one. Both cannot be right.

The issues are real. The emotions are intense. The solutions are problematic. From the courthouse to the White House, religious interests play for high stakes. But just as they influence American politics, parties and politicians move them like pawns on the political chessboard. From any perspective, religion no longer plays its intended role on America's political stage.

## THE THEORETICAL ROLE OF RELIGION IN SOCIETY

What role does or should religion play in society? The generally recognized founder of sociology, Émile Durkheim, stated that "nearly all the great social institutions have been born in religion. . . . If religion has given birth to all that is essential in society, it is because the idea of society is the soul of religion."[3] Looking at religion in the American context, sociologist Robert Bellah says that "every movement to make America more fully realize its professed values has grown out of some form of public theology."[4] To Bellah religious and moral values serve as glue bonding society together, producing "both a basic cultural legitimation for a society which is viewed as at least approximately in accord with them, and a standard of judgment for the criticism of a society that is seen as deviating too far from them."[5]

In America these religious and moral understandings have moved along a continuum from uniformity to diversity and from simplicity to complexity. For example, when Harvard College was founded, its charter expressed this purpose: "Everyone shall consider the main end of his life to know God and Jesus Christ which is eternal life."[6] Harvard's purpose then reflected a much more homogenous society than Harvard's purpose now. In his 1978 Harvard University commencement address, Aleksandr Solzhenitsyn described an escalating conflict between the historical Christian faith and an emerging faith of humanism: "The humanistic way of thinking . . . started Western civilization on the dangerous trend of worshipping man and his material needs."[7] Echoing Solzhenitsyn's analysis, although opposed to his position, John Dunphy predicted in 1983 that "the classroom . . . will become an arena of conflict between the old and the new—the rotting corpse of Christianity . . . and the new faith of humanism."[8] So it is that stark contrast and strident conflict have emerged regarding America's religious and moral understandings.

Because "the past is prologue," understanding the future of religion in American politics requires an analysis of how and why the divisions originated that now mark the political landscape. An examination of four eras—the founding, the Civil War, the New Deal, and the modern—reveals seven propositions in a theory that explains the continuing interaction of religion and politics in the twenty-first century.

1. Fundamental differences and similarities between conservative and liberal religious interests affect how, why, and when they influence politics.
2. Economic, political, social, and religious issues are interdependent.
3. Religious unity is closely related to economic, political, and social unity.
4. Religious influence on politics and society follows a cyclical pattern of action and reaction.
5. Educational institutions significantly help to determine the dominance of a religious viewpoint in politics and society.
6. The religious moderation of the American people together with their political moderation diminishes the strength of deviating religious points of view.
7. Presidents and other political leaders reflect rather than direct religious influences on politics and public policy.

The theory's objectives are both to examine the emotion-charged relationships of religion and politics in a dispassionate and objective manner and to provide a framework for analyzing their relationships. Put another way, the theory explores the links between politics and religion, suggests new ways of thinking about them, and simplifies the seeming complexity that surrounds them.

## THE FOUNDING ERA

In origin, was America a secular state, as many contend, or a Christian nation, as others argue? Today most scholars see the founding of American government as secular in nature. First, the Federalist papers, the fundamental explanation of the government established, contain no references to God or to the Bible. Second, the only person of major significance during the founding era to refer to the Bible, Thomas Paine, was obviously not a Christian. Third, James Madison and Thomas Jefferson, leading architects of America's founding, generally refrained from invoking the Bible in their writings. Fourth, the U.S. Constitution contains no references to the Deity, while the Declaration of Independence contains only a few references. Fifth, the founders generally emphasized "natural law" rather than "divine law," believing that man has rights just because he is man and not because he is a creature of God.

Convinced of the deficiency of today's dominant secular explanation of the founding era, a minority of scholars counter with these arguments: First, men like John Jay, one of the three authors of the Federalist papers, were of ardent conservative Christian convictions, and other prominent founders, like James Madison, received strongly conservative religious educations that influenced how they perceived government. Second, conservative religious beliefs significantly influenced leading deists of the day, such as Thomas Jefferson and Benjamin Franklin, who recognized and responded to the dominant conservative religious influences of their time. Third, the term "law of nature," or "natural law," used by Jefferson in the Declaration of Independence came from William Blackstone's *Commentaries on the Laws of England*, where the term clearly referred to the laws of God and was not intended to be distinct from "divine law." Fourth, today's scholars, generally of a secular persuasion, understandably explain the founding era from their own set of biases, extolling the contributions of Benjamin Franklin, George Washington, John Adams, James Madison, and Thomas Jefferson but overlooking the significant contributions of many founders of conservative religious persuasion, including William Livingston, John Hancock, John Witherspoon, George Mason, John Dickinson, Richard Henry Lee, Fisher Ames, John Jay, Rufus King, Gouverneur Morris, Elbridge Gerry, Benjamin Rush, John Rutledge, James Wilson, and C. C. Pinckney. Putting the issue in context, Daniel L. Dreisbach notes that "the near exclusive focus on a select few virtually deified famous founders impoverishes our understanding of the American founding. It also departs from the canons of good scholarship. The demands of honest scholarship require scholars to give attention to the thoughts, words, and deeds of not only a few selected demigods but also an expansive company of men and women who contributed to the founding of the American republic."[9] Fifth, scholars in the nineteenth century tended to look on America's founding more from a Christian point of view than scholars of the twentieth and twenty-first centuries.

Some take a middle position on the issue in one of two ways. First is the view that the Declaration of Independence, written by Thomas Jefferson and strongly influenced by other deists, like Samuel Adams and Thomas Paine, reflects a secular origin, whereas the U.S. Constitutional Convention, attended by many delegates of conservative Christian convictions, reveals a significant Christian influence. Second is the view that the Declaration of Independence, possessing several references to the Deity, affirms a conservative religious heritage, whereas the U.S. Constitution, absent any references to the Deity or the Bible, affirms a secular heritage.

Regardless of the position taken, the issue is exceedingly important. If America began as a Christian nation, as some argue, then we have removed ourselves far from the religious precedents of the founding, and in the process, we have created a government decidedly contrary to the founders' intentions. If, on the other hand, America began as a secular state, as others contend, then we have given undue deference to religious issues and too much protection to religious causes.

## Origins of Conflict

Political scientist Kenneth W. Thompson draws from two of America's greatest journalists, Walter Lippmann and James Reston, in arguing that America's moral and political tradition are the "forgotten foundations of democracy" and that the liberties we cherish today originated with "that remarkable group of eighteenth century American political leaders who took their conception of man from the central religious tradition of Western civilization."[10] Emphasizing Thompson's point, Robert Bellah states, "The Bible was the one book that literate Americans in the 17th, 18th, and 19th centuries could be expected to know well. Biblical imagery provided the basic framework for imaginative thought in America up until quite recent times and, unconsciously, its control is still formidable."[11] And, seeing a clear link between the founders' biblical view of man and the fundamental political decisions of the founders, such as those in the U.S. Constitution, historian Richard Hofstadter says of the founders,

> To them a human being was an atom of self-interest. They did not believe in man, but they did believe in the power of a good political constitution to control him. . . . From a humanistic

standpoint there is a serious dilemma in the philosophy of the Fathers, which derives from their conception of man. They thought man was a creature of rapacious self-interest, yet they wanted him to be free—free, in essence, to contend, to engage in an umpired strife. . . . They had no hope and they offered none for any ultimate organic change in the way men conduct themselves. The result was that while they thought self-interest the most dangerous and unbrookable quality of man, they necessarily underwrote it in trying to control it.[12]

Among the founders, James Madison referred to the "degree of depravity in mankind which requires a certain degree of circumspection and distrust," the "caprice and wickedness of man," and the "infirmities and depravities of the human character." Alexander Hamilton wrote of the "folly and wickedness of mankind," while John Jay saw man as governed by "dictates of personal interest."[13] Even Thomas Jefferson wrote, "Free government is founded on jealousy, not in confidence; it is jealousy and not confidence which prescribes limited constitutions, to bind those we are obligated to trust with power. In questions of power, let no more be heard of confidence in man but bind him down from mischief by the chains of the constitution."[14]

This very strongly held biblical view of the nature of man, it may be argued, helped influence the type of government they established: one limited by checks and balances of power among the several branches and characterized by protection of the individual from capricious exercise of governmental power through the Bill of Rights. Their distrust of the nature of man helped lead them to create a government in which the people directly elected only the members of the House of Representatives, with the president and membership in the Senate and the courts being indirectly elected by the people. As Alexis de Tocqueville wrote, "The greatest part of British America was peopled by men who, after having shaken off the authority of the Pope, acknowledged no other religious supremacy: They brought with them into the New World a form of Christianity which I cannot better describe than by styling it a democratic and republican religion."[15]

The congressional Thanksgiving Day proclamations of 1780 and 1782 illustrate the prevailing strength of conservative religious influences. In 1780, Congress proclaimed the desire to "cause the knowledge of Christianity to spread over the earth," and in 1782 "that the religion of our divine Redeemer, with all its divine influences, may cover the earth as the waters cover the seas."

From a conservative religious perspective, the founders intended that the U.S. Constitution and the Bill of Rights would protect the populace from undue governmental interference in their lives. The First Amendment, for example, had as its goal the prevention of a "state church" superior to other churches. To them, the separation of church and state did not mean the exclusion of prayer and Bible reading from the public schools; indeed, they encouraged both in many ways. In early American history, 75 percent or more of public school education centered on the Bible. Only later, through the influence of such men as Unitarian Horace Mann in the nineteenth century and humanist John Dewey in the twentieth century, did biblically based education decline from its zenith in the days of the McGuffey Readers.

Deist religious influence, although different from the prevailing conservative religious influence, was geographically isolated in the northeastern United States and was hardly the religion of the general populace. It differed from the prevailing religious ethos of the day principally on the matter of the deity of Christ. With respect to God, however, deist and conservative theology had much in common, sharing a view that God acts directly in the affairs of men. The principal deist political leaders, Thomas Jefferson and Benjamin Franklin, held this view. Franklin said, "I never doubted, for instance, the existence of the Deity; that He made the world and governed it by His Providence; that the most acceptable service of God was the doing of good to men; that our souls are immortal; and that crime will be punished, and virtue rewarded either here or hereafter."[16] And Jefferson asked, "Can the liberties of a nation be thought secure, when we have removed their only firm basis, a conviction in the minds of the people that these liberties are the gift of God? That they are not to be violated but by His wrath? Indeed, I tremble for my country when I reflect that God is just; that His justice cannot sleep forever."[17]

The covenant idea of the conservative religious environment also significantly influenced governmental structures during the founding of the American government, as illustrated in the Mayflower Compact, which reads, "We . . . do by Presents, solemnly and mutually in the Presence of God and one another, covenant and combine ourselves together into a civil Body Politick." Based on the biblical concept of God's covenant with man, governments were to reflect the idea of the people covenanting together under God to form a government responsible to God and his law. As Daniel Elazar has pointed out,

> The constitutions of the American states in the founding era were perhaps the greatest products of the American covenant tradition. . . . The creation of new states, even new towns, across the United States throughout the 19th century reflected the covenanting impulse.
>
> As a consequence of these many uses of covenant, the American "instinct" for federalism was extended into most areas of human relationships, shaping Americans' notions of individualism, human rights and obligations, business organization, civil association, and church structure as well as their notions of politics. . . . For Americans, covenant provided a means for a free people to form political communities without sacrificing their essential freedom and without making energetic government possible.[18]

Along with the idea of covenant, another idea, that of the social contract or compact, greatly influenced the founders, especially through John Locke's *Two Treatises on Government*. Although generally considered secular in origin, social compact thought, like the covenanting impulse, bore the earmarks of limited government, federalism, and protection of the rights of man. But often overlooked are Locke's religious views, as voiced in *The Reasonableness of Christianity* (1695): "As Christians we have Jesus the Messiah for our King, and are under the law revealed by Him in the Gospel."[19] Locke also stated that "the law of Nature stands as an eternal rule to all men, legislators as well as others. The rules that they make for other men's actions must . . . be conformable to the law of Nature—i.e., to the will of God."[20] In this regard, William Blackstone, the most significant influence on American law, said, "As man depends absolutely upon his maker for every thing, it is necessary that he should in all points conform to his maker's will." Carefully distinguishing natural law from the law of nature, he said, "The revealed law is (humanly speaking) of infinitely more authority than what we generally call the natural law. Because one is the law of nature, expressly declared so to be by God himself; the other is only what, by the assistance of human reason, we imagine to be that law."[21]

Viewing the contribution of conservative religious influences on America's founding, Harvard University historian Samuel Eliot Morison noted,

> Puritanism was a cutting edge which hewed liberty, democracy, humanitarianism, and universal education out of the black forest of feudal Europe and the American wilderness.
>
> Puritan doctrine taught each person to consider himself a significant if sinful unit to whom God had given a particular place and duty, and that he must help his fellow men.
>
> Puritanism is an American heritage to be grateful for and not to be sneered at because it required everyone to attend divine worship and maintained a strict code of moral ethics.[22]

Also significant to the founding era were such schools as Harvard and Yale, which provided essential leadership. Michael Novak has pointed out,

> Schools in the colonies were founded around the same purpose. Even the great universities, which subsequently were secularized, had evangelistic roots. Harvard College [was] founded in 1636 to train ministers of the gospel....
>
> Yale was constituted in 1701 in recognition of the fact that the colonies had been established "both to plant and under the Divine Blessing to propagate in this wilderness, the blessed reformed Protestant religion, in the purity of its order and worship, not only to their posterity, but also to the barbarous natives."[23]

Colonial charters in this era exhibited the marks of Protestant, and particularly Puritan, Christianity. The Fundamental Orders of Connecticut (1638–1639) boldly declared its goal: "To maintain and pursue the liberty and purity of the gospel of our Lord Jesus which we now profess, as also the discipline of the Churches, which according to the truth of the said gospel is now practiced amongst us."[24]

Common to many colonies were established churches, Puritan

or Congregational churches in the North and Anglican in the South. Among the thirteen colonies, seven had established churches—Connecticut, Georgia, Maryland, Massachusetts, New Hampshire, South Carolina, and Virginia. Six did not—Delaware, New Jersey, New York, North Carolina, Pennsylvania, and Rhode Island. Also widespread among the colonial charters and early state constitutions were religious tests for holding office. Pennsylvania, the most pluralistically tolerant state, required in 1776 that legislators take this oath: "I do believe in one God, the creator and governor of the universe, the rewarder of the good and the punisher of the wicked. And I do acknowledge the Scriptures of the Old and New Testament to be given by Divine inspiration." The Delaware Constitution mandated in 1776 that officeholders take this pledge: "I do profess faith in God the Father, and in Jesus Christ His only Son, and in the Holy Ghost, one God, blessed for evermore; and I do acknowledge the holy scriptures of the Old and New Testament to be given by divine inspiration."[25]

Requirements for church membership were high, resulting in far higher figures in the colonies for church attendance than for church membership. Religious influence pervaded colonial society. Tiny Jewish and Roman Catholic populations ensured that Protestant Christianity's domination was not monolithic. Pluralism rather than unity typified Protestant Christianity. Found among the colonies were Baptists and Moravians, Quakers and Presbyterians, Mennonites and Congregationalists, Anglicans and Methodists, and others. Meanwhile, the deism of Thomas Jefferson and Benjamin Franklin contributed yet another dimension. Although deism did not have a large number of adherents, its influence extended far beyond what its numbers would suggest. Generally well educated and often well placed politically, deists exercised considerable power and prestige. Deists and Protestants disagreed on many religious doctrines, such as the divine inspiration of the Bible and the Deity and the virgin birth of Jesus Christ, but they agreed on two exceedingly important issues of faith and freedom: opposition to the establishment of a national church and affirmation of individual freedom.

Identifying yet another difference between secular and conservative religious influences during the founding, Robert Bellah points out that "neutral deistic language warmed the hearts of none and by itself and unaided, it could hardly have provided the imaginative basis of a national consciousness without which the new nation could easily have shattered into the divisions and fragments that continually threatened it. What civil religion unaided could not accomplish became possible with the help of a burgeoning revivalism. Cold external forms could be filled with a warm inner life, appropriated and impressed into the imaginative life of the people." Bellah argues that deists of the founding era laid the foundation of today's civil religion, which seeks to unify all religious people, Protestant, Catholic, and Jew, around inoffensive and neutral religious words and symbols, such as God and prayer. Conservative religious influences, on the other hand, provided the spirit of nationalism that also helped to unify the country.[26] For example, the deist Thomas Jefferson, in his second inaugural address, revealed the religious impulse of nationalism by likening America to biblical Israel when he said that he would need "the favor of that Being in whose hands we are, who led our forefathers, as Israel of Old, from their native land and planted them in a country flowing with all the necessaries and comforts of life, who has covered our infancy with His providence and our riper years with His wisdom and power."[27]

The strongly separatist theology of the Old and New Testaments contributed to the nationalistic and separatist character of American foreign policy for many generations. Israel, for example, always received God's blessing in the Old Testament so long as it did not succumb to the alien influences of foreign nations and religions. In the New Testament, the themes of "what fellowship hath light with darkness" and "ye are the light of the world" influenced the belief that America was a "city set on a hill," in the words of John Witherspoon. America's foreign policy avoided entangling alliances but had a "white man's burden" to export its religious, social and governmental heritage to the world. Alexis de Tocqueville spoke to the influence that Christianity exercised over the American mind and public policy before, during, and after the founding of American government: "In the United States religion exercises little influence upon the laws and upon the details of public opinion; but it directs the customs of the community, and by regulating domestic life, it regulates the state."[28] He explained,

> It was religion that gave birth to the English colonies in America. One must never forget that. In the United States religion is mingled with all the national customs and all those feelings

which the word evokes. For that reason it has a peculiar power. . . . Christianity has kept a strong hold over the minds of Americans, and . . . its power is not just that of a philosophy which has been examined and accepted, but that of a religion believed in without discussion. . . . Christianity itself is an established and irresistible fact which no one seeks to attack or to defend.[29]

The religious prelude to the founding of American government occurred during the Great Awakening, from about 1720 to 1760. This religious event crystallized both a religious and a political unity among the colonists that paved the way for the successful writing and acceptance of the Declaration of Independence, which, although written by Jefferson, received the careful scrutiny of religiously conservative persons. Even though the result was the Revolutionary War, the founders initially intended not to revolt from the mother country but to secure their rights as Englishmen. The founders resented taxation by Parliament without representation in Parliament. For example, Samuel Langdon proclaimed to the Congress of Massachusetts in 1775, "Because we refuse submission to the despotic power of a ministerial Parliament, our own sovereign, to whom we have been always ready to swear allegiance—whose authority we never meant to cast off . . . has given us up to the rage of his ministers."[30]

From a conservative religious perspective, the Declaration of Independence demonstrated that the colonists under God had rights that English parliamentary tyranny had abridged; that is, "All men are created equal, that they are endowed by their Creator with certain unalienable rights." Had England not abridged the God-given rights of the colonists, then the colonists would have had no other stipulated reason for revolt. Even with the abridgement of their rights, many colonists (the Tories) remained loyal to the mother country.

The Revolutionary War, therefore, occurred in part as a conservative religious undertaking premised on the colonists' biblical understanding that a people have no right to revolt against an established government unless that government violates their divinely endowed rights. As stated in the Declaration of Independence, "whenever any form of government becomes destructive to these ends, it is the Right of the People to alter or to abolish it, and to institute new government."

The liberal deist pen of Jefferson, though evident in the Declaration of Independence, seems to have bowed to the prevailing conservative religious convictions of others. Indeed, at their insistence, Jefferson added several references to God in the Declaration of Independence. His states' rights political party, the Jeffersonian Republicans, provides even further evidence of this conservative religious consciousness and also an ironic touch that the deist Jefferson led a party substantially populated by persons of conservative religious convictions, who supported states' rights within the federal system. Among them was a Baptist preacher, John Leland from Virginia, who significantly influenced James Madison to fight for what became the first part of the First Amendment: "Congress shall make no law respecting an establishment of religion nor prohibiting the free exercise thereof." Jefferson's deism, mild when compared with European deism of his day, generally did not conflict with the prevailing conservative religious influences on political matters that had begun to dominate the national mind through the Great Awakening, prior to the Declaration of Independence and the Revolutionary War.

English parliamentary tyranny threatened the colonists' political and religious rights by imposing taxation without representation and by threatening the loss of their religious liberty. Joseph Emerson, a Congregational minister, stated in 1776, "For they [the colonial leaders] saw, while our civil liberties were openly threatened, our religious shook; after taking away the liberty of our taxing ourselves, and breaking in upon our charters, they feared the breaking in upon the act of toleration, the taking away of liberty to choose our own ministers, and then imposing whom they [Parliament] pleased upon us for spiritual guides, largely taxing us to support the pride and vanity of diocesan Bishops."[31]

Later, when the founders adjourned the 1787 Constitutional Convention in Philadelphia without incorporating a bill of rights, especially the right to freedom of religion, conservative and secular forces joined hands to insist on the addition of a bill of rights.

### An Enduring Tension

The principal political issues of the American founding, the Declaration of Independence, the Revolutionary War, the U.S. Constitution, and the Bill of Rights had their roots deeply embedded in the political philosophy of conservative religious interests that generally coincided with a mild American brand of deism held by a small minority of men, such as Franklin and Jefferson.

From these two religious roots emerged an increasingly hostile tension during the rest of American history, notably the Civil War era, the New Deal era, and the modern era. While the founders emphasized both liberty and equality, they placed emphasis on the former. Liberal religious interests, on the other hand, have increasingly emphasized equality more than liberty, especially in the twentieth and twenty-first centuries. Thus the increased tension between the two has prompted increasing conflicts between liberty and equality and debate about whether America's origins are Christian or secular. In 1801 Yale College president Timothy Dwight, the grandson of Jonathan Edwards, who preached the classic sermon "Sinners in the Hands of an Angry God" in 1741, foreshadowed the increasing tension between the two and the gradual demise of religious conservatism: "You must take your side. There can be no halting between two opinions. . . . Between them and you there is, there can be, no natural, real, or lasting harmony. . . . Will you imbibe their principles? Will you copy their practices? Will you teach your children, that death is an eternal sleep; that the end sanctifies the means? that moral obligation is a dream? Religion a farce? . . . Will you burn your Bibles? Will you crucify anew your Redeemer? Will you deny your God?"[32]

## THE CIVIL WAR ERA

Great persons and great ideas mold history. Or at least they reflect in their greatness the transformation of history and a bridge to the future. Why has American government grown substantially in size and power during the twentieth and twenty-first centuries? The answer fundamentally rests with what happened prior to the Civil War in the lives of certain individuals and their ideas about equality. Why did liberal denomination church organizations and religious interest groups, such as the National Council of Churches, establish their presence earlier in the twentieth century than conservative religious groups, such as the Moral Majority, the Christian Coalition, and Focus on the Family? Once again, the answer fundamentally resides in the Civil War era. The beachheads of America's religious warfare became clearly defined during this epoch.

## Conservative and Liberal Beachheads

Whereas liberty and limited government stood out as hallmarks of the founding era's religious and political ferment, equality and social reform became hallmarks of the new "perfectionist" emphasis of conservative theology and of transcendental and Unitarian theology during the Civil War era. John Thomas explains, "The transformation of American theology in the first quarter of the nineteenth century released the very forces of romantic perfectionism that conservatives most feared. . . . As it spread, perfectionism swept across denominational barriers and penetrated even secular thought."[33]

While still holding to the essential features of conservative theology, leading conservative theologians and evangelists, such as Charles Finney of Oberlin College, began to emphasize the sanctification or perfection of man after salvation. Finney and others, including William Lloyd Garrison, provided substantial leadership in the fight to abolish slavery. Finney and Garrison, however, differed in their approaches. Finney, who brought Garrison into the limelight of the abolitionist movement, later broke with him on an important question. To end slavery, should the abolitionists function as a political interest group to bring about governmental and social reform?

Because Finney believed that without the regeneration of the heart, governmental and social reform would have no enduring value, he placed primary emphasis on the proclamation of the gospel. To the contrary, Garrison argued that the abolitionists should actively participate in politics as an interest group to abolish slavery. Finney asserted, "If abolition can be made an appendage of general revival, all is well. I fear no other form of carrying this question will save our country or the liberty or soul of the slave."[34] Garrison countered, "I shall strenuously contend for the immediate enfranchisement of our slave population. . . . I will be as harsh as truth, and as uncompromising as justice. On this subject, I do not wish to think, or speak, or write, with moderation."[35]

Although Garrison stands out in history books, primarily because of his aggressive methods, Finney preached against slavery to tens of thousands of persons in his mammoth crusades, and he trained antislavery leaders through his Oberlin College position. In the final analysis, perhaps both the direct and indirect approaches were necessary to condition the public mind about slavery. Their contrasting positions together with the assessments of religion and politics during the founding era by Alexis de Tocqueville, Samuel Eliot Morison, Robert Bellah, and others highlight six historical differences between conservative and liberal religious interests:

- that the biblical message is primarily personal and individual rather than social and national;
- that the gospel message has personal application with national implication; that is, the effective alteration of the external circumstances of life ultimately depends on changing the internal condition of the heart;
- that meaningful social and government reform should be first of all a product of personal regeneration; that is, regeneration of the soul before reformation of society;
- that indirect political action is in the long run more efficacious than direct political action; that is, moral suasion is more effective than legal sanction;
- that regenerated man needs to recognize his limitations in imposing his will on finite and fallen society;
- that divine or natural law is fundamental to American law and government.

Transcendentalists, far more liberal than either the deists of the founding era or the eighteenth-century Unitarians, also advocated slavery's abolition. Transcendental theology stressed the presence of the divine within man as a source of truth and a guide to action, denied the biblical doctrine of sin, looked on man as innately good, optimistically viewed the future of man, and generally believed in eliminating restrictions on man's freedom.

Herein is an irony of liberal transcendental theology. Its leaders, such as Ralph Waldo Emerson and Henry David Thoreau, emphasized the freedom of man from coercion, but as the abolitionist cause developed, they began to believe that the cause merited coercive governmental action. Contrast Emerson's dilemma on this matter in these quotations:

The root and seed of democracy is the doctrine, Judge for yourself. Reverence thyself. It is the inevitable effect of the doctrine, where it has any effect (which is rare), to insulate the partisan, to make each man a state. . . .

Democracy, Freedom, has its root in the sacred truth that every man hath in him the divine Reason, or that, though few men since the creation of the world live according to the dictates of Reason, yet all men are created capable of so doing. That is the equality and the only equality of all men. To this truth we look when we say, Reverence thyself; be true to thyself. . . .

I waked at night [he recorded in his journal] and bemoaned myself, because I had not thrown myself into this deplorable question of Slavery, which seems to want nothing so much as a few assured voices. But then, in hours of sanity, I recover myself, and say, "God must govern his own world, and knows his own way out of this pit, without my desertion of my post, which has none to guard it but me. I have quite other slaves to free than those negroes, to wit, imprisoned spirits, imprisoned thoughts, far back in the brain of man,—far retired in the heaven of invention, and which, important to the republic of Man, have no other watchman, or lover, or defender, but I."[36]

Just as transcendentalists sometimes had difficulty reconciling their emphasis on freedom from coercion with taking direct action to abolish slavery, so too not all of conservative theology opposed slavery, especially in the South. Whereas the conservative religious current in the North actively supported slavery's abolition, in the South it reinforced the institution of slavery. Although the South had much in common with the dominant conservative religious tendencies of the North and Midwest, it refused to allow the "perfectionist" emphasis of Finney and other conservative religious leaders to challenge slavery or other governmental and social traditions of the region.

## Beachhead Strategies and Strengths

What then can we say about the impact of religious tension during the Civil War era? First, without the voices of Finney, Garrison, and others in conservative religious circles and Emerson, Thoreau, and Theodore Parker in the liberal religious circles of transcendentalism and Unitarianism, the abolitionist movement would likely have fizzled and the political base for abolition and the public consciousness of slavery would have incurred incalculable damage.

Second, social reform through the use of governmental power began to emerge as a tool for religious action. In the twentieth and twenty-first centuries, liberal religious interests have increasingly built on this foundation of direct governmental action in the interest of social reform.

Third, conservative theology in the twentieth century, especially until the late 1970s, generally followed the Finney model of trying to influence public policy indirectly, through preaching the salvation and regeneration of man. The conversion and regeneration of man, Finney argued, would thereby bring about social reform in the way that John Wesley's preaching had produced significant social reform in England.[37]

Fourth, as gleaned from the second and third conclusions, the religious tension of this epoch laid the foundation for direct influence on government by liberal religious interests and the continued emphasis by conservative religious interests on indirect influence. As a result, in the twentieth century until the late 1970s, the principal church lobbies in Washington were primarily those of liberal religious persuasion, such as the National Council of Churches, and others from mainline and liberal denominations like the Methodist and Episcopal.

Fifth, as the church became transformed, especially in liberal religious circles, from predominantly a spiritual institution to a more secular organization, it acquired characteristics of an interest group that competed with other groups to influence public policy. Rather than functioning separately from the interest group conflict, it began to function on an equal footing with other interest groups in seeking to influence public policy. To conservative theologians, this trend, which became greatly accentuated during the twentieth century, removed the church from its prophetic pinnacle and reduced its political power. Alexis de Tocqueville's observation that, although the church in the late 1700s and early 1800s exercised little direct influence on public policy, it did direct "the customs of the community, and by regulating domestic life, it regulates the state,"[38] reveals the significance of the conservative point of view. Namely, the church has more political power when it is less political.

Sixth, this was the last time in American history that conservative and liberal religious interests had significant common public policy aims. Despite the religious tension between them during the founding and Civil War eras, they could agree on certain major common goals, except in the South. But in the twentieth century, as liberal theology departed more from its roots in conservative theology, they had little if any agreement on either the means or the ends of public policy. Modest efforts to bring them together during the late twentieth and early twenty-first centuries have occurred, but not with universal success. However, through the influence of Jim Wallis and others, the Democratic Party began efforts to build bridges to evangelical Christians.[39]

Seventh, the emphasis of liberal theology on direct influence may also explain in part why liberal Protestant denominations enjoyed greater representation in government, such as in the U.S. Congress, throughout much of the twentieth century. In conservative religious circles, preaching has enjoyed a higher calling than political vocations have, whereas laymen in liberal religious circles have received more encouragement to have a political vocation. Other factors, such as education and geography, also help to explain this difference.

Eighth, by raising the issues of equality and social reform, the Civil War era provided substantial impetus to the later growth of big government, as political party platforms began to emphasize social reform and the equal protection clause of the Fourteenth Amendment served to justify governmental action in domestic, social, and economic life. Much of the reason for twentieth-century governmental expansion may rest at the doorstep of the religious fermentation prior to the Civil War. As Harvey Mansfield points out, "A society of natural equals then needs government of unlimited scope, that is, an enormous inequality of political power, in order to protect its equality."[40] Although equality played a role in the founding era, particularly in the Declaration of Independence, it occupied a status inferior to liberty's. The rise in the significance of equality during the Civil War era set the stage for a continuing twentieth-century tension between liberty and equality in the making of public policy.

Ninth, the Civil War era's religious emphasis on economic, social, and governmental reform contributed to greater attention to these subjects in political party platforms. Previously, party platforms generally lacked the clarion calls for reform that subsequently punctuated the platforms of such third parties as the Populist and Progressive as well as the two major parties.

Tenth, whereas the preservation of constitutional government served as a hallmark of conservative religious interests throughout the twentieth century, the call for democratic action in the interest of economic, social, and political reform became a hallmark of liberal religious interests as a result of the legacy of the Civil War era. Indeed, during the twentieth century, many persons of liberal religious persuasion viewed the checks and balances and division of power within the American constitutional system as unnecessary obstacles to democratic action and social reform.

Eleventh, without the catalyst of the slavery crisis, liberal religious interests would probably never have had the success they achieved in the twentieth century. Slavery provided a point of protest that prompted the promulgation of liberal theology. Then, in the twentieth century, the Great Depression provided even more opportunities for liberal religious interests to influence public policy by advocating economic, political, and social reforms.

Twelfth, the prelude to the influence of Jewish and Roman Catholic religious interests in American public policy occurred during the Civil War era with the immigration of large numbers of both groups, especially German Jews and Irish Catholics. The fountainhead not only of Protestant liberalism but also of Jewish liberalism occurred in Germany; hence the influx of German Jews brought a natural tie to liberal economic, ideological, political, and social movements in America. Roman Catholic theology, on the other hand, has generally adapted to the social and political realities of the culture in which it finds itself; thus the bulk of Roman Catholic immigrants, who were generally less well off economically and tended to be big-city residents, gradually began to identify more with the Democratic Party and labor unions during the twentieth century.

Thirteenth, emancipation of black Americans during this era paved the way for their identification first with the Republican Party of Abraham Lincoln and then with the Democratic Party of Franklin Roosevelt, whose social and economic policies and big government tendencies benefited them more.

### The Heritage of the Civil War Era

During this era, Charles Finney observed that "the world is not growing worse but better."[41] This optimistic religious spirit served as a backdrop for the optimism of the League of Nations, the United Nations, the New Deal, and many other economic, political, and social programs. Government, which became the key instrument to achieve these goals, naturally grew in response to the pressure placed on it. Not until the 1970s did this spirit of optimism come crashing down, when the programs designed to usher in a better world lost their luster in the ashes of dissent and discontent about their actual achievements.

## THE NEW DEAL ERA

The New Deal era marked a significant escalation in the conflict between conservative and liberal influences that resulted in the clarification of their differences; the marked decline of conservative Protestant dominance; the changed role of the church, especially in liberal religious circles, from spiritual interests to secular interest-group activism in government and politics; and the inclusion of new religious groups with substantial influence on public policy issues. In hindsight, the New Deal era looks like a skirmish prior to full-scale warfare between conservative and liberal religious interests during the last third of the twentieth century and into the twenty-first century.

### Emerging Liberal Religious Interests

Early in the twentieth century and long before the New Deal, the social gospel movement began to propose agendas for governmental action on social and economic issues, looking to the government to establish "the kingdom of God on earth." During this period, as liberal religious forces gradually captured control of major denominations, such as the Methodist, Presbyterian, and Episcopal, churches that had played the major role in social welfare prior to the twentieth century began to remove themselves from this function. After the New Deal, of course, social welfare became largely the work of government. Robert Alley explains, "During [Roosevelt's] long term in office the churches began the upsurge in theology which came to flower in 'Neo-orthodoxy' under the brilliant leadership of Reinhold Niebuhr and Paul Tillich. By 1940 Niebuhr had become an enthusiastic Roosevelt Democrat. The interplay between FDR's 'brain trust' and Niebuhr is best documented in the statement of George Kennan, who said Niebuhr was 'father to us all.' His realism tempered with the ethic of Jesus undercut the Gospel of Wealth and established the standard of social justice for theologians of the forties and fifties. He became the theologian of the New Deal."[42]

The New Deal appears in history books as a response to overwhelming economic and social dislocations, and in a narrow sense this is true. But in a much larger and more accurate sense, the social and economic ideas of the New Deal had their origins in the halls of liberal theology. For example, as Berton Dulce and Edward Richter have pointed out, "In Wilson's social legislation, the 'social gospel' achieved recognition on a new scale. Here was the birth of the new concept for a new society that eventually found full expression in the programs and philosophy of the New Deal." These professors also note that "in his 1937 Inaugural Roosevelt . . . echoed the fusion of the social gospel and the predominant strain of Wilsonian democracy, declaring, 'The test of our progress is not whether we add more to the abundance of those who have too much; it is whether we provide enough for those who have too little.' He saw 'one-third of a nation ill-housed, ill-clad, ill-nourished.'"[43]

During the New Deal era, liberal religious and political interests began to change their views of the Bible and the Constitution. Prior to this time they generally accepted the Bible as "the word of God," meaning that it has no errors, but through the influence of liberal religious interests, the common view in the leading denominations and seminaries changed to "the Bible contains the word of God," signifying that it has errors or is only partially God's word and that advances in knowledge and a changing society require new scriptural interpretations. Gradually, man became more important and God less important, as man became, in effect, judge of what the word of God means. This erosion of the prevailing view of scripture preceded a similar erosion in the conservative view that the U.S. Constitution contains language whose meaning remains consistent from generation to generation and that any alteration in its meaning should occur only via amendment, not via reinterpretation of words and ideas agreed on by the founders. Liberal religious interests supported both biblical and constitutional reinterpretations.

In inaugural addresses and Thanksgiving proclamations, presidents began to emphasize the work of man on earth rather than the grace and activity of God in the affairs of men. Contrast, for example, the beginning of George Washington's Thanksgiving Day proclamation with that of Franklin Roosevelt:

• Washington: "Whereas it is the duty of all nations to acknowledge the providence of Almighty God, to obey His will, to be grateful for His benefits, and humbly to implore His protection and favor."[44]

- Roosevelt: "In traversing a period of national stress our country has been knit together in a closer fellowship of mutual interest and common purpose. We can well be grateful that more and more of our people understand and seek the greater good of the greater number. We can be grateful that selfish purpose of personal gain, at our neighbor's loss, less strongly asserts itself. We can be grateful that peace at home is strengthened by a growing willingness to common counsel. We can be grateful that our peace with other nations continues through recognition of our own peaceful purpose."[45]

Roosevelt's proclamation stands out as the first to break with Washington's emphasis on the providence and grace of God, emphasizing instead the works of man. One of the liberal religious purposes of government became clear during this era, namely to utilize government as the principal tool to bring happiness to humans who could not achieve it on their own.

Although the founders wanted to strengthen the federal government in relation to the states, they still envisioned a national government with limited powers. As James Madison observed in Federalist paper no. 45,

The powers delegated by the proposed Constitution to the federal government are few and defined. Those which are to remain in the state government are numerous and indefinite. The former will be exercised principally on external objects, as war, peace, negotiation, and foreign commerce; with which last the power of taxation will, for the most part, be connected. The powers reserved to the several states will extend to all the objects which, in the ordinary course of affairs, concern the lives, liberties, and properties of the people and the internal order, improvement, and prosperity of the state.[46]

### Emerging Liberal Political Interests

As an intellectual architect of the New Deal, Rexford Guy Tugwell stated that to reduce liberty and to increase equality in public policy, the New

Deal had to undermine the intentions of the founders by reinterpreting constitutional language:

> The intention of the eighteenth and nineteenth century law was to install and protect the principle of conflict; this [principle], if we begin to plan, we shall be changing once for all, and it will require the laying of rough, unholy hands on many a sacred precedent, doubtless calling on an enlarged and nationalized police power for enforcement. We shall also have to give up a distinction of great consequence, and very dear to a legalistic heart, but economically quite absurd, between private and public or quasi-public employments. There is no private business, if by that we mean one of no consequence to anyone but its proprietors; and so none exempt from compulsion to serve a planned public interest.[47]

Some years later, reflecting on delays in achieving this objective, Tugwell remarked, "Organization for these purposes was very inefficient because they were not acknowledged intentions. Much of the lagging reluctance was owed to the constantly reiterated intention that what was being done was in pursuit of the aims embodied in the Constitution of 1787 when obviously it was in contravention of them."[48]

What happened? The meaning of the Constitution's very words changed, not by amendment but by reinterpretation. Justice Felix Frankfurter, for example, said that words in the Constitution are "so restricted by their intrinsic meaning or by their history or by tradition or by prior decisions that they leave the individual justice free, if indeed they do not compel him, to gather meaning not from reading the Constitution but from reading life."[49] Justice Oliver Wendell Holmes made much the same point: "When we are dealing with words that also are a constituent act, like the Constitution of the United States, we must realize that they have called into life a being the development of which could not have been foreseen by the most gifted of its begetters."[50] This point of view triggered substantial changes in interpretation that significantly increased the power of the national government in relation to that of the states.[51]

### The Significance of the New Deal Era

For a variety of reasons, liberal religious and political interests dominated the New Deal era. First, conservative religious and political interests did not make common cause in the way that liberal religious and political interests did, in part because of conservative religious leaders' emphasis on the spiritual rather than the material aspects of life. Moreover, conservative southern Protestants maintained their solid allegiance to the Democratic Party. Later in the twentieth century, they broke from the Democratic Party, thereby allowing conservatives to build substantial strength in a theretofore untapped region.

Second, liberal churches clearly identified government as the principal agent they needed to influence in the pursuit of their goals, and they organized through the National Council of Churches and denominational interest groups to influence public policy. Conservative religious interests, lacking this organizational interest and capacity, found themselves shorthanded.

Third, perhaps more than any other single cause, the Great Depression served as a catalyst to highlight the liberal view of government. Without it, the liberal position could hardly have held sway. The Great Depression created a problem that liberal religious interests could utilize in their efforts to enlarge the scope of government to new economic, social, and political areas.

Fourth, because liberal religious interests controlled the major denominational seminaries, particularly in the North, they had a significant advantage in shaping the public mind, namely from the pulpit, which theretofore conservative religious interests had controlled.

Fifth, science and the forces of urbanization and industrialization began to attack the heart of conservative strength. Science challenged biblical teachings about the origins of man and the earth while urbanization and industrialization broke down the dominance of America's agrarian society, in which conservative religious interests had flourished. The big cities contributed to a de-emphasis on conservative religious convictions and the depersonalization of American society.

Sixth, President Franklin Roosevelt used the increasing influence of radio and newspapers to promote the New Deal. Absent these avenues of leadership, he would have had considerable difficulty in achieving his objectives. The media provided a way for him to crystallize public support.

Seventh, the emergence of Roman Catholic, Jewish, and African American voters in large numbers in the big cities, combined with traditional southern Protestant support, allowed the president sufficient leverage to win both personal victories at the polls and programmatic victories in Congress. Ironically, liberal Protestant thought could not have won without the overwhelming support of these new groups of voters that were generally alien to their religious influence except as it had political impact.

But more was at stake. First, the New Deal era presented a clear contrast between conservative and liberal purposes for government. The conservatives' religious respect for constitutional government, meaning a limited national government role, versus the liberals' respectful rejection of constitutional government, denoting a liberal democratic state that emphasized the pragmatic application of political power in the pursuit of liberal religious and political goals and the enlargement of the national government, escalated the stakes for which the two sides were fighting. George McGovern describes this difference with great clarity in his autobiography, *Grassroots*:

> The study of these men [Hegel and Marx] forced me to think seriously about the political process, but neither of them captured my interest with anything approaching the enthusiasm I experienced in discovering "the Social Gospel." This effort to find in the New Testament and the Hebrew prophets an ethical imperative for a just social order strongly appealed to me. To know that long years of familiarity with the Bible and the idealism nurtured in my public-school years were resources that I could direct to humane political and economic ends was a satisfying discovery. Religion was more than a search for personal salvation, more than an instantaneous expression of God's grace; it could be the essential moral underpinning for a life devoted to the service of one's time. Indeed, one's own salvation depended upon service to others.[52]

Second, the political slogans of the New Deal era, such as "New Deal" and "Fair Deal," revealed a changed emphasis from the responsibilities of man to the rights of man and government's role in securing those rights. These slogans and programs spoke more of what government should do for people rather than what the people should do for themselves. America began to shift from a responsibility-based society to a rights-based society.

Third, securing control of the national government and reorienting the goals of government allowed liberal religious and political interests to maintain effective control over public policy into the 1980s. In the process greater political power shifted to the national government until challenged by President Reagan's efforts to alter the allocation of governmental power between national and state governments.

Fourth, the New Deal magnified the idea of equality by placing it on a par with liberty or perhaps even eclipsing liberty in importance. In so doing the New Deal enhanced the powers not only of the national government but also of the presidency. Both the contemporary presidency and cooperative federalism generally mark their genesis with the New Deal.

Fifth, while conservative religious and political interests have usually favored nationalism, liberal religious and political interests have favored internationalism. Social gospel and neo-orthodox theology encouraged internationalism by laying the cornerstones for Wilson's League of Nations and Roosevelt's United Nations. The realpolitik of Reinhold Niebuhr's neo-orthodox theology also helped to undergird the cold war policies of several administrations.

Sixth, the defeat of Prohibition during the New Deal era symbolized the weakened conservative Protestant position in American society and foreshadowed a reduced emphasis on this type of personal morality issue until the 1970s, when abortion, homosexuality, and other issues arose. A significant portion of liberal Protestants and the overwhelming number of Roman Catholic and Jewish voters opposed the conservative Protestant position on Prohibition.

Whereas conservative and liberal religious interests had generally maintained common bonds and goals in public policy during the founding and Civil War eras, the New Deal era severed those bonds, setting the stage for a post–New Deal reassertion of conservative religious and political interests. The liberal rout of politically lethargic conservative Protestantism during the New Deal era perhaps inspired liberal forces to muster more weaponry for even greater victories through the Fair Deal, New Frontier, and Great Society programs. Subsequent efforts to achieve more liberal victories, however, provoked a latent reaction of conservative religious and political interests and fractured the South's unquestioning loyalty as a member of the liberal religious and political coalition of the New Deal. Gradually a conservative coalition of political and religious forces began to form to engage in full-scale war with the liberal coalition.

## The Modern Era

On the eve of the modern era, the death of Prohibition foreshadowed a dramatic decline in the dominance of conservative Protestant Christianity. The demise of several decades-old traditions illustrates this decline, including Sunday closing laws, Bible reading and prayer in the schools, nativity scenes on public property, sermons by clergy at baccalaureate services, and prayers before athletic events at public schools. Combined with the legalization of abortion and the legal recognition of homosexuality, conservative Protestant Christianity found itself on the defensive on many fronts.

Using their increased and better-educated numbers, Roman Catholics helped to elect the first Roman Catholic president in 1960 and to secure financial aid for parochial schools in the Elementary and Secondary Education Act of 1965. Averse to the dictates of Protestant culture on such issues as opposition to alcohol consumption and gambling and observance of Sunday as the Lord's day, Roman Catholics and Jews accelerated the decline of the historically dominant, conservative Protestant culture.

The 1960s enabled liberal Protestants, Jews, and Roman Catholics to participate in the American civil rights movement, working closely with its best-known leader, Baptist preacher Martin Luther King Jr. Also in the 1960s, the American Civil Liberties Union, with many liberal Protestant and Jewish members, successfully challenged the cherished traditions of America's conservative Protestant culture in the courts on such issues as prayer and Bible reading in the schools.

Opposed to the passing of America's historically Protestant culture, conservatives counterattacked. During the late 1970s, conservative leaders and interest groups began massive organizational efforts to challenge liberal Protestantism. In addition to their organizational and media efforts on television and radio, they started Christian schools in large numbers to oppose the secularizing influences of the public school system. Among their better-known endeavors are the Christian Broadcasting Network, Regent University, and Liberty University.

But conservative Protestants were not alone in feeling alienated from American culture. Also during the 1970s, conservative Roman Catholics sensed challenges to their own doctrinal beliefs on such issues as abortion and homosexuality. By the late 1970s and early 1980s, conservative Protestants and Catholics had begun to fight for common interests, joining in 1980 to help elect Ronald Reagan as president. White Protestants in the South and conservative Catholics in the North migrated from the Democratic Party to the Republican Party. On the interest group scene, many conservative religious groups formed, including the Catholic-inspired Eagle Forum and the Protestant-inspired Moral Majority and Christian Coalition, to challenge the National Council of Churches and other liberal religious interest groups.

Conservative Protestant resurgence, largely the product of fundamental, charismatic, Pentecostal, and evangelical denominations and organizations, paved the way for rapid church growth, including the megachurch movement, which spawned scores of churches in the thousands of members. The fastest-growing churches included independent, fundamental Baptists; Southern Baptists; charismatics and Pentecostals, such as the Assemblies of God and Church of God; and Mormons, although historically they are not considered a Christian denomination.

The Roman Catholic Church, divided between conservatives and liberals by the changes of Vatican II during the 1960s, experienced its own conservative growth under the leadership of a conservative pontiff, John Paul II. Conservative religious orders, such as the Legionnaires of Christ, experienced dramatic growth, while liberal religious orders, such as the Jesuits, suffered large losses. The charismatic movement also penetrated the Roman Catholic community. As Catholics dramatically increased their influence economically, politically, and socially in American society, they set the stage for the "Catholic moment" in America, an opportunity to eclipse Protestant cultural dominance.

Contemporary political conservatism, which features Ronald Reagan in its centerfold, rose from the ashes of defeat and despair during the debacle of 1964, when Republican presidential candidate Barry Goldwater won only six southern states, to political preeminence during the late twentieth century and early twenty-first century—so much so that the principal candidates for the Democratic presidential nomination in

2008 developed strategies and hired staff to woo evangelical Protestants and conservative Catholics away from the Republican Party.

Religious and political conservatives face two challenges. First, evangelical Christians have begun to divide into at least two camps, traditional evangelicalism, which focuses more on the eternal by emphasizing the proclamation of the gospel, and emerging evangelicalism, which directs more energy to the temporal by placing greater emphasis on the environment and other issues. This division could diminish the political clout of evangelicals as liberals and Democrats appeal to the temporal side of emerging evangelicalism. Second, as E. J. Dionne argues in "The Liberal Moment," the ideological pendulum, which swung decidedly in favor of conservatives during the past thirty years, may now swing back in favor of liberals, given as he believes that American political history reflects significant swings in the ideological pendulum. So, if true, the liberal moment is upon us.[53]

Since the 1960s, conservative and orthodox branches of Judaism have enjoyed significant growth as more Jews have begun to take historical Judaism seriously. Additionally Jews discovered new allies among fundamental and evangelical Protestants and conservative Catholics, whose biblical views inspired their support for Israel. Despite Republican Party entreaties, however, Jews have generally remained loyal to the Democratic Party. Republicans might have had more success in these appeals had they not offended Jews by their highly visible cultivation of conservative Protestants and Catholics.

As we have seen, African Americans, overwhelmingly Protestant, shifted their allegiance during the 1930s from the Republican Party of Abraham Lincoln to the Democratic Party of Franklin Roosevelt, where they remain, usually giving 90 percent or so of their votes to Democratic Party presidential candidates. The Civil Rights Act of 1964, the Voting Rights Act of 1965, and Jesse Jackson's presidential candidacies in 1984 and 1988 solidified African American allegiance to the Democratic Party. Jackson's close ties to the American Muslim community, however, alienated many Jews who had vigorously supported the civil rights movement. Ironically, the civil rights movement depended greatly on Jewish financial, intellectual, and political assistance. Increased economic success and conservative positions on such issues as abortion and homosexuality could reduce African Americans' identity with the Democratic Party, but the rise of Barack Obama may negate this possibility.

Today, with the rapid rise of Islam in America, American pluralism has become more pronounced. Once known as the church of American presidents, the Episcopal Church now has fewer adherents than Islam. Although Muslims have not yet established a significant political presence, they have sufficient numbers and finances to begin influencing American values and moral understandings. Yet another rapidly growing movement contributing to the diversity of American values and moral understandings, the New Age movement poses even more challenges to the cultural influences of both Protestants and Catholics, who emphasize the importance of God in creation and human existence. The New Age movement stresses that life exists separately from the external reference point of God and revealed scripture. Manifested in spiritual, pagan, occult, and metaphysical writings, New Age books possess a large presence on the shelves of major trade bookstores.

Ever increasing religious pluralism has generated an ever greater variety of values. First, immigration contributed to pluralism as Catholics, Jews, and other immigrant groups challenged Protestantism's dominance. Second, divisions within Protestantism, especially the advent of liberal Protestantism and the increasing number of Protestant denominations, added impetus to pluralism. Third, the power of traditional Protestantism gradually receded under the challenges brought about by immigration and division. Fourth, whether the current resurgence of conservative Protestantism is anything other than a brief reassertion of a lost past remains an open question. Fifth, likewise, whether Catholicism can eclipse Protestantism's influence, making this the Catholic moment in America, remains unclear. Sixth, the rise of Islam and the New Age movement illustrate other pluralist forces contributing to diversity and division among American values and moral understandings.

The modern era not only climaxes a long history of changes in American values and moral understandings but also points to the importance of discerning the emerging significance of religion in American politics. Robert Bellah argues that "any coherent and viable society rests on a common set of moral understandings about good and bad, right and wrong, in the realm of individual and social action."[54] During the founding era, religion served as the glue holding society together, but now it appears to be a sharp knife tearing society apart, raising the question of whether America can survive as a free democratic society without generally accepted moral and religious values. Solzhenitsyn observes,

> In early democracies, as in American democracy at the time of its birth, all individual human rights were granted on the ground that man is God's creature. That is, freedom was given to the individual conditionally, in the assumption of his constant religious responsibility. Such was the heritage of the preceding one thousand years. Two hundred or even fifty years ago, it would have seemed impossible, in America, that an individual be granted boundless freedom with no purpose, simply for the satisfaction of his whims. Subsequently, however, all such limitations were eroded everywhere in the West; a total emancipation occurred from the moral heritage of Christian centuries with their great reserves of mercy and sacrifice. . . .
>
> We are now paying for the mistakes which had not been properly appraised at the beginning of the journey. . . . We have placed too much hope in political and social reforms, only to find out that we were being deprived of our most precious possession: our Spiritual life.[55]

Those from a conservative religious viewpoint would generally side with Theodore White, who said, "Although Christianity has never been the guarantee of a democratic state anywhere in the world, no democracy has ever thrived successfully for any period of time outside of Christian influence."[56]

To the contrary, others such as former Yale University president A. Bartlett Giamatti would argue that, given its increasingly pluralistic society, America must now tolerate a wide array of divergent moral and religious values. In that regard he denounces the religious Right: "Angry at change, rigid in the application of chauvinistic slogans, absolutistic in morality, [the antihumanists or the religious Right] threaten through political pressure or public denunciation whoever dares to disagree with their authoritarian positions. Using television, direct mail and economic boycott, [they] would sweep before them anyone who holds a different opinion."[57]

Under these circumstances, can the American mainstream function as the magnet in the middle, pulling the extremes to the center and

unifying America in a common ground of moral and religious understandings? History says no. If history is the best predictor of the future,
the mainstream may moderate the excesses of America's religious and
political differences, but the messiness of muddling through will always
mark their resolution.

## NOTES

Epigraph: *Economist*, November 3–9, 2007, 21.

1. Stanley Rothman and Amy Black, "Elites Revisited: American Social and
Political Leadership in the 1990s," *International Journal of Public Opinion Research* 11, no. 2 (1999): 180.

2. Pew Forum on Religion and Public Life, "Many Americans Uneasy with Mix of Religion and Politics," August 24, 2006, http://pewforum
.org/docs/?DocID=153.

3. Durkheim quoted in Robert N. Bellah, *On Morality and Society* (Chicago: University of Chicago Press, 1973), 191.

4. Robert N. Bellah, "Religion and Legitimation in the American Republic," *Transaction* 15 (1978): 21.

5. Robert N. Bellah, *The Broken Covenant: American Civil Religion in Time
of Trial* (New York: Seabury Press, 1975), ix.

6. Quoted in Michael Novak, *Choosing Our King* (New York: Macmillan,
1974), 114.

7. Aleksandr I. Solzhenitsyn, *A World Split Apart* (New York: Harper and
Row, 1978), 49, 53.

8. John Dunphy, "A Religion for a New Age," *Humanist* 43 (January–February 1983): 26.

9. Daniel L. Dreisbach, "Founders Famous and Forgotten," *Intercollegiate
Review* 42, no. 2 (2007): 11.

10. Kenneth W. Thompson, *The Moral Issue in Statecraft* (Baton Rouge:
Louisiana State University Press, 1966), xii.

11. Bellah, *Broken Covenant*, 12.

12. Richard Hofstadter, *The American Political Tradition* (New York: Knopf,
1948), 16.

13. Alexander Hamilton, James Madison, and John Jay, *The Federalist Papers*, ed. Clinton Rossiter (New York: New American Library, 1961), 346, 353,
231, 471, 40.

14. [Thomas Jefferson], "Resolution Relative to the Alien and Sedition
Laws" (1798), in *Basic Writings of Thomas Jefferson*, ed. Philip S. Foner (New
York: Wiley, 1944), 330.

15. Alexis de Tocqueville, *Democracy in America* (New York: Vintage Books, 1954), 311.

16. Franklin quoted in Robert N. Bellah, *Beyond Belief: Essays on Religion in a Post-Traditional World* (New York: Harper and Row, 1970), 173.

17. Jefferson quoted in *Our American Heritage*, ed. Charles Wallis (New York: Harper and Row, 1970), 51.

18. Daniel J. Elazar, "Political Theory of Covenant: Biblical Origins and Development," *Publius* 10, no. 4 (1980).

19. John Locke, "An Essay Concerning the True Original, Extent and End of Civil Government," in *The Philosophical Works*, ed. J. A. St. John (London: Bell, 1908), 5:1–13.

20. John Locke, "The Reasonableness of Christianity as Delivered in the Scriptures," in *The Works of John Locke* (London: Tegg, 1823), 5:135.

21. William Blackstone, "Of the Nature of Laws in General," in *Commentaries on the Laws of England* (Oxford: Clarendon, 1765), 39, 42.

22. Morison quoted in Wallis, *Our American Heritage*, 53.

23. Novak, *Choosing Our King*, 114, 115.

24. *The Federal and State Constitutions, Colonial Charters and other Organic Laws of the United States*, ed. Benjamin Perley Poore (Washington, DC: U.S. Government Printing Office, 1877).

25. For these quotations and a selection of other founding documents, see Charles W. Dunn and James David Woodard, *The Conservative Tradition in America* (Lanham, MD: Rowman and Littlefield, 1996), 132–35, and Poore, *Federal and State Constitutions*.

26. Bellah, *Broken Covenant*, 45.

27. Jefferson quoted in Winthrop S. Hudson, *Nationalism and Religion in America* (New York: Harper and Row, 1970), 33.

28. Tocqueville quoted in Robert S. Alley, *So Help Me God* (Richmond, VA: John Knox Press, 1972), 21.

29. Tocqueville quoted in Ellis Sandoz, "Classical and Christian Dimensions of American Political Thought," *Modern Age* 25 (Winter 1981): 21.

30. Langdon quoted in *The Pulpit of the American Revolution*, ed. John Wingate Thornton (New York: Franklin, 1970), 21.

31. Emerson quoted in *Religion and the Coming of the American Revolution*, ed. Peter N. Carroll (Waltham, MA: Ginn-Blaisdell, 1970), 87, 88.

32. Timothy Dwight, *A Discourse on Some Events of the Last Century, Delivered in the Brick Church in New Haven on Wednesday, January 7, 1801* (New Haven: Read, 1801), 17–23, 28–30, 32–34, 45–47.

33. John L. Thomas, "Romantic Reform in America," *American Quarterly* 17 (1965): 658.

34. Finney quoted in William G. McLoughlin, *Revivals, Awakenings and Reform* (Chicago: University of Chicago Press, 1978), 130.

35. Garrison quoted in Vernon L. Parrington, *Main Currents in American Thought*, vol. 2, *1800–1860* (New York: Harcourt, Brace, 1930), 354.

36. Emerson quoted in ibid., 392, 399.

37. A. Skevington Wood, *The Burning Heart: John Wesley, Evangelist* (Grand Rapids, MI: Eerdmanns, 1967).

38. Tocqueville quoted in Alley, *So Help Me God*, 21.

39. See Jim Wallis, *The Soul of Politics* (New York: Orbis Books, 1994), and Jim Wallis, *God's Politics: Why the Right Gets It Wrong and the Left Doesn't Get It* (San Francisco: HarperSanFrancisco, 2005).

40. Harvey C. Mansfield, *The Spirit of Liberalism* (Cambridge, MA: Harvard University Press, 1978), 39.

41. Finney quoted in McLoughlin, *Revivals*, 130.

42. Alley, *So Help Me God*, 21.

43. Berton Dulce and Edward J. Richter, *Religion and the Presidency* (New York: Macmillan, 1962), 63, 102.

44. *A Compilation of the Messages and Papers of the Presidents, 1789–1897*, ed. James D. Richardson (Washington, DC: U.S. Government Printing Office, 1896), 1:64.

45. *The Public Papers and Addresses of Franklin D. Roosevelt*, ed. Samuel I. Rosenman (New York: Random House, 1938), 4:449.

46. Alexander Hamilton, James Madison, and John Jay, *The Federalist*, ed. Henry Cabot Lodge (New York: Putnam, 1902), 290.

47. Rexford Guy Tugwell quoted in *New Deal Thought*, ed. Howard Zinn (Indianapolis: Bobbs-Merrill, 1966), 89.

48. Rexford Guy Tugwell, "Rewriting the Constitution," *Center Magazine* 1, no. 3 (1968): 20.

49. Frankfurter quoted in Carl Brent Swisher, *The Growth of Constitutional Government* (Chicago: University of Chicago Press, 1963), 77.

50. Holmes quoted in Alpheus T. Mason, *The Supreme Court from Taft to Warren* (New York: Norton, 1964), 15.

51. In 1936, the Supreme Court declared that the general welfare clause of Article I, Section 8, permitted Congress to appropriate funds for just about any purpose it chose. As the Court put it, "The power of Congress to authorize expenditure of public moneys for public purposes is not limited by the direct grants of legislative power found in the Constitution" (*United States v. Butler* [1936]). In 1937, "interstate commerce" (Article I, Section 8) was defined as anything that substantially affected the flow of interstate business, whether or not it actually crossed state lines (*National Labor Relations Board v. Jones and*

*Laughlin* [1937]). In 1942, the Court held that the federal government could regulate a product even if the producer did not intend to sell it, because the product could still affect interstate commerce. If a producer keeps what he or she produces, substitute products are not necessary, and interstate commerce is therefore affected (*Wickard v. Filburn* [1942]). More recently, the clauses of the Fourteenth Amendment guaranteeing "equal protection of the laws" and "due process of law" have been used with increasing frequency to establish national regulation in matters dealing with education and criminal law. For more than one hundred years, these subjects had generally been within the jurisdiction of the states.

52. George McGovern, *Grassroots* (New York: Random House, 1977), 34.

53. E. J. Dionne, "The Liberal Moment," *Chronicle Review*, September 7, 2007, B6–B9.

54. Bellah, *Broken Covenant*, ix.

55. Solzhenitsyn, *World Split Apart*, 21, 23, 49, 51, 57.

56. White quoted in Wallis, *Our American Heritage*, 53.

57. Giamatti quoted in *New York Times*, September 1, 1981, 1.

# RELIGION IN THE PUBLIC SQUARE

## Jean Bethke Elshtain

"God talk," at least as much as "rights talk," is the way America speaks. American politics is unintelligible if severed from America's religions, most important of these being Christianity, in its multiple Protestant and its Catholic versions. The greatest impact flows from the Protestant direction, given the course of American history.

### HUMAN LAW AND NATURAL LAW

None of this is a surprise. American democracy from its inception was based on principles derived from a long tradition of reflection on the laws of God and the ways in which human societies should reflect God's laws as available to human beings in the form of natural law. That is, human law should conform to the natural laws available to human beings through reason and, many Christians would add, through grace. America was, and remains, a land of religious seekers and believers who found and find in communal liberty—in free exercise—the freedom to be religious rather than freedom from religion.

One must be careful in making historical claims, of course, as there are always those who rush to the fore proclaiming that the founders, to a man, were deists who had little or no interest in "organized religion." (I've always found that a curious locution, by the way. What is the contrast? Disorganized religion?) Be that as it may, it is my general impression, based on the historical scholarship, that the deist argument is unsustainable as it is usually put. But that isn't the most important question, surely. What we should concentrate on is what the founders helped to unleash when they combined nonestablishment with free exercise. America's founding was not "sacral" in anything resembling a theocratic sense, but neither was it scrubbed clean of providential meaning and purpose. Adams, Washington, and others wrote of this often, of their certainty that the hand of Providence was at work in the extraordinary events of the American Revolution.

## Religion and Politics in the Church versus State Debate

Given the complexities of nonestablishment and free exercise deeded to us by the Constitution and the Bill of Rights, it is unsurprising that a substantial chunk of American jurisprudence, over the past sixty years or so, once the federal government moved into the terrain occupied previously by the states, has been devoted to the often inaptly named "church-state debate." I leave it to the constitutional lawyers to tend to the contradictions, tensions, muddles, and so on derived from jurisprudence. As a civic philosopher, I have the task of pointing out that we make a real mess of things if we equate the fluid world of religion and politics to the legalistic and jurisprudential terms of the so-called church-state debate.

When someone opines with great assurance that our churches, synagogues, and mosques should not be in the business of social provision or open advocacy on controversial issues because this violates the separation of church and state, he or she makes a huge mistake. Rather, what is going on is a dynamic cooperative arrangement between religion and civic forces to promote the common good, first, and, second, to encourage civic participation by church members: one can scarcely think of a more quintessentially "American" activity. We rush too quickly nowadays to the courts for, well, damn near everything because we want a nice, clean definitive answer and because we want to shut some people down, often pesky people of the religious sort. Democratic politics doesn't work like that—or shouldn't. Tidiness is bound to distort rather than to clarify.

So although ours is not and never has been a theocracy or a nation with an official religion, religion and politics have always interacted in ways direct and indirect. This was a theme advanced by the great French observer of American democracy, Alexis de Tocqueville, when he toured the fledgling American republic in the Jacksonian era. The result of that travel was the masterwork *Democracy in America*. Tocqueville found that the religiously formed and shaped democratic egalitarianism and the associational enthusiasm he witnessed were new under the political sun. His own experience had been one of a nation with a tight alliance between throne and altar—France's ancien regime—and then the horrific and violent wrenching of the French Revolution, the Terror (in which members of his own family perished as victims of the guillotine). Was religious freedom the upshot? Not at all. Instead, the French revolutionaries devised an official religion of the state: they worshipped at the idol of their own projects. Tocqueville depicted the terrible draining away of a people's systems of meaning and purpose when their faith was wrenched violently from them.

In the American republic, by contrast, people could be believers and citizens, members of a church, citizens of the state. The terrain in which they met, most of the time, was that realm of institutional and associational life we call civil society. So, to repeat, it is a serious error to map the legalistic terms of the church-state debate onto the more fluid, complex, and nuanced world of religion and politics. Church-state and religion-politics are not identical, not synonymous.

## THE LOGIC OF ENGAGEMENT

That church and state are separate—ours is a secular government—does not now mean and never has meant that ours is a thoroughly secularized society. In March 2000, the ninety-sixth American Assembly, a venerable effort initiated some sixty years ago and designed to bring together citizens to honestly confront major issues of public life, met to consider religion and American civil culture. As one of the leaders of this assembly, I had the tasks of gaining the widest possible representation of America's religions and helping to steer our diverse group toward a statement we could all sign on to concerning the place of religion in American life. Fifty-seven men and women representing sixteen religious orientations attended. Here are four key sentences from the document that we produced at the culmination of our intense three-day meeting: "We reject the notion that religion is exclusively a private matter relegated to the homes and sacred meeting places of the faithful, primarily for two reasons. First, religious convictions cannot be severed from their daily lives. People of faith in business, law, medicine, education, and other sectors should not be required to divorce their faith from their professions. Second, many religious communities have a rich tradition of constructive social engagement, and our nation benefits from their work in such var-ied areas as social justice, civil rights, and ethics."

This suggests a logic of engagement for religion in the public square that clashes with one powerful argument that often prevails in academic disputes nowadays and is, in turn, picked up in jurisprudential circles. One might call it strict separationism on the level of citizen engage-ment. To oversimplify, the argument is that, if you are religious, your convictions need to be translated into a strictly secular civic idiom when you take part in political deliberation. Make this translation or remain silent. This position assumes a single vocabulary for political debate and civic deliberation. When pressed, however, such advocates find it very difficult to explain to us exactly what this abstract discourse of politi-cal deliberation looks like or sounds like. Arguments along these lines not only cut against the grain of American civic culture but are draco-nian in their attempt to inhibit the speech of persons religious in the public square. One reason that America's religious institutions remain the heart of our civil society—we have an abundance of evidence on this score—lies in the fact that religion in America was never required, at least not officially, to privatize itself, despite efforts along those lines over the years.

In strong separationism there is an animus against faith communi-ties sustaining schools, civic advocacy efforts, health-care institutions, and the like. A strong separationist finds the idea of public religion—not established religion—noxious and a threat to civic life, as the strong separationist believes that believers, deep down, want to sacralize the public sphere, want some sort of theocracy, whatever their deeds, what-ever their words, whatever their disclaimers.

It follows that Christians, Jews, Muslims—any person or group with a faith commitment—should not, when speaking as citizens, give rea-sons for their support for, or opposition to, a policy, proposal, or situ-ation in terms that incorporate a religious reference or an imperative derived from their faith. Instead, they are to deploy some purportedly neutral civic language. Only in this way, claim strong separationists, can America achieve a workable civic consensus. But this makes little sense historically and civically. We have been chugging along rather remark-ably for such a diverse—and religious—society for over two centuries and thus far have not been overtaken by dangerous clerics out to steal all our liberties.

## CONFESSIONAL PLURALISM AND SOCIAL PLURALISM

So, for a change, let's refract the concerns that surface in this debate from the standpoint of religious belief. If we do, the problem looks quite different: what becomes evident is a problem with narrowing our understanding of politics and civic life rather than with the bringing of religious commitments to politics; nevertheless, it is religion that is put on the defensive consistently. In his book *The Dissent of the Governed*, the distinguished Yale constitutional scholar Stephen Carter reminds us that tolerance is not simply "a willingness to listen to what others say. It is also a resistance to the quick use of state power . . . to force dissenters and the different to conform." As an example of this phenomenon, Carter points to pro-life protest and the ways in which attempts to quash this form of legitimate protest and public advocacy have proceeded apace with the blessings of the courts in applying the Racketeer Influenced and Corrupt Organizations Act (RICO) to pro-life dissent. Where were the civil libertarians when this was going on? If RICO had been deployed against antiwar protesters or protesters decrying any effort to limit pornography on the Internet as an assault on free expression, the hue and cry would have been overwhelming. But pro-life protesters are politically incorrect, so we must find some way to shut them down. The link, in most cases, between pro-life and religious faith is, then, part of the explanation for the animus against this form of civic dissent—hence Carter's referencing of crackdowns on pro-life protest as an example of the intrusive use of state power.

Because confessional pluralism and social pluralism have gone hand-in-hand in America, measures that exert a chilling effect on the appearance in the public square of citizens armed with religiously derived convictions would, if undertaken systematically, undermine one of the glories of our republic—our pluralities, our creedal differences that, at their best, are occasions for engagement rather than opportunities for using the courts to make civic pariahs of certain groups. Perhaps we can understand part of what lies behind the strong separationist position if we recall how many important political philosophers in the history of the West insisted that loyalty to the state must trump all other loyalties; that there cannot be strong authorities within a state that are not controlled by the state. Thus Jean-Jacques Rousseau, in his famous *Social Contract*, required reading for all students of political thought, opines that Christianity is a terrible civic religion because it may put people at odds with themselves, in conflict, when it comes to what is required of them by public authority. He calls for an official state or civic religion to which all citizens must conform. There cannot be a civic life in which citizens are complex beings with multiple, overlapping loyalties that often cooperate but, at times, may come into conflict.

Surely, however, this is what our founding fathers bargained for when they endorsed free exercise. They were not so naive as to assume that there would always be an identity—a perfect congruence between—political authority and religious belief. They surely also understood that religious arguments are not, as often alleged, of such a nature that they are unassailable by definition, for someone else from a particular faith community will likely pop up and say, "I have a different interpretation of what sacred scripture or doctrine requires." Religion is no monolith, despite dreams and fears that it might become such.

Looking back, we are enormously grateful that figures embodying a prophetic witness position have emerged in our history. We celebrate each January the birthday of Martin Luther King Jr., whose every utterance was a civic sermon and whose eloquent voice was testimony to the bringing of religious conviction into direct conflict with unjust law and ill use of political authority. "Let justice roll down like a mighty river," the beauty of the cadences of the prophet Amos flowed off King's tongue as millions uttered, "Amen, and again, amen." Most of the time at this juncture someone pops up and says, "For every MLK I'll give you a rogue who claimed to be a prophet but said and did evil things"—although, now that I think about it, an opponent would likely not use the word "evil," as it is surely too "religious"! My response to such charges is that, of course, any strong conviction can be put to ill use. We do not venerate John Brown, a zealot who murdered people, although he, like King, was an antislavery, anti–racial bigotry advocate. Currently, we have laws to deal with those who claim religious inspiration as they commit crimes.

Not too long ago, in a question-and-answer session following one of my lectures at a small college, an interlocutor queried, in a manner that always frustrates me, "But what you're saying means some guy could drive his car into a crowded sidewalk café and kill a bunch of people and say that God made him do it." After I said things like, "Oh come on, now," I pointed out that none of us are obliged to accept the first-person claim of each and every person that God personally made him, or her, commit some horrible crime. But how dare the questioner—or anyone else—equate the prophetic witness of a King to a deranged murderer, as if, in making provision for King's testimony, we pave the way for the wicked and the criminal. This is errant nonsense, but one hears it all the time.

## CONTEXTUAL ENGAGEMENT

Now, to be sure, we must remain alert to misuse of religion. But civic advocacy is not a misuse; rather, it is a task of citizenship incumbent on the faithful, whose faith calls them to public life. This invites a position I call "contextual engagement," a stance that urges citizen-believers to offer a nuanced assessment of the ways in which religion enters civic discourse depending on the nature of the issues involved—what are the stakes here?—and depending on what arenas or spheres of human social life are affected and how. How should those implicated in any given situation address the issues at stake and express their concerns to their fellow citizens?

My working assumption is that, in a pluralistic society such as our own, with its politics of negotiation and compromise, it will—most of the time—be the case that the engagement of religious believers with politics will not involve an earth-shattering dilemma. The lines are not—most of the time—drawn in the sand. I also assume that it is not the task of Christianity or any religion in a society premised on non-establishment, as well as free exercise, to underwrite any single political ideology, agenda, or platform. There are bound to be some issues—euthanasia, abortion, cloning, stem cells, capital punishment—that call on a religious believer to "go all the way down" in her argument. That is, she may be obliged to offer the fullness of religious reason giving, including the theological anthropology at work, to explain fully the force of her position. If you are committed to the dignity of the human person, the moral equality of all God's children, this invites an understanding of that dignity in relation to our duties and our rights on grounds that may not be exclusively theological but are importantly so. It is a draconian exercise and a prejudicial demand if, using the courts and coercion, I oblige you to separate the depth of your beliefs from the reasons you proffer publicly for the stance you take.

There are times when Christians, and other persons religious, will want to make it absolutely clear where they stand, and why, but these moments are not likely to be the stuff of everyday politics—of most of the straightforward and rather boring work done in our legislatures and our courts. At other moments, however, a matter of grave concern may be involved. The key moral questions are likely to be, Who is placed inside or outside the boundary of moral concern if this policy or law goes forward? Is this a common-good question? And so on.

I suggest, therefore, that we flip the usual question on its head. The usual question is, How much religion can or should politics accommodate? What is acceptable or not from the political side where the public presence and voice of religion are concerned? Do we allow religion to play a robust civic role? As theologian Robin Lovin has argued, there is a strangely hypothetical and abstract quality to this way of thinking. Instead, we should pay attention to how things actually work on the ground and reframe matters, for a change, from the point of view of religion: What sort of politics does religion require in order to play the role that religious commitments demand? Perhaps the problem with many of the arguments we've been hearing is that a too-narrow understanding of politics is involved rather than a dangerously intrusive religion.

The interaction of religion and politics is a continuing tension. But, as Reinhold Niebuhr pointed out many years ago now, religious judgments are always in danger of being dismissed, ridiculed, or even persecuted, but it is vital—essential—to the health of our civil society, as Robin Lovin insists, following Niebuhr, that "religion continue to provide the critical self-limitation" that keeps a political system from overreach. American civic life is a world of many voices and idioms, including their religious varieties. This is as it should be. And, out of all this, if things are working well, we manage—with all the messiness—to articulate visions of how we can come to know a good in common that we cannot know alone.

# ON THAT "SUPERINTENDING PRINCIPLE" THAT WAS THERE BEFORE THE LAWS

*Hadley Arkes*

I would like to take, as my opening portion of text, that admonition sagely offered by G. K. Chesterton when he remarked on those people who come to love one strand in Catholicism more than they love Catholicism itself. And that produces, in each case, a notable disfiguring. If they come to appreciate a soul, apart from our bodily existence, they may cultivate a contempt for the body and for life. They neglect the cardinal point that we are souls embodied, that bodily life is a good, that death does not stand on the same plane as life as a good to be chosen, and so they may fall into rituals of collective suicide, all done in the name of the "spiritual life." As Chesterton put it, this person "takes one idea out of the thousandfold throng of Catholic ideas; and announces that he cares for that Catholic idea more than for Catholicism. He takes it away with him into a wilderness, where the idea becomes an image and the image an idol. Then, after a century or two, he suddenly wakes up and discovers that the idol is an idol; and, shortly after that, that the wilderness is a wilderness. If he is a wise man, he calls himself a fool. If he is a fool, he calls himself an evolutionary progressive."[1]

## THE SUPERINTENDING PRINCIPLE

Now I would like to draw on that same sense of neglecting the whole for the part, because that sense of things comes into play in the understanding of the Constitution, as people fasten, say, on the Bill of Rights, or

47

the First Amendment, as more important than the Constitution itself, so that it becomes, for them, the whole of the Constitution. And what is missed is a deeper truth that leads us back, as Alexander Hamilton said, to that superintending principle, as he called it, the Governor of the universe, the Author of the laws of nature, including that moral law that is immutable and the same in all places. It was the awareness of that moral law, and the Author of that law, that provided the very ground for the Constitution: it affirmed in the first place that there were principles of moral judgment, principles of right and wrong, that could be used to test the rightness of the laws or the Constitution.

What brought all of this to mind was a letter from a friend at another university. I had spoken at his place on Constitution Day and used the occasion to recall the serious argument, during the development of the Constitution, on the wisdom of adding a bill of rights. That there was a serious argument seems to come as news even to many lawyers and judges. The concern among some of the founders, such as James Wilson and Alexander Hamilton, was that a bill of rights would misteach the American people about the ground of their rights. It would impart the sense that the rights that were mentioned, or written down in the text, were somehow more fundamental, more logically prior, than the rights that the framers neglected to set down. And do we not find the evidence all about us, as in that familiar line, heard quite often, when people invoke those rights they have "through the First Amendment"? Do they imply that in the absence of that amendment they would not have had those rights to speak and assemble?[2] My friend at another university raised a familiar question in retort: Wouldn't that right to speak, however, to engage in criticism of the government and debate over the laws—wouldn't that freedom to speak be far more central or fundamental than other rights? But this is again, I think, a problem of taking one strand detached from all of the rest—for we run the risk now of losing the larger cluster of principles, the character of the regime, its animating principles—and the moral laws that lie behind it.

John Marshall famously said that anyone who published a libel in this country may be sued or indicted—he may be sued for damages or indicted for a criminal offense.[3] Marshall understood that words could be the source of harms inflicted without justification, and when that happened the law could reach these kinds of wrongs, carried out with words, as it reached other kinds of wrongs. It could bar threatening phone calls, acts of extortion and intimidation, and verbal assaults of all kinds, as well as the symbolic assault of burning crosses.

When the Bill of Rights was proposed, the crusty Theodore Sedgwick asked, Why don't you specify my right to walk down the street, my right to get up in the morning? The pitch was, Why would you think that, in a regime of freedom, you didn't have the right to speak or assemble?[4] In the understanding of the Federalists, people had a right to all dimensions of their freedom, no matter how prosaic, and the burden fell to the government in justifying the restriction of personal freedom. My friend Robert Bork, in one of his interesting opinions as a federal judge, extended the First Amendment to cover the freedom of a sculptor in crafting a piece of sculpture. And yet it was a serious stretch. The First Amendment, as we know, was brought forth for the sake of protecting political speech and the freedom of religion. Sculpture was not exactly among the things that the First Amendment was crafted to protect, and as the judges followed that limited understanding, they also contrived a distinction between political speech and commercial speech. And yet it was not at all a stretch to cover sculpture under the original Constitution, as understood by Federalists such as Sedgwick. For in their understanding, this was a regime of freedom, and we would have a presumptive claim to all dimensions of our freedom—whether we were advertising our wares, doing sculpture, or walking down the street. And on the other hand, none of these things were insulated from the reach of the law when they were vehicles for wrongdoing.

In our own day, of course, the "first freedom," the most decisive freedom, has been redefined by many people to be not the freedom of religion or of speech but the freedom, and the right, to order an abortion. That freedom has become, for many, an anchoring right, meant to secure a large portion of freedom in matters sexual—freedom from the moral reproaches and judgments cast by others, and cast most critically in the form of laws that forbid or refuse to honor. But we know that this move has been seen as striking because it has replaced the strand of the First Amendment that really has been seen as the first freedom. If we are to take apart strands, then there has been a powerful case made over the years for freedom of religion as the strand that truly stands as the first freedom.

## Religion as a First Freedom

But we need to remind ourselves that the case for religion as a first freedom did not reside simply in a claim for tolerance. In one of his most luminous political essays, James Madison made the explicit connection between religion and a constitutional order. I refer, of course, to his "Memorial and Remonstrance against Religious Assessments" in Virginia in 1785. In our own day, people may have a view of religion so wide, so anxious to avoid invidious distinctions, that they would take in some rather vague notions of "forces at work in the universe." But as Madison and his generation understood the matter, religion involved "the duty which we owe to our Creator and the manner of discharging it." Religion involved, that is, the obligations that flowed to the Creator of the universe, the Author of those laws of nature that encompassed the distinct nature of human beings, with a capacity to reflect on moral obligations and the origin of all things. (As Chesterton once remarked, only human beings have a religious sense—when was the last time you heard of a cow giving up grass on Fridays?) The existence of that Creator and the Author of the moral laws alerted us at the very least to a law outside ourselves. As Madison put it, "It is the duty of every man to render to the Creator such homage and such only as he believes to be acceptable to him. This duty is precedent, both in order of time and in degree of obligation, to the claims of Civil Society. Before any man can be considered as a member of Civil Society, he must be considered as a subject of the Governour of the Universe: And if a member of Civil Society, do it with a saving of his allegiance to the Universal Sovereign."

James Wilson insisted that, contrary to William Blackstone, the American law began by actually incorporating a principle of revolution.[5] It began, that is, by recognizing the possibility that revolution could be justified because even a decent government could turn itself into a tyranny. For the American law began with the recognition that there could be an unjust law: that the positive law could be made with all of the trappings of legality, while the law itself lacked the substance of justice. But the American law could have that quality only because it began with the understanding of natural rights—began, that is, with an understanding of a body of principles, of right and wrong, that could be invoked at any time to measure the rightness or wrongness of those policies enacted through the positive law.

## PRIMACY OF THE MORAL LAW

That is to say, we began with the understanding of a moral law in place even before the Constitution and the laws made under that Constitution, and that moral law was given its surety by the presence of the Author of that law. That moral law furnished the understanding of the moral grounds on which we committed ourselves in the first place to a regime of law. At the same time, that moral law marked limits on what the positive law in any place could rightly command. Or to put it another way, it marked an awareness of the things that the sovereign people could not rightly will even in their position as a people ruling themselves. As Plato taught us, there is the most elementary distinction between a person who recognizes a law outside himself and one who recognizes no law beyond his own appetites. For many in that first generation, and in ours, the awareness of that moral law, and the Author of that law, furnished the moral ground for respecting other laws—and for respecting, in the first instance, the difference between a regime of law, a regime that bound both rulers and citizens to a common law, and a despotism, a regime with no law beyond the will of the rulers.

Quite apart from everything else, the absorption of that moral sense made the most profound difference for citizens in a republic. For if we were establishing in America, for the first time, the right of a people to govern themselves, it was even more critical to cultivate in ordinary people a sense of obligation to respect the laws made by their fellow citizens, in contrast with laws propounded by princes with all of the trappings and majesty of royalty.

But that sense of the centrality of the religious understanding came out most dramatically in the argument over the Bill of Rights. As James Wilson tellingly observed, the purpose of this new government was not to create "new rights by a human establishment" but rather "to acquire a new security for the possession or the recovery of those rights" we already possessed by nature.[6] Blackstone had famously said that we give up the full range of rights we possessed in the state of nature, including, as he said, our "liberty to do mischief," and we exchange those unqualified rights for a more compressed or contracted set of rights under civil society—call them "civil rights"—but those diminished rights are rendered more secure by the advent of a government that can protect and secure those rights.

James Wilson responded to that argument with one of those tell-ing Talmudic questions: "Is it part of natural liberty," he asked, "to do mischief to anyone?"[7] In other words, to translate the question into the terms of Thomas Aquinas or Abraham Lincoln, when did we ever have a "right to do a wrong"? If we follow the clues left us by Wilson, we recognize that, even in the state of nature, we never had a right to mur-der, to rape, to assault. And so as we entered civil society, the laws that restrained us from murder and rape did not restrain us from anything we ever had the right, the rightful liberty, to do. What rights then did we give up when we entered this government, under this Constitution? The answer tendered by the Federalists was none. As Alexander Hamilton put it in Federalist paper no. 84, "Here, in strictness the people surren-der nothing"; they surrender none of their rights.[8]

The Federalists, such as Hamilton and Wilson, can be understood here only as they rejected the moral understanding of Thomas Hobbes in his construction of the state of nature and, indeed, in his construction of the moral world. As Hobbes put it in *Leviathan*, "The desires, and other passions of man are in themselves no sin. No more are the actions, that proceed from those passions, till they know a law that forbids them: which till laws be made they cannot know." That is, before the existence of law and civil society, we cannot expect men to know the difference between right and wrong, or to treat that difference as one they can af-ford to respect.

That was an understanding evidently—and decisively—rejected quite clearly by James Wilson in his commentaries, when he observed that we had no right to do a wrong even in the state of nature. But in that vein, no one made the rebuttal of Hobbes more explicit than the nine-teen-year-old Alexander Hamilton, in his revolutionary pamphlet *The Farmer Refuted*, written when he was still a student at King's College in New York. The young Hamilton offered this account: "[Hobbes] held . . . that [man in the state of nature] was . . . perfectly free from all restraints of law and government. Moral obligation, according to [Hobbes], is derived from the introduction of civil society; and there is no virtue, but what is purely artificial, the mere contrivance of politicians, for the maintenance of social intercourse." And the young Hamilton was no less precise in touching, at once, the central point of corruption in the argument: "The reason [Hobbes had] run into this absurd and impious doctrine, was, that he disbelieved the existence of an intelligent superintending principle, who is the governor, and will be the final judge of the universe. . . . Good and wise men, in all ages, have embraced a very dissimilar theory. They have supposed, that the deity, from the relation we stand in, to himself and to each other, has constituted an eternal and immutable law, which is, indispensibly, obligatory upon all mankind, prior to any human institution whatever."[9]

What has to be said, if we look seriously at the record, is that the references to the Creator who endowed us with rights were no mere rhetorical flourishes. The understanding of the laws of nature and of nature's God placed us within a cosmos with a moral structure. And it explained then why those bipeds who conjugated verbs were by nature the bearers of rights.

As Aristotle explained, that creature had the capacity not just to emit sounds to indicate pleasure or pain but to give reasons over matters of right and wrong.[10] Even in this age of animal liberation, we do not sign labor contracts with our horses or cows or seek the informed consent of our household pets before we authorize surgery on them. But we continue to think that those beings who can give and understand reasons deserve to be ruled with a rendering of reasons in a regime that elicits their consent.

## THE GROUND OF NATURAL RIGHTS

Still there is an enduring question as to whether we can run deeper than that and speak of beings who have an intrinsic dignity, which becomes the source in turn of rights that the rest of us must be obliged to respect. In my book *Natural Rights and the Right to Choose*, I recalled some of my colleagues at Amherst who had taken as their signature tune that line of Nietzsche's, amplified by Dostoyevsky, that God is dead and everything is permitted. They are people of large liberal sympathies, and when they focus on that homeless person in the gutter, the man who has broken his own life, they are still inclined to say that he has an essential dignity or even sanctity. For some of my colleagues this is sanctity without the sacred: they will speak of the importance of avoiding plagiarism as a sacred obligation among academics. What they mean is that the sacred is that which elicits their strongest passions; we ourselves endow something with the standing of the sacred as we invest our passions in it. By this construal, that man in the gutter who has broken his own life has a certain sanctity only because we have conferred it on him. That is strikingly different from the understanding revealed by Justice John McLean in his dissenting opinion in the Dred Scott case, when he leaned in to say, You may think that black man is chattel, but "he bears the impress of his Maker, [he] is amenable to the laws of God and man; and he is destined to an endless existence."[11] That is to say, he has a soul, which will not decompose when his material existence comes to an end. Now my colleagues in the academy are, as I say, people of generous disposition and large natures, but even they have to admit that they cannot give the same account of the wrong of slavery, or the wrong of the Holocaust, that McLean was able to give. McLean's understanding still comes closer to the understanding of most Americans, because most Americans have not detached themselves from the religious tradition. It made a profound difference in the past when we understood that even the most diminished among us were creatures made in the image of something higher. That explained why they were bearers of rights, why they bore an intrinsic dignity that the rest of us were obliged to respect. As Chesterton once put it, the church has never said on behalf of democracy, or said within his time, what Jefferson or Lincoln said about democracy, but "there will be a rending of all religious peace and compromise, or even the end of civilization and the world, . . . before the Catholic Church would admit that [even] one single moron, or one single man 'is not worth saving.'"[12]

A telling test on this point rang in for me a few years ago during a talk I was doing at Villanova. One student, after listening to me discourse, remarked that, in his own experience, people were driven in their motives mainly by self-interest—rather than these highfalutin notions that I was retailing. And he asked me what I would say to that. I said that I would want to know something more about him then, to draw him out on that subject: I invited him to cast his gaze around the room, containing about seventy-five to a hundred students, and I asked him whether he agreed with Harry Jaffa, that these people around him bore an intrinsic dignity, the source of rights of an intrinsic dignity that he was obliged to respect. Or did he regard himself as fully willing to give the ascendance, as he said, to self-interest, and regard himself as wholly free to sell these people out—to sacrifice their freedom and even their lives—as it suited his interests? I remarked that his answer to that question had to have the most profound bearing on the question of whether I would think it justified or even safe to share with him the power over my life by sharing with him the right to vote in shaping the government and the laws. (The questions elicited one of the rarest reactions I've ever encountered: he rather lit up with a recognition and, smiling, said "thank you." Not, as I say, the kind of reaction I usually receive.)

The firefighters on September 11, poised at the threshold of the World Trade Center, wove into their lives the assumption that they were equally obliged to save every soul they could reach in those buildings. Once again, we could understand that point more readily when we believed that humans were made in the image of something higher. But can reason furnish itself the materials of that understanding?

My dear friend Robert George at Princeton stands, at once, as a serious Catholic and serious philosopher, and he has insisted that there is no need to make the appeal to revelation on this, the most critical point at the root of political life. His own approach to this problem puts the accent on creatures "of this nature." The human embryo is not in a position to exercise the capacities that are built into its nature as a human being. It does no syllogisms; it shows no penetrating insight or arresting wisdom, nor does it show bravery or a willingness to subordinate its inclinations out of a respect for moral obligations. But we would not put this embryo into a soup even if it would make the soup more interesting. As unprepossessing as the embryo is, even people not very reflective have a sense that that "is not what it is made for." It is not so trifling that it belongs in salads or soups, or deserves to be treated on the plane of ordinary animal matter. There is something of immeasurable depth contained in that smallest of beings, which is far yet even from looking the way human beings typically look. When we see beings of that kind in a maturity of competence, we recognize that they should not be governed without their consent. When we see beings of that kind, too young or too infirm to be in command of their powers, we are summoned to treat them with a special care, and to be in awe yet of what they are, even if they are diminished in their powers.

George may be quite right, and we may say enough, in explaining the ground of "natural rights," the rights that are grounded in the enduring nature of humans, by appealing mainly to the understanding of creatures of this nature—much in the way that Immanuel Kant would contend that any proposition with the standing of a real moral principle could be drawn from the very idea of "a rational creature as such." And yet does that understanding carry us over to an understanding of sanctity—does it carry us to the understanding, as Chesterton says, that even the least among us has a life worth respecting?

## RELIGIOUS TRADITION AND THE TRADITION OF MORAL PHILOSOPHY

We may come here to that point at which our religious tradition is so woven in with the tradition of moral philosophy that the two become difficult, even impossible, to disentangle. The church, and our religious centers, have become the main enclaves in our own time to sustain natural law reasoning, even after the schools of philosophy have grown skeptical that reason has any serious claim to the knowledge of moral truths.

Several years ago Cardinal Jean-Marie Lustiger came in from Paris to do the Erasmus Lecture for us in New York under the Institute for Religion and Public Life. In the course of his lecture, the cardinal touched on that aphorism of John Stuart Mill's that has become a reigning slogan of what has been called "liberal" philosophy: that my personal freedom finds its limit at the point at which I begin to inflict injuries on other people. Lustiger raised the question, Do we assume that this principle covers any other person? All other persons? Do we assume that everyone out there counts, including people whose identity and character we could not know? Would it be plausible to alter that liberal slogan to make it read in this way: Our liberty ends as soon as we begin to injure, or affect adversely, those persons who count? And with a wink we may grasp just who doesn't count.

What Lustiger was pointing out then was this: Even the most familiar cliché of liberalism had apparently absorbed the premise that all men are created equal. But if that proposition, as Lincoln called it, was not indeed a truth—and important segments of liberal opinion have denied, after all, that this or any proposition could constitute a moral truth—then the most elementary dogmas of liberalism dissolve in their meaning. For why should we care that people we don't know may be injured or affected adversely by our acts? Can liberalism itself account for why we would ascribe moral worth to every person, even without knowing who that person is?

The answer was wholly explicable when it was said in the past that they are all children of God, or as Locke put it, that we are "all the workmanship of one . . . wise Maker . . . sharing all in one community of nature."

But as we trace things out in this way, I wonder if we come to the simple, inescapable truth of the compound we are—we are souls embodied, we are the only creatures with a religious sense, just as we are the only creatures that can bring forth law and moral judgment. No one who tries to give an account of the ground of polity and laws, no one who tries to give an account of this Constitution, can do that without, very quickly, running into the kinds of questions posed by Lustiger, or posed even by the firefighters if they had paused at the threshold to the World Trade Center and asked, Just why are we obliged to save any soul we can reach? We cannot give an account then of this Constitution, or the most elementary things in our law, without drawing ourselves back to the nature of that being who is both the subject and object of the laws. And we cannot give an account of that being without drawing on the mysteries running deep in that nature—like the mystery of why we have that capacity that the Greeks called *epistemonikon*, the capacity to grasp universals, along with propositions, like the law of contradiction, not bounded by space or time. It is the very capacity that made the human understanding, as Aristotle said, approach the divine. If we were made in the image of God, it was not because God had arms or legs or suffered from the maladies that afflict our bodies. It was the gift of reason that brought us closer than anything to the mind of the one who made us. (In that vein, I think of Ronald Knox's musing about the tendency to name scientific laws after those insightful men who discovered them. But as Knox remarked, if it took a considerable mind to discover that law, it must have taken a considerable mind to put it there in the first place.)

## RELIGION AND THE FUTURE OF AMERICAN POLITICS

The question has been posed seriously about the future of religion in America, for we have not seen, in my lifetime, such a measure of hostility to the religious—quickly reviled as "theocrats"—and we have seen a new passion to stamp the religious tradition as unwholesome in a republic. What other construction could be placed on that movement that springs up in all parts of the landscape, as though animated by the same persuasion, and by something akin to a religious zeal, to use the levers of the law to drive religion out of the public square: to remove exemptions on taxes for churches, to forbid religious agencies of adoption to respect the moral teachings of their churches, to bar certain groups from public parks, or even to treat as a species of hate speech what may be said in the pulpit.

To ask about the future of religion in America is to ask, at the same time, about the future of popular government—it is to ask whether there is a serious prospect for constitutional government when people lose the sense that these creatures about us have a certain sanctity, which explains why we regard them as rights-bearing beings. Or when we lose the sense that there is, behind the laws, a moral law, which stands as a test of the rightness of and the justification for those laws. If those convictions, sprung from the religious tradition, become ever more attenuated, we should not be surprised to see people acting out the conventions of a democracy—going through the familiar motions of voting and taking part in assemblies—and yet something will have vanished from the substance of their understanding. They will not be able to explain why anyone around them bears any sanctity as a rights-bearing being, on any other ground than the assumption that we have invested them with that standing—that we ourselves have decided to regard them in that way, as though we ourselves were the source of an ersatz sanctity that we were conferring on them. In short, these people could not explain why those around them should not be treated, say, as simply larger, former fetuses—human, to be sure, but not lives that we need to respect when it no longer suits our interest. We may have around us many spirited, engaging people. But a people delivered in this way from the religious understanding that once shaped our people have made of themselves the most infirm allies for us, for they cannot give a moral account any longer of our rights, or the regime that secures them, and we would be foolish to rest serenely on the assumption that we can rely on people constituted in this way to protect our rights or our lives.

As Woody Allen used to say, I'm sorry I can't leave you with something positive—would you accept two negatives? But to be clear-headed about our situation may be a way of preparing the ground of hope—and resolution. And so as Lincoln said, let us go forward with manly hearts.

## NOTES

1. G. K. Chesterton, "The Thing: Why I Am a Catholic," in *The Collected Works of G. K. Chesterton* (San Francisco: Ignatius Press, 1990), 3:317.

2. For a fuller treatment of the concern, held by some of the Federalists, for the critical misteaching of a Bill of Rights, see my chapter "On the Dangers of a Bill of Rights: Restating the Federalist Argument" in *Beyond the Constitution* (Princeton, NJ: Princeton University Press, 1990).

3. John Marshall, "Address on the Constitutionality of the Alien and Sedition Acts," in *The Political Thought of American Statesmen*, ed. Morton J. Frisch and Richard G. Stevens (Itasca, IL: Peacock, 1973), 113.

4. *Annals of the Congress of the United States, 1789–1824*, 1st Cong., August 15, 1789 (Washington, DC: U.S. Government Printing Office, 1834), 1:731.

5. "A revolution principle certainly is, and certainly should be taught as a principle for the constitution of the United States, and of every State in the Union." James Wilson, "First Lecture on the Law," in *The Works of James Wilson*, ed. Robert Green McCloskey (1804; repr., Cambridge, MA: Harvard University Press, 1967), 1:79.

6. James Wilson, "Of the Natural Rights of Individuals," in *Works of James Wilson*, 2:585.

7. Ibid., 587.

8. Alexander Hamilton, James Madison, and John Jay, *The Federalist Papers* (New York: Modern Library, n.d.), 558. In the same vein, Dr. Benjamin Rush commended the framers for avoiding the incoherence of attaching a Bill of Rights to the Constitution: "As we enjoy all our natural rights from a pre-occupancy, antecedent to the social state," it would be "absurd to frame a formal declaration that our natural rights are acquired from ourselves." Rush quoted in Herbert J. Storing, "The Constitution and the Bill of Rights," in *How Does the Constitution Secure Rights?* ed. Robert A. Goldwin and William A. Schambra (Washington, DC: American Enterprise Institute, 1985), 30.

9. Alexander Hamilton, *The Farmer Refuted* (February 1775), in *The Papers of Alexander Hamilton*, ed. Harold C. Syrett (New York: Columbia University Press, 1961), 1:86–87.

10. Aristotle, *The Politics*, 1253a.

11. *Scott v. Sandford*, 60 U.S. 393 (1857) at 550.

12. Chesterton, "Thing," 151n1.

# IS AMERICA A CHRISTIAN NATION?

*Hugh Heclo*

There are no guarantees, but sometimes research actually can help us think more clearly about hot political topics. Recent research studies show that religious polarization in the American electorate is real and important, but not all-important. The nation's overall religious cleavages have remained largely unchanged for at least the past quarter century. Politically and religiously speaking, it is the vast and moderate middle that continues to hold ultimate power. This is true even when one includes conservative Protestants in the picture.[1]

Polarization in Republican and Democratic voting has, however, grown at the far ends of the spectrum, where Americans are either extremely "religious" or extremely "nonreligious" (as defined in terms of regular attendance at religious services). This is not because masses of Americans have been becoming religiously and politically polarized. It is because the choices presented by party activists in recent years have been more effective in sorting fervent religious and secular believers into opposing party camps.[2] Though the vast moderate middle holds ultimate power, these extremes hold immediate rhetorical power. In these opposing minorities are the managers and shock troops of the culture wars. Our public talk is now infested with scary claims and counterclaims. Godless secularists are threatening to destroy our Christian nation, while theocracy-minded Christianists are threatening to destroy our secular republic.[3] What is a citizen to think?

If we look below the surface of publicists' self-serving hyperbole on this subject, what we mainly find are politicians and activists using religion, not religious conflicts driving our politics. Few Americans care about the venerable religious differences over Christology, the means of salvation, infant baptism, and the like. Christian Americans, and even conservative white Protestant Christian Americans, are a many-splintered thing, but they can be organized as "values voters" (subtext: everyone else lacks values?). That work is done by professional political managers who are adept at such organizing and manipulation. Conservative culture activists are not busying themselves in simply upholding the Christian tradition, which, by biblical standards, would have to give equal time to preaching against divorce, greed, fornication, and indifference to the poor. Likewise, liberal culture activists are not interested in understanding Christianity in its political dimensions. Activists on both sides of the culture war have a vested interest in misrepresentation. As Andrew Greeley and Michael Hout put it, "If they can puff up the otherness of the opposition, they can rally their base. And by exaggerating how strange the religious right is, demagogues can assure themselves that they will run afoul of very few real people." Typically, what is at issue in the political culture war is not religion but which side is more skilled in its demagoguery.[4]

We can expect politicians and political activists to sow confusion on major issues, especially around election time (which now seems to be all the time). But we should expect better from the professional keepers and transmitters of the American memory. The distinguished authors of a new American history textbook tell students that the United States "has never been a Christian nation." The equally distinguished history professor reviewing this textbook says that "on the contrary, the United States in its essence has always been a Christian nation, and this should be apparent to anyone with half a brain."[5]

This is not much help for a generation that needs all the help it can get in trying to think straight about who we are and who we hope to be. The problem is not that someone doubting whether this is a Christian nation lacks half a brain. The problem is that in today's rabidly partisan conflicts, the average, historically clueless American is whiplashed from both sides with reckless claims about American nationhood, Christianity, and political agendas. Religious and secular partisans alike have a vested interest in drowning out any sensible consideration of the subject. The resulting disinformation is an invitation to thoroughly benighted public debate.

Then should we just drop the subject, relegating one more important but complex issue to the modern dark hole of "whatever"? We should not. Understanding the legitimate difficulties involved in addressing this question can offer deeper insights into the subject. The complexity is really an opportunity to gain a better perspective on our current condition, even if this means simply realizing that our contemporary uncertainties are nothing new. Younger Americans, in particular, need to learn the value of facing down the oversimplifications peddled by today's sloganeers in the public square. The message to them is, Take care, but also take heart.

Is America a Christian nation? What follows can be thought of as seven answers in search of a better question.

To begin clearing the conceptual underbrush and, hopefully, to give some comfort to the perplexed, we might start with what appears to be a moment of utter clarity—a declaration from the Supreme Court that "this is a Christian nation." It is one of the few Supreme Court decisions that today's religious Right likes to cite in its campaign to "take back America for Christ." It is also a Supreme Court decision that these cultural warriors take quite out of context.

## PUTTING THE QUESTION

It is nothing new for this nation of immigrants to be resentful toward immigrants. Following the Civil War, much of America's booming railway system in the West was being constructed by the hands and on the backs of Chinese workers. In 1885, Congress passed a law making it illegal for American employers to prepay the transportation costs or in any way assist the migration of any foreigner "to perform labor or service of any kind in the United States."[6] The main targets of this legislation were the Chinese workers supposedly taking jobs from Americans. But the iron law of unintended consequences soon kicked in. By paying the costs to bring the English Reverend E. Walpole Warren to be its rector and pastor, the Holy Trinity Church of New York did exactly what this law forbade. Thus the issue was, had this utterly respectable Christian church violated the law against immigration assistance?

When the case came before the Supreme Court, the justices had little trouble reaching a decision. After showing that Congress clearly intended the law to deal with "cheap, unskilled labor," the Court went on to argue that Congress could not possibly have intended this law to apply to American churches. The reason was that since "this is a religious people," no intended action against religion could be imputed to any piece of national or state legislation. Citing a mass of organic laws and cultural practices, the Supreme Court issued its unanimous decision in 1892, including a summary observation that "these, and many other matters which might be noticed, add a volume of unofficial declarations to the mass of organic utterances that this is a Christian nation." That the Court's central argument is not about religion or Christianity but a common-sense approach to interpreting congressional intent is indicated in the ruling's final words:

> [The congressional statute] . . . is a case where there was presented a definite evil, in view of which the legislature used general terms with the purpose of reaching all phases of that evil; and thereafter, unexpectedly, it is developed that the general language thus employed is broad enough to reach cases and acts which the whole history and life of the country affirm could not have been intentionally legislated against. It is the duty of the courts, under those circumstances, to say that, however broad the language of the statute may be, the act, although within the letter, is not within the intention of the legislature, and therefore cannot be within the statute.[7]

The author of the Court's decision was Justice David J. Brewer, the son of a Congregationalist missionary to Turkey and grandson of a New England Congregationalist minister. In later years, Brewer would go on in public addresses to reflect on the coming end of the nineteenth century and to offer hopeful predictions about the spread of Christianity in the twentieth century.[8] He was a representative figure of the time, a full-fledged expression of a Protestant establishment that possessed dominant cultural authority. Brewer's identification of America as a Christian nation at the end of the nineteenth century prompted scarcely a ripple of public comment, because there was little need to explain what this claim might mean. It expressed an accepted truism. The truism was historical, demographic, and cultural in nature. America had been and was a nation composed mostly of Christians and, thus, a nation giving evidence of their beliefs. As a descriptive statement about the nation, it was factually accurate, and the Court decision presented an abundance of evidence to show that truth.

However, this Supreme Court decision was not identifying American nationhood with the Christian religion. Efforts of today's religious Right to exploit the *Holy Trinity Church* decision to that end are misleading, intentionally or otherwise. The point of Justice Brewer's discussion was to adduce evidence for a common-sense interpretation of the anti–immigrant assistance law. On behalf of the Court, he was pointing out that the people being represented in the legislature's passage of this law were, and had been from the beginning, a people self-declared to be Christian. Thus it made no sense to think that Congress had passed a law intending to prohibit Christian churches from paying the travel costs of prominent religious leaders. Nor, as the Court decision said, would the nation's commitment to religious liberty permit an interpretation of the law as intending to outlaw travel assistance for rabbis or any other non-Christian religious leaders journeying to America to serve their flocks.

We have good grounds for judging what Brewer meant. He was not saying that America as a nation was created or exists for the sake of advancing the cause of the Christian religion. He was not saying that the nation should reflect solely the concerns and beliefs of Americans who are Christians. We can know these things because later, in a 1905 book, Brewer made clear what he meant. There he emphasized that America is not a Christian nation in the sense that anyone should be compelled by the government to support Christian doctrines, or that every American was in fact or in name Christian, or that profession of Christianity should be a condition for being politically or socially recognized in American public life. More to the point, America's being a Christian nation certainly did not mean that Christianity was a religion that should be established through state power. As he put it, "The government as a legal organization is independent of all religions."[9] America was a Christian nation because the people being represented in this nation's system of self-government were overwhelmingly if vaguely and diversely Christian. Therefore, the law in question could not have been intended to prevent a Christian church from paying the ocean fare of an English cleric coming to America.

Fast-forward a hundred-plus years to today and it is obvious that even asking, Is America a Christian nation? amounts to something approaching fighting words. If today's Supreme Court produced such a ruling, we can be sure there would be much more than a ripple of public comment.

Accordingly, we can begin to appreciate how much the provocativeness of the question depends on the context of the times. The question being posed is politically provocative in our own times because we have reached a stage of contesting the fundamentals of knowing who we really are. This contest, identified in shorthand as the culture wars, is not a struggle among ordinary, politically inactive Americans pondering their "we-ness." It is an ideological contest among America's public intellectuals and political activists. One side sees the rejection of America as a Christian nation to be a good thing, signifying intellectual openness and democratic inclusiveness. The other side sees it as a bad thing, signifying the loss of America's traditional identity and moral compass.

Underlying the views of both sides—and thus digging deeper the trench warfare—is the presupposition that America must be one thing or the other. America is or is not, was or was not, a Christian nation. This all-or-nothing thinking serves the partisan interests of today's religious and secular political activists alike, because both, oddly enough, are following the structure of the same well-worn script.

Politically active Christians on the conservative right typically claim that they are on the defensive against powerful secular forces undermining the religious character of our laws and culture. In a sense, the religionists' answer to our question is that America has been a Christian nation, but misguided people today are trying to change that.

By contrast, politically active secularists on the liberal left typically claim that they are on the defensive against an aggressive Christian conservative movement and its narrow-minded moralizing. In this sense, the secularists' answer to our question is that America is not a Christian nation, but misguided people are trying to change that.

Thus the script presented by both religious and secular political activists seeks to claim possession of one of the most powerful of all political narratives—the story of decline, resistance, and restoration. Each side finds the other useful to keep the partisan juices pumping.

My purpose in asking, Is America a Christian nation? is not simply to talk about how one might "explore" the subject but to work through the conceptual underbrush to actually answer the question. Academics often spend a great deal of time talking about how important it is to appreciate the complex and uncertain nature of a subject, savoring the tentativeness of any possible answer. Such intellectual carefulness is, of course, praiseworthy. But too often, our carefulness turns into an intellectual fussiness that never gets around to answering the question.

Academics tend to forget that the objective in asking a question is not just to seek answers but actually to find them.

So what is the answer: Is America a Christian nation? The answer is yes—no—no—no—sort of—sort of—and no way.

I begin with a premise: the Christianness being talked about in public debates is a variable, and it is the nature of a variable to vary. The applicability of the term "Christian" varies among the different domains in terms of which people can reasonably try to understand the word.

This is not postmodern relativism, where Christianity can mean anything we want it to mean. It is saying that one needs to be clear about the different contexts within which meanings of the term "Christian" are to be understood. The following discussion covers seven domains that are particularly relevant for talking about America as a Christian nation. The quality of the data, particularly from opinion surveys and sociological studies regarding Americans' deepest religious beliefs, leaves much to be desired (to put it mildly). While I would not fight hard to defend any given data point, I think the evidence I cite does indicate rough orders of magnitude in the direction of the conclusions I have tried to draw.

## CHRISTIANITY AS AMERICANS' SELF-IDENTIFICATION

The first domain to consider is relatively straightforward. Demographically speaking, how do Americans identify themselves religiously when asked?

In that context, at the beginning of the twenty-first century, over 80 percent of all adult Americans told pollsters they were Christians (down slightly from 89 percent in 1947, when this Gallup poll question was first posed). In a more comprehensive 2001 survey, when asked, "What is your religion, if any?" 76 percent of adult Americans classified themselves as Christian (down from 86 percent in 1990).[10] Those identifying with non-Christian religious groups made up 3.7 percent of the adult population. At the same time, 14 percent did not subscribe to any religious identification; in other words, 29 million out of 208 million adult Americans in 2001 fell into the self-professed category of "no religion" (with a final 5 percent refusing to answer the question).[11]

In this context of dominant Christian self-identification, about nine out of ten adult Americans say they never doubt the existence of

God, and eight out of ten say prayer is an important part of their daily lives. These and similar statistics one might muster show a level of self-identified Christianity far above that of other developed nations. Large majorities of Americans report that their religious faith is very important in their lives and describe themselves as "deeply spiritual." Even among the minority of Americans reporting "no religion," a majority say they believe in a personal god and/or believe that the Bible was divinely inspired.[12]

If one pushes harder on admittedly soft data to ask whether Americans view their outlook on life to be essentially religious or secular, the self-professed religious orientation in today's America remains dominant. In 2001, 37 percent were clear in regarding their outlook as "religious," and only 10 percent equally clear in regarding their outlook as "secular." Another 38 percent of Americans described their outlook as "somewhat religious," and only 6 percent as "somewhat secular" (9 percent either said they did not know or refused to answer).[13]

At this point, it is not fair to continue torturing the data. Generally speaking, in a world at the beginning of the twenty-first century that is one-third Christian, one-fifth Muslim, one-sixth nonreligious, and one-seventh Hindu, the United States clearly falls in the statistically Christian family of nations.[14] What Brewer observed a hundred years ago remains true today: Americans think of themselves as religious, and in being religious, they think of themselves as predominantly Christian. So yes, in the domain of demographic self-identification, America is a Christian nation.

### CHRISTIANITY AS AMERICANS' SOURCE OF MORAL GUIDANCE

Beyond their religious self-identification, there is the matter of Americans' reliance on the Christian religion for moral guidance. How do Americans regard the relevance of Christianity to their everyday lives?

Although roughly four-fifths of American adults identify themselves as Christians, only 45 percent of Americans strongly agree that the Christian faith is relevant to their lives these days. Only about one-fourth of Americans say they base their own moral decision making primarily on the principles and teachings of their religion. This average 25 percent applies to attendees of mainline Protestant churches. For self-professed Catholics, it drops to 16 percent. Even among "born-again"

Christians, only 40 percent say they rely on biblical or church teachings as their primary source of moral guidance. Where, then, do most Americans look for moral guidance? Mainly, it seems, they look to personal, utilitarian calculations. Slightly over six out of ten Americans report that their moral guidance comes from considering what will bring the most pleasing results to themselves or other persons.[15]

A similarly modest view of the claims of the Christian religion appears in responses to questions about Americans' views of success in their personal lives. When asked how they define a successful life for themselves, almost 60 percent of American adults give priority to a healthy family life or some tangible accomplishment such as financial or education goals. Another 14 percent point first to various kinds of emotional fulfillment (a prestigious job, a sense of satisfaction with life). Only 7 percent of Americans view spiritual wholeness and development as the first factor defining a successful life. This is about the same proportion of Americans who define successful living as a matter of enjoying good physical health.[16]

Hence, while roughly four out of five Americans identify themselves as Christians, most also appear rather lukewarm about this religion's relevance to their daily lives. Only 42 percent of Americans say they are absolutely committed to the Christian faith. If polls are to be believed, 38 percent of Americans say they have confessed their sins and accepted Christ as their savior, but a majority of all Americans (60 percent) say they think there is no single religion that has all the answers to life's questions.[17] When survey questions that include the word "Bible" ask if there are absolute moral truths applicable to all people and times, most Americans (68 percent) agree. But when asked without the "Bible" prompt in the pollster's question, the vast majority (78 percent) agree instead that moral truths are changeable depending on personal circumstances, or admit that they have never thought about the matter. Among born-again Christians—the presumably hard core of "fundamentalist" Christians—two-thirds say they do not believe there is such a thing as absolute moral truth.[18]

More-qualitative sociological studies in recent years point in the same general direction. Most Americans may identify themselves as Christians, but most Americans, and most American Christians, do not appear to submit to the Christian religion for authoritative moral guidance in their lives. Instead, the prevailing commitment in matters of ultimate significance is to the individual as judge of what is right and wrong for him or her, but never judgmentally in relation to others. The sociologist Alan Wolfe says this outlook has gained widespread currency since the 1960s and calls it the idea of "moral freedom." As he puts it, "The ultimate implication of the idea of moral freedom is not that people are created in the image of a higher authority. It is that any form of higher authority has to tailor its commandments to the needs of real people."[19] Wolfe's studies of middle-class Americans do not describe libertines who feel they are unbound by moral rules. If his studies are representative, most Americans believe that there is a difference between right and wrong and that there are standards by which a person should try to lead a good and meaningful life. The point is that each person is viewed as rightly deciding for himself what those moral standards are to be. On this basis, America is "one nation after all" regarding the agreed source of moral guidance. That source is the autonomous individual making choices in a condition of moral freedom and treating all views with equal respect.

So what shall we say? Is America a Christian nation? No, not in the sense that a majority of Americans regard Christianity as the major force for guiding their moral decisions and defining success in their daily lives. In answering the question in this way, I do not think one is setting the bar unrealistically high. The issue here is not whether most Americans abide by the religion they profess (something that few adherents of any religion probably do very well). The issue is whether most Americans claim to be guided by the religion they profess. By self-report, the answer is negative. Most Americans may be well meaning, kindly, and generally humane, but wanting to be or being nice does not translate into America's being a Christian nation. At most, it amounts to an echo of the historical Christian religion sounding in the sentiments of people trying to be good while rejecting any moral authority superior to their own self-validating choices.

## AMERICANS' BELIEF IN THE DOCTRINES OF CHRISTIANITY

This third domain might be called the confessional standing of Americans as a Christian nation. I am not referring to the 2,500 or so separate Christian denominations in the country. I am talking about the core doctrinal content that unites Catholic, Protestant, and Orthodox churches into Christianity as such—the beliefs that make Christianity Christian rather than something else.[20] This is important for addressing our question, because of all the world religions, Christianity is inherently and fervently doctrinal in nature. It has been so from the beginning, that is to say, from the days of Paul, Peter, and the early disputes in the Council of Jerusalem regarding the hold of Jewish law on gentile Christians.

This enormous emphasis on doctrine is not because Christianity is essentially a checklist of doctrines. It is because this religion's centerpiece is a very odd person, a person who in a key sense is the religion. The essence of Christianity's good news (i.e., its gospel) is that this fully human man Jesus was equally the only begotten son of God, that he died for believers' sins as foretold by the Jewish scriptures, that he was dead and buried, and that he was raised again by God his Father and was seen alive by his followers.[21] The fantastic claims and actions surrounding this peculiar person could not help but give rise to fundamental questions that demanded answers. In the early centuries of the Christian religion, these answers were being sought not in the first instance by unbelievers but by believers in Jesus, and not by believers who had touched and known the man but by the following generations of Christians, who were going on and trusting in those earliest personal reports, which were gradually assembled into the text of the Bible's New Testament.

Doctrine emerged from addressing the questions any rational person (not the person of blind faith that the early church fathers warned against) would have when confronted by these reports. How are we to understand this person in whom we are believing? How can God have a son? In what sense or senses was Jesus both God and human? How can it be just for God to kill Jesus Christ to pay for humans' sinfulness? What logic allows God to be one and three? Core doctrines of Christianity emerged along the horizon where the astonishing facts claimed by and about this person Jesus were translated so far as possible into intellectual terms for human understanding. To be sure, many doctrinal divisions among Christians could never be settled. But as Jaroslav Pelikan demonstrated through a lifetime of scholarship, the creedal core of the Christian tradition—"what the church of Jesus Christ believes, teaches and confesses on the basis of the Word of God"—remained remarkably constant over two thousand years.[22] Nor is there today any lack of clear, straightforward explications of what this core thing called traditional Christianity is, however rich its forms of variation may be.[23]

If one assesses America as a Christian nation in light of belief in this venerable doctrine of the Christian tradition, the result is clear. Recent research is unanimous in concluding that far from affirming, much less understanding and delighting in, their religion's doctrines, American Christians have very little idea of, or interest in, what those doctrines are. Alan Wolfe, for example, has described how most of today's Americans live their faith in such a way that issues of doctrine and theology have virtually disappeared in favor of tolerance of divergent views.[24] To be sure, in comparison with secular Europe, Americans remain hyperactively religious. But their activity is little interested in seeking a God of theological truth, and very interested in seeking out a religious community that serves their personal needs (both utilitarian and aesthetic). Where theological debates once raged, the hottest disputes are now typically over preferences for styles of worship music.

Scholars have sought various ways to describe this overall trend. One speaks of a "spirituality of seeking" replacing the "spirituality of dwelling" provided by traditional religion. Another sees competition in America's religious marketplace being won by self-expression values— "the pursuit of self-realization through personal quests for spiritual insight and fulfillment." A third describes the general trend of "shrinking transcendence." In this process, the "little transcendences" experienced by seekers of spirituality displace the "great transcendences" of salvational religion and its promise to bridge the divide between God and man. A fourth speaks of Americans' "quiet faith" of religious individualism, whereby today's Americans focus on their personal needs rather than on submission to an outside power.[25] There are many things that might be said about this pervasive American devotion to personal spirituality. That it is Christian is not one of those things. None of it amounts to a commitment to traditional Christian doctrine as recognized for over two millennia.

To take some specific doctrinal issues, surveys of American public opinion make clear that Jesus has what is called a very high approval rating. However, about half of Americans believe Jesus sinned during his life on earth, a character fault that fits poorly with someone who was not only fully human but also fully God, as Christian doctrine has historically taught. Ninety percent of Americans say they own a Bible, and a large majority claim to know all of its basic teachings. But three-fourths of Americans also wrongly believe that the Bible teaches that God helps those who help themselves. Of those Americans who have a view on the subject, a majority believe that a person will earn salvation if he or she is generally good or does enough good things for others. In effect, a vague, triune view of salvation prevails, with entry to eternal heavenly life gained through three gates: by completing a critical mass of good deeds, by accepting God's grace through Jesus Christ, or by counting on God's love for all people. Three-quarters of Americans believe in the intrinsic goodness of human beings, thus denying the basic Christian doctrine of original sin and doing away with any plausible need for a savior to pay for their sins before a holy God. This muddled theology of salvation is not surprising, since about half of Americans who say they are Christians also say they believe that all religious faiths teach the same basic principles.[26] None of this corresponds to the authoritative teachings handed down through two thousand years as to what the Christian religion has held to be true. It does, however, correspond to the ancient teaching that without knowledge of God and his perfections, man will seem good to himself.

The exact meaning of any of these statistics—not to mention the wording of polling questions—is obviously something one could debate at great length. The larger picture, however, seems clear enough. Americans are more interested in having religious faith than in understanding the doctrines that define the meaning of their faith. So while the overwhelming majority of Americans describe themselves as being seriously concerned about matters of "spirituality," exactly which spirit, saying what, is left open to one's personal preferences. Since the concern with spirituality is essentially self-referential, the odds are stacked against any spirit claiming to impose obligations from outside, as one chooses to define these duties.

So is America a Christian nation? In terms of knowledgeable creedal commitments to this religion, the answer is no.

Nor should this be surprising. A noncreedal Christianity fits very well with the larger American culture that endorses individual choice, tolerance of different truths, and distrust of anyone's party line about what morality ought to be. Reciting the traditional Christian creed at a worship service, and really meaning it, is a countercultural act.

American social scientists have pointed out the advantages for civic life of Americans' noncreedal Christianity. Again, for example, Alan Wolfe commends modern Americans' approach to religious faith because "the more we refrain from treating religion as if it has some status that makes it different from everything else in the world . . . the greater our chances of avoiding religion's ugly legacies while still being able to appreciate its benefits for the individuals who practice it and the democratic society they inhabit. . . . Believers who prefer a God of love to a God of truth are not going to kill for their beliefs or to give their support to those who do."[27]

Such observations may be true of religion in general, but from its earliest beginnings, Christian doctrine has said nothing about killing for its beliefs. From Calvary onward, it has said a very great deal about suffering and dying for its beliefs. Restraining American Christians from killing nonbelievers is hardly the issue. If we are to assess America as a Christian nation, the more relevant issue is whether Americans behave like a people who are committed to the Christian religion. If Christianity is not something "different from everything else in the world," then never mind killing for it—such a religion clearly cannot be held by its believers to be something worth living for, much less dying for. This brings us to the behavioral domain concerning America as a Christian nation.

## CHRISTIANITY AS EXPRESSED IN AMERICANS' BEHAVIOR

In a fourth sphere, we come to matters of conduct, the area where Christian scripture commands believers to be not only hearers but also doers of the word, a people known by their fruits.

Obviously, there are many types of virtuous behavior that might be more or less indirectly associated with America's being a Christian nation. Among developed nations for which we have such data, Americans tend to stand out in terms of giving to charities, volunteering for civic good works, and the like. But clearly, statistics on churchgoing are the best known and most relevant behavioral measure that sets the religiosity of Americans apart from that of other developed nations. Indeed, for decades it has been taken as one of the key markers of American exceptionalism.[28] In terms of attending organized religious services (i.e., at times outside popular religious holidays), polls repeatedly show that about 40 percent of Americans report attending a worship service in the previous week. Given the demographics noted earlier, most of these are obviously Christian worship services. Thus, while most Americans identifying themselves as Christians may not appear "well churched"— in the sense of being under the doctrinal teaching of their religion's tradition—a very large minority appear quite "churchy" in the sense of regularly attending houses of worship.

However, closer examination indicates that this self-reported church-going is often—probably over half of the time—a lie. According to independent validation by head counts, time diaries, and the like, the percentage of Americans actually attending any place of worship in the previous week is probably closer to 20 percent rather than the widely publicized self-reported figure of 40 percent. The overreporting appears to be greatest among committed believers and active church members. A particularly careful case study of one well-established suburban evangelical church in the Deep South showed a 59 percent rate of attendance overreporting in 1996, not by the general public but by church members. If one assumes that by "attending church" in the last week respondents meant attending their church's actual worship service (versus social affairs, committee meetings, etc.), the overreporting or lying rate was 83 percent. The rate of overreporting for Sunday school attendance was 57 percent.[29]

In terms of behavior that significantly affects the pocketbook, approximately 17 percent of adult Americans claim to have tithed to churches and related ministries in the past year, but again, there is evidence of Americans' bearing false witness to their pollster. A study of financial records showed that two-thirds of these people were lying about their financial giving and that the actual figure was closer to 6 percent. For regular church attendees as well as born-again Christians claiming to tithe, the rate of false claims was about 63 percent.[30] Along the same lines, 92 percent of American households are said to own at least one copy of the Christian Bible, but only about one-third of adults say they read their Bible (outside church services) during the week.[31] Given the rate of Americans' false reporting about churchgoing and tithing, it is fair to surmise that the actual proportion of Bible readers is a small minority of Americans.

The data on behavior outside church walls are especially difficult to gather, but they all point in essentially the same direction. A recent review of evidence from a wide variety of sources concludes that not only American Christians in general but also born-again evangelicals "are as likely to embrace lifestyles that are every bit as hedonistic, mate-rialistic, self-centered, and secularly immoral as the world in general."[32] It is important to note that the terms "born-again" and "evangelical" designate those whom the larger culture would generally regard as the most traditional and fundamentalist Christians. One researcher identi-fies born-again Christians as those who say they have made a personal commitment to Jesus Christ that remains important in their lives and believe they will go to heaven because they have confessed their sins and accepted Christ as their savior. In 2006, 45 percent of American adults made such a declaration to a pollster, while a much smaller subset of the born-again—9 percent of American adults—met the researcher's stricter criteria for being evangelical.[33] In either case, the distinguished evangelical preacher and Bible expositor James Montgomery Boice pre-sumably knew his coreligionists as well as anybody. Shortly before his death, Boice observed in 1996 that "the sad truth is that they [evan-gelicals] perhaps even more than others have sold out to individualism, relativism, materialism and emotionalism, all of which are the norm for the majority of evangelical church services today. Evangelicals may be the most worldly people in America."[34]

If such observations apply to the "hard core" of American Christians, what shall we say about the characteristics of America as a Christian nation in a more general cultural sense? By any reasonable concep-tion of what might constitute a Christian nation, the general American population exhibits behavior pointing in exactly the opposite direction. In recent decades, American popular culture has moved toward the widespread acceptance of behaviors never associated with Christian-ity—gambling, public lewdness, foul language, mass consumption of pornography, and the like. For example, in the last quarter of the twenti-eth century, legalized gambling changed from an isolated and rare phe-nomenon to a pervasive activity. At the end of the century, 68 percent of adults reported gambling in the past twelve months (1998), losing $50 billion in legal gambling.[35] Gross gambling revenues (amounts wa-gered minus winnings returned to players) rose from about $1 billion in 1980 to over $78 billion in 2004. Only two states now lack some form of legalized "gaming," an activity confined to criminal enterprises only a generation ago but today a significant funding source for state and local governments. In 2004, 80 percent of adults viewed casino gambling as an acceptable activity for themselves or others, 76 percent viewed casinos as an important part of a community's entertainment and tourism options, and slightly over a quarter of adult Americans had gone to gambling casinos in the previous year.[36]

To take another perhaps too obvious example, one estimate is that Americans now annually spend more on pornographic activities—oddly enough known as "adult entertainment"—than on professional football, baseball, and basketball combined, or something roughly equivalent to Hollywood's total box office receipts in the nation. American spending in strip clubs exceeds the combined revenue of Broadway theaters, regional and nonprofit theaters, and symphony orchestra performances. The $12 billion in annual revenues from Internet online pornography now equals the combined annual revenue of the ABC, NBC, and CBS television networks. It is true that in recent years, the revenues of traditional commercial enterprises in the sex industry (such as magazines) have declined. However, this is because technology in the form of videotapes, cable and satellite TV, the Internet, and personal communication devices has allowed universal and discreet access to hard-core pornographic material. And vast numbers of Americans have responded with a huge demand for an ever increasing and varied supply of such material. In the late 1980s, roughly 1,600 new hard-core adult videos were released to the market annually; by 2000, the number had reached 11,000. Beyond porn commerce, there has been an ever increasing supply of amateur pornography, with some 300,000 Web sites at the beginning of the twenty-first century offering sexually explicit content for free. In 1998, there were 14 million individual pornographic Web pages, and in 2004, there were some 420 million such Web pages. The growth of wireless cell phone media tells the same story. By 2005, pornography constituted half of the multimedia traffic carried by U.S. wireless operators from outside their own portals.[37]

A survey at the beginning of the twenty-first century found that 32 percent of men and 10 percent of women in the country had visited a sexually oriented Web site. That is no doubt a major underestimate if there is the same extent of lying on this subject as there is about church attendance and tithing. At the same time, the largest group of consumers of Internet pornography was the next generation of Americans, youths twelve to seventeen years of age. Another survey in 2000 by the evangelical magazine *Christianity Today* found that 27 percent of America's pastors said they had sought out pornography on the Internet, anywhere from "a few times a year" to "a couple of times a month or more."[38] Quite apart from pornography, since the mid-twentieth century, the crude sexual content of the general culture has grown beyond the bounds of any traditional Christian understanding of the sanctity of the human body.[39]

One is left with the obvious question, With a population that claims itself to be three-quarters to four-fifths Christian, who is making this popular culture popular? It is certainly not simply that remnant 14 percent of Americans claiming to have "no religion." It must be the overwhelming majority of nominal American Christians.

So back to the question, Is America a Christian nation? In the behavioral terms that make up the functioning everyday culture in this nation, no, the evidence simply does not support the charge. Again it might be claimed that I am setting too demanding a test. How many believers in any religion actually abide by that religion day in and day out in all aspects of their lives? I would not presume to know the answer, but that is not the issue here. The issue here is the overall behavioral tendencies, the main cultural drift of things produced by millions of Americans deciding to live one way or another. In this sense, there does not seem to be even a prima facie case for twenty-first-century America's being a Christian nation.

## CHRISTIANITY IN AMERICANS' POLITICAL INSTITUTIONS

Given the cultural milieu of Protestant Christianity from which this nation originated, it would be extraordinarily strange if this religious background had *not* left a significant imprint on the legal and institutional arrangements constituting American nationhood.[40] As we shall see shortly, Christian precepts were embedded in the common law and often enforced through civil authorities, as in laws respecting the Christian Sunday Sabbath, blasphemy, and the like. However, this is not to say that U.S. political institutions and measures for the rule of law were created and developed for the sake of advancing Christianity as such or that the system of self-government was framed to represent only Christian interests. It is to say that Americans' constitutive political thinking was necessarily entwined with strands of Christian thinking. And nowhere was that more evident than in the institutional thinking about church-state relations.

Thus, in trying to understand democracy in America, Alexis de Tocqueville laid great emphasis on the influence of the English Puritan colonies of New England. Theirs was more than a passing regional or historical presence. Tocqueville argued that the foundation of Puritan principles—fervent Christian piety, democratic self-government, and republican freedom—spread its influence to gradually enlighten "the whole American world."[41] Tocqueville considered this a monumental achievement. It overturned the dominant European mind-set. A vibrant Christianity and democratic freedom could be mutually supportive, not contradictory to each other. Even New England's "puritanical" laws criminalizing immoral conduct carried the seeds of freedom and self-government, because these were laws voted by the free agreement of self-governing communities of citizens.

However, the Christian influence cut deeper into the institutional template of America than issues of congregational self-government among equals. It went to the fundamental issue of individual religious liberty, the ground for all other liberties. As a patchwork of colonies, America began life as a seventeenth-century remnant of European "Christendom," a term denoting centuries of close, mutual ties of power between western Europe's religious and civil rulers. English colonists in the New World found themselves wedged precariously between powerful versions of that ideal of Christendom, with the Spanish to the south, the French to the north, both nations claiming vast areas to the west, and a weaker version of Christendom in the mother country's official Church of England across the Atlantic to the east.

The key point here is that before the colonists were Americans, they were, in a culturally pervasive way, Protestant Dissenters. Understood historically, this term means more than merely someone who dissents or protests. Dissenters were dissenters because they were first of all affirmers. In the religious history out of which America emerged, Puritan Dissenters affirmed what they claimed to be a purified Christianity. Theirs was a Christianity whose truth claims did not depend on traditional intervening church-state structures but on the Bible's truths shown forth through the Holy Spirit to individual believers in voluntary association with each other.

Certainly America's Puritan forefathers were not religiously tolerant as we would understand that concept today. The struggle over the place of official religion in America's laws and institutions was long and complex.[42] The essential point for our purposes is that by the time American independence was won, it was the Protestant Dissenting mentality that had prevailed. The clarion call of Dissenters as a religious people building the institutions of the American state can be characterized as "no preference and no penalty." Christian belief, to be authentic, had to exist without the helping hand of state power—no establishment of religion. And Christian belief, to be authentic, also had to exist without the threatening frown of state power—free exercise of religion. And so it was that we ended up with a First Amendment in the Bill of Rights that says the things it says: "Congress shall make no law respecting an establishment of religion"—no preference—"nor prohibiting the free exercise thereof"—no penalty. American politics was liberated to be religiously moralistic precisely because the government was prohibited from involving itself in the higher matters of theological doctrine and sectarian differences.

The dominance of this Christian, Dissenting Protestant way of thinking (first at the national level and with time at the state government level) explains why there is no contradiction between two official proclamations now being used in the culture wars. As noted at the beginning, the Supreme Court in 1892 declared that "this is a Christian nation." Almost a hundred years earlier, the very Christian President John Adams signed and U.S. senators (founding fathers all) approved a treaty with the Muslim powers of Tripoli stating, "As the government of the United States of America is not in any sense founded on the Christian religion—as it has in itself no character of enmity against the laws, religion or tranquility of Moslems—and as the said States never have entered into any war or act of hostility against any Mehomitan nation, it is declared by the parties that no pretext arising from religious opinions shall ever produce an interruption of the harmony existing between the two countries."[43] The treaty's reference is to the "government" of the United States, not the people, and this observation takes us back to the essential point. Christianity was not established by law as the legal religion of the state, but it was the religion of the people. Far from these two facts' being contradictory, they were logically connected. Insofar as institutional separation of church and state in America was based on principle (and not just a practical necessity in the religiously pluralistic colonies), it was more a product of Christian thinking than of any secular or deist Enlightenment philosophy (which was at best confined to small elite circles in the colonies).[44] Following from John Locke, Roger Williams, and others, in a more or less straight line through to James Madison's Virginia remonstrance against Patrick Henry's proposal for state taxes to support religious education, and on to the drafting of the Constitution's First Amendment, the restraint on government for the sake of religious liberty was a religious and a Christian argument. Religious liberty was anchored in a deep appreciation of transcendent duty. It was man's duty to his Creator that produced the individual's inalienable right to freedom of conscience over against secular powers.[45] It is not too much to say that from this flowed the sensibility to all the other rights of life, liberty, and the pursuit of happiness that perceptive foreigners came to call the "American creed." This same fountainhead has done much to feed the modern emphasis on individual choice as its own self-justifying norm and a cultural end in itself, but that subject is not the issue here. The larger point is that the way to the American creed and its associated political institutions passed through Christianity, not secularism.

Is America a Christian nation? Its legal and institutional structures vigorously deny any such official endorsement, but in so doing, these structures are also drawing heavily on the deep capital of the nation's Dissenting Protestant Christian heritage. In this rather backhanded way, America is a Christian nation, sort of.

## CHRISTIANITY AND AMERICANS' POLITICAL ETHOS

A sixth domain for addressing America as a Christian nation focuses not on demographic identities, religious doctrine, behavior, institutional arrangements, and the like, but on something more intangible—the political ethos of the nation. This term "ethos" tries to capture something that is obviously elusive. But it is not therefore anything less real and is possibly even more important because of its very taken-for-grantedness. A political ethos is the persisting tone of public affairs, their moral and aesthetic style and mood.[46] A people's ethos is their evaluative stance, a common "attitude" in enacting their public life.

As talk of culture wars began to grow in the early 1980s, three notable historians of American religion (themselves Christians) investigated the claims of the religious Right that America at its founding was a Christian nation that had changed under the pressures of modern secular humanism. The conclusion of these scholars was to challenge and moderate the premise. In its founding era, the American nation was not predominantly Christian in any theologically rigorous or evangelical meaning of that term, but the American character was generally religious in a vaguely Christian sense.[47] In other words, anyone seeking an accurate historical understanding of America as a Christian nation really should feel obliged to abandon all-or-nothing thinking and be willing to live with some inherent ambivalence.

It is certainly true that a desire to protect and advance the Christian faith was stated as a primary goal in the early English settlements of America (e.g., the charters of Virginia, 1606, 1609, 1611; New England, 1620; Massachusetts Bay, 1629, 1691; Maryland, 1633; Rhode Island and Carolina, 1663). Likewise, after the Revolution of 1776, constitutions of the original U.S. states typically gave direct recognition to the Christian religion—sometimes authorizing public funds to support public worship and Christian educational institutions (e.g., Massachusetts, Connecticut, New Hampshire, Maryland), sometimes making profession of Christianity or Protestantism a condition for holding public office (e.g., Pennsylvania, Delaware, New Hampshire, North and South Carolina, New Jersey, Massachusetts, Connecticut, Vermont, Maryland). And invariably, state and local governments had laws and court interpretations of the common law that gave special protection to things held sacred by Christians, such as the sanctity of the Sunday Sabbath and marriage as well as prohibitions against public blasphemy.[48]

But it is also true that these official endorsements of Christianity were mostly hortatory and enforced with diminishing success in such a mobile, westward-pushing and fractious society. In the post–Civil War years, one can continue to find a few official endorsements of Christianity in state constitutions and laws, but in doing so, one is really sifting for remnants. The long-term story has been one of the gradual abandonment of such direct endorsements. The Revolutionary War broke the hold of the Church of England establishment in Virginia and elsewhere; in Connecticut (1817) and Massachusetts (1833), the disestablishment of the Congregational "standing orders" brought the last official state churches to an end. Soon states such as New York were constitutionally enshrining the principle of the separation of church and state, largely to make a statement against the masses of new Catholic immigrants. Dismantling "anti-sin" legislation has been a longer-term trend, and in doing so, Americans have typically appealed to that principle—the "sanctity" of the individual and his or her free choice—that Dissenting Protestant Christians had themselves implanted in the culture. Current controversies over antisodomy laws and same-sex marriage are only the latest examples.

Working out the political implications of America's vaguely Christian heritage has been a long-term, complex project, and the residue is a distinctively American ethos. Precisely because the religiously inspired institutional separation of church and state was taking root by the time of the struggle for political independence, America's political culture in the decades after 1776 was set free to generate a vibrant intermixture of the people's religious views and their politics. As the European impulse to legislate theology and legally establish an official Christianity was set off-limits in America, the free play of competition in the religious and political marketplaces became not merely less dangerous to social order but positively inviting. Here, the strands of Christian and republican thinking in the young nation fit together nicely to produce a highly moralistic but safely nontheocratic attitude toward political life. On the one hand, the strong pull of Puritan and Protestant thinking more generally—where every mundane activity was to be regarded as coextensive with serving and glorifying God—served to deny any separation between religious commitments and public activity. On the other hand, the nation's self-understanding of its political founding was premised on the mixture of moral reasoning and political action. Americans were continually reminded of this foundational patriotic heritage—they had become a people by launching a political revolution against their monarch precisely on the grounds that his laws and the actions of his agents were morally reprehensible and a violation of God's natural order of human rights.

Sealing this nonseparation of religion and politics was the common recognition that republican self-government required a virtuous citizenry and that this, in turn, required the moral underpinnings provided by religion in general and Christianity in particular. This pervasive view in America has been called the moral calculus of republicanism.[49] Tocqueville in the 1830s was expressing what had become and remained the widely accepted view when he said that Christianity in America was the first of its political institutions. It had that status because this religion taught a democratic people the art of being free.[50]

Thus for religious historians to say that the early American republic's character was generally religious and vaguely Christian is to say that this was a nation being built by people who mostly believed—however crude their Christian theology and behavior might be—that the temporal sphere of daily life was shot through with meaning of eternal, godly significance. A person, a citizen, was not understood to be inhabiting two separate realms of life, one religious spiritual sphere separate from the world and another political-temporal sphere safely living in only the here and now. Neither was the political society to be understood in that dualistic way. The result is a public ethos that Americans take for granted and Europeans find, to various degrees, galling and laughable. It is moralistic and crusading, benevolent and providential. We can briefly consider each feature in turn.

Until well into the twentieth century, the moral energy propelling America's many social reform movements was primarily religious rather than secular. This applied to the antislavery and early women's movements, to prison and orphanage reform, to the "social gospel" seeking to apply moral norms to the new forces of industrialism, and to a series of "godly insurgencies" under the banner of populism. The same ethos also fueled moral crusades against immigrants, mixing of the races, and various forms of "un-Americanism."[51]

Fortunately, the dark side of crusading moralism has always had to contend with what might be called the rule of benevolence in America's public ethos. This, too, was a residue of the nation's vaguely Christian heritage, and it flowed from the religious duty to seek the good of others. This Christian command for benevolence fit well with the idea of virtue in republicanism to seek the common good, and both united to become deeply embedded in the approved attitude toward public life. Of course, this stance has opened up generations of reformers to charges of being hypocritical busybodies and do-gooders, though the participants have preferred to see themselves as "those who hunger and thirst after righteousness." But the force contained in such charges of hypocrisy is itself testimony to a deeply moralistic attitude toward public life—otherwise why not accept false dealing as a natural feature of politics about which one should be sophisticated rather than complaining? In any event, the call to benevolence has been a powerful element of our political ethos. It has instilled in American public life an odd expectation. It is the expectation that rather than being merely powerful, smart, effective, and all the other attributes the world expects, one should in the first place be good.

At this point, we are brought into contact with a final feature of America's political ethos that I am calling providential. It is a sense that in enacting life on the political stage, Americans are engaged in aligning the nation (or misaligning it) with a larger, God-given moral order that lies beyond itself and a God-directed plan for history that lies behind its performance. Some have understandably called this America's "public religion" or civil religion.[52] This is fine so long as we do not mistake the same term for, say, the official secularism of the French government's civil religion or the atheistic public religion of official communism in the former Soviet Union or today's China. America's idea of public religion is thoroughly providential and rich in Christian themes and symbolism. As generations of Americans came to understand it, the nation's Revolution of 1776 was never simply about taxation without representation or mere political independence. It was about fulfilling God's plan for human freedom and ordered liberty through self-government, first in this new nation and ultimately for all mankind. It was on those same terms that Abraham Lincoln taught Americans to understand the even more devastating upheaval of their Civil War. This, too, was the public teaching about America's fateful role in the world wars, then in the long cold war against communism, and now in the twenty-first-century contest with jihadist terrorism. Throughout these momentous affairs, the tonal quality of America's public ethos has been providential. In its central line of thinking, America has envisioned itself as a redeemer nation whose story is not simply a self-made narrative but the reflection of a God-inspired mission with decisive meaning for all mankind.[53]

Partisans of today's religious Right can understandably claim that contemporary America is only a pale reflection of its Christian past, if by that one means a time when many state laws directly endorsed the Christian religion and its moral precepts. But that pattern had faded long before the 1940s, when the Supreme Court (through interpretation of the Fourteenth Amendment) began applying the First Amendment's religious nonestablishment and free-exercise clauses to state governments. America's political ethos is another matter. Pale or not, there is a continuing reflection of something in our public life that is generally religious and vaguely Christian. This remained the case even in the political upheavals of the 1960s. It is true that the vision of a redemptive community experiencing individual and collective rebirth was now denominated into a thoroughly secular cultural framework. However, at their best, 1960s activists affirmed the traditional values of authenticity, "of faith and deeds, of civic virtue and redemptive sacrifice."[54] The venerable American tradition of moralizing politics was far from abandoned; it was now invoked in matters of race, gender, class, the environment, consumer protection, sexual preference, and other movements. The tradition of benevolent problem solving for the good of others was carried forward, with 1960s moralists now defining this good to be the liberation of self and others from oppressive structures of authority. Faith was not rejected, but the object of faith changed, from transcendent standards that would judge a person's choices and preferences to faith in the individual and one's personal search for authenticity and self-expression.

And so too today, the traditional moral calculus of republicanism remains quite active in the American mind, even though, as we saw, over three-quarters of Americans say they do not believe there is such a thing as unchanging moral truth. At the beginning of the twenty-first century, three out of four Americans also told pollsters that they were worried about the moral condition of the nation and ranked it as one of the top two or three priorities that needed to be addressed. (This same view was held by two-thirds of America's younger generation, ages seventeen to thirty-five, as well as by 41 percent of atheists.) And what is to be done? Here again, the old moral calculus of republicanism clicks into place. In light of the perceived moral threat to the nation, 70 percent of Americans in 2001 said they wanted to see religion's influence on American society grow.[55] And three-quarters of these concerned Americans said it did not matter to them which religion it is that becomes more influential. This is hardly a ringing endorsement of Christianity as such. However, it is the continuation of a political ethos that is more vaguely religious than rigorously Christian. Americans continue to define political life in heavily moralistic terms and to see religion as of primary importance for reviving its deplorable moral condition.

This sixth domain—concerned with an overall political ethos—is by its very nature heavily symbolic. But since symbols matter to human beings, it is no less important because of that. Here, in a general figurative sense appropriate for speaking of such things, my conclusion is that

America does meet the loose descriptive attributes in its political ethos for being sort of a Christian nation.

By now we are rounding our way toward home, not to the answer, but to answers. Having come this far, we can see that any single answer to the question, Is America a Christian nation? must inevitably be misleading, and that in discerning multiple answers to the question, we can move toward a closer approximation of the truth of things. Demographically, America is a Christian nation. In terms of a majority of Americans' being morally guided by, doctrinally committed to, or behaviorally faithful to Christianity, America is not a Christian nation. America's political institutions (especially in a legal separation of church and state) and America's political ethos (especially in its moralizing, redemptive character) carry the imprint of the nation's Christian heritage, making America still today a derivatively "sort-of" Christian nation.

## CHRISTIANITY'S VIEW OF THE QUESTION

Finally, we might turn the question to a different, more fundamental angle. One need not be a Christian to ask whether the question of America as a Christian nation makes any sense within the framework of Christianity itself. In this case, it is not so much the answers but the question that is put on trial. How Christian is it to view America as a Christian nation?

Obviously, there are bookshelves of theology and interpretation one could consult on this subject, not least St. Augustine's account of two cities coexisting in the world—the city of God, composed of Christ's elect who love God, and the earthly city, founded on love of power and self. However, all of this can be safely bypassed if we simply turn to the essence of the matter—namely, the understanding given by the central figure of this Christian religion. Jesus' words deal our question a fatal blow. Americans in the collective, as one of the nations of this world, cannot be Christian. Nor can any other people, as the world defines such political, ethnic, or cultural categories. In judging our question, there is a clear verdict produced by the biblical narratives recounting all the engagements between the originator of this religion and the powers of this world. Consider those two engagements that bracketed the earthly ministry of this religion's central figure.

The first engagement is said to have taken place at the outset of

Jesus' public ministry, with Satan's climactic temptation. The Tempter is described as finally offering the world to Jesus: "Once again the devil took him to a very high mountain, and from there showed him all the kingdoms of the world, and their magnificence. 'Everything there I will give to you,' he said to Jesus, 'if you will fall down and worship me'" (Matthew 4:8).[56]

For our purposes, the interesting thing is that Jesus does not dispute that it is in Satan's legitimate power to offer all the kingdoms of the world to him. The current proprietorship is not in dispute, or as John later puts it, "The whole world lies under the sway of the wicked one" (1 John 5:19). Instead of disputing the validity of the offer, Jesus shifts the focus onto a different plane altogether by quoting Deuteronomy: "Away with you, Satan. The Scripture says, For You shall worship the Lord your God and him only shall you serve."

The final engagement on this issue of religious nationhood occurred about three years later, before the Roman Empire's representative, Pontius Pilate (John 18:33–36). With the desertion of not only the fickle crowds but also apparently of all family, friends, and disciples who know him best, Jesus' public ministry is in ruins.

> Pilate: Are you the King of the Jews?
> Jesus: Are you asking this of your own accord, or have other people spoken to you about me?
> Pilate: Do you think I am a Jew? It's your own nation who handed you over to me. What have you done?

At this point, using a different term, Jesus' response seems aimed precisely at transforming this idea of his own "nation" into a different "kingdom."

> Jesus: My kingdom is not founded in this world. If it were, my servants would have fought to prevent my being handed over. But in fact, my kingdom is not founded on all this.

Christianity is a very peculiar religion, perhaps, by conventional standards, not even a religion at all. Its essence is not a set of moral guidelines, or creeds, or sexual and other behavioral rules. Its essence is a person. This person says he is a king, a ruler, but not the ruler of a nation. Rather, he is the ruler of a kingdom manifested in the world—notice Jesus makes a direct connection to how his followers behave in this world—but a kingdom that is not of this world. Here is the Christian pilgrim's ordained path on the narrow ridge between being in and not of this world. Success on this journey is not measured by outcomes necessarily visible in the world, not by collective achievements, numbers of converts and churches, good deeds, political victory, or even national survival. Christian success is measured only by individual faithfulness.

Thus, as ideas occupying the same sentence, Christianity and the American nation are not so much incompatible as they are incommensurate. Seen from the perspective enunciated by the central figure of this religion, the question tempts one to exalt the relative into an absolute. Claims of patriotism, valid as they are, remain inferior to reality. They threaten to lure well-meaning but shallow American Christians into making commensurate what is Caesar's and what is God's. It was worry about this error that led the Christian scholar Richard Niebuhr to warn seventy years ago, "The foes we need to defend ourselves against are always those in our own household, for these deceive us as the foreign foe cannot."[57] And over fifteen hundred years before Niebuhr, it was the same Christian outlook that led Augustine to insist on the distinctions, priorities, and loves separating the city of man and the city of God, even as they shared the same space in time.

So we have come to the end of our attempt at conceptual clarification. Is America a Christian nation? First, yes, America is a Christian nation in a very broad sense of its formal, demographic identity. Second, no, America is not a nation of Christians in any strong traditional meaning of that term—not in moral guidance, not by doctrinal creed, not by cultural behavior. Third, yes, sort of, America is a nation powerfully influenced by Christianity, both in its legal institutions and its political ethos. And as many founding fathers hoped, in the free marketplace of religious competition, America might someday become a nation of more rather than fewer Christians.[58] Fourth and finally, as judged by Christianity itself, America is not and cannot be a Christian nation. The scripture that believers in this religion call holy indicates that only people, one at a time, and not collective entities, can be Christian. America, like every other worldly power, is an incommensurate, inferior thing. Hence, if one takes this religion seriously as it presented itself in human form, the answer to this article's question is no way.

What then shall we say? We live in a time—not rare in our history—when a significant number of Americans regard being superpatriotic and super-Christian as the same thing. Pollsters find that today's conservative Protestants have more pride in America than any other religious or nonreligious social group. Among the roughly one-quarter of Americans who belong to conservative Protestant churches, a large majority (77 percent of conservative white Protestants and 87 percent of self-identified evangelicals) see America as founded on Christian principles, and most of these people think that Christian morality should be the law of the land.[59] What such answers to these simplistic polling questions might actually mean politically covers, as the Bible says, a multitude of sins.

Hopefully, clearing the underbrush of "Christian nation" blather will encourage more serious attention to the vital relationship between Christianity and our American democracy. Since it is a relationship between many Americans' Christianity and everybody's democracy, the stakes are high. "Serious attention" means thinking with care, like grownups, and not succumbing to the emotional sloganeering that dominates our public shouting matches on this subject. The Christian Right's effort to identify its country with its faith both distorts patriotism and cheapens Christianity. Likewise the secular Left's scare tactics about theocracy and insistence on separating all religion from politics is an appeal to emotions, not rational citizenship. Sensible citizens need to know how to answer, with due diligence, the question about America's being a Christian nation. Otherwise, the abuse of the religion beloved by sincere Christians and the abuse of reason prized by secularists will continue to thrive, thanks in large part to the professional practitioners of low rhetorical cunning.

## NOTES

This chapter first appeared as an article in *Political Science Quarterly* 122 (Spring 2007).

1. These and other reality checks on exaggerated claims about the Christian Right's impact on election outcomes are contained in Andrew Greeley and Michael Hout, *The Truth about Conservative Christians: What They Think and What They Believe* (Chicago: University of Chicago Press, 2006), 39–68, and Pietro S. Nivola and David W. Brady, eds., *Red and Blue Nation? Characteristics and Causes of America's Polarized Politics* (Washington, DC: Brookings Institution Press, 2006).

2. Morris P. Fiorina, *Culture War? The Myth of a Polarized America* (New York: Pearson Longman, 2006), 130–32, 179–81.

3. The battle cry for Christians to mount the barricades against secular humanists can be found throughout the media of the evangelical subculture, as in any number of products supported by the Coral Ridge Ministries of Reverend D. James Kennedy. For examples of the recent hysterical fears from the secularist side, see Michelle Goldberg, *Kingdom Coming: The Rise of Christian Nationalism* (New York: Norton, 2006); Kevin Phillips, *American Theocracy* (New York: Viking, 2006); and James Rudin, *The Baptizing of America: The Religious Right's Plans for the Rest of Us* (New York: Thunder's Mouth, 2006). A more thoughtful account is Damon Linker, *The Theocons* (New York: Doubleday, 2006).

4. Greeley and Hout, *Truth about Conservative Christians*, 66. For an account of Republican skill on this score, see Thomas B. Edsall, *Building Red America: The New Conservative Coalition and the Drive for Permanent Power* (New York: Basic Books, 2006). In pushback mode, political liberals have launched a vigorous counterattack for the "values voters." See Michael Lerner, *The Left Hand of God: Taking Back Our Country from the Religious Right* (San Francisco: HarperSanFrancisco, 2006); Bob Edgar, *Middle Church: Reclaiming the Moral Values of the Faithful Majority from the Religious Right* (New York: Simon and Schuster, 2006); Obery M. Hendricks Jr., *The Politics of Jesus: Rediscovering the True Revolutionary Nature of the Teachings of Jesus and How They Have Been Corrupted* (New York: Doubleday, 2006); and Brian D. McLaren, *The Secret Message of Jesus: Uncovering the Truth That Could Change Everything* (Nashville, TN: W Publishing Group, 2006).

5. David Edwin Harrell Jr., Edwin S. Gaustad, John B. Boles, Sally Foreman Griffith, Randall M. Miller, and Randall Bennett Woods, *Unto a Good Land: A History of the American People* (Grand Rapids, MI: Eerdmans, 2005); Bruce Kuklick, "Text Messages: Misplaced Priorities in the Teaching of American History," *Books and Culture* 12 (July–August 2006): 30–32.

6. *Alien Contract Labor Law, U.S. Statutes at Large* 23 (1885): 332.

7. *Holy Trinity Church v. United States*, 143 U.S. 457 (1892), accessed at http://supreme.justia.com/.

8. David J. Brewer, *The Twentieth Century from Another Viewpoint* (New York: Revell, 1899).

9. David J. Brewer, *The United States: A Christian Nation* (1905; repr., Powder Springs, GA: American Vision Press, 1996).

10. Summary estimates are given in Gregg Esterbrook, "Religion in America: The New Ecumenicalism," *Brookings Review* 20 (Winter 2002): 45–48. More detailed studies of Americans' religious self-identification are in the 1990 National Survey of Religious Identification conducted by Barry A. Kosmin, Seymour P. Lachman, and associates at the Graduate School of the City University

of New York, which was followed by their 2001 American Religious Identity Survey, accessed at http://www.gc.cuny.edu.

11. Only 2 million of 208 million adult Americans stated their beliefs to be atheist, agnostic, humanist, or secular. The other 27 million in the "no religion" category could not or would not identify themselves with any religion by name. American Religious Identity Survey.

12. George Barna, "Seven Paradoxes Regarding America's Faith," December 17, 2002, accessed at Barna Research Online, http://www.barna.org/.

13. American Religious Identity Survey, exhibit 3.

14. *World Christian Encyclopedia: A Comparative Survey of Churches and Religions in the Modern World*, 2nd ed., ed. David B. Barrett, George T. Kurian, and Todd M. Johnson (Oxford: Oxford University Press, 2001).

15. George Barna, "Practical Outcomes Replace Biblical Principles as the Moral Standard," September 10, 2001, accessed at Barna Research Online.

16. George Barna, "Family and Personal Accomplishments Lead People's List of Success Determinants," November 6, 2002, accessed at Barna Research Online.

17. George Barna, *The Index of Leading Spiritual Indicators* (Dallas: Word, 1996), 14.

18. George Barna, "Americans Are Most Likely to Base Truth on Feelings," February 12, 2002, accessed at Barna Research Online.

19. Alan Wolfe, "The Final Freedom," *New York Times*, March 18, 2001. Wolfe's findings are elaborated in *One Nation, after All* (New York: Viking, 1998) and *Moral Freedom* (New York: Norton, 2001).

20. See *The Rule of Faith: Scripture, Canon and Creed in a Critical Age*, ed. Ephraim Radner and George Sumner (Harrisburg, PA: Morehouse, 1998).

21. In his letters to the young churches, Paul recounts the shorter version of this gospel doctrine repeated by the first small congregations of Christian Jews, "that Christ died for our sins according to the scriptures; and that he was buried, and that he rose again the third day according to the scriptures" (1 Corinthians 15:3–4).

22. Jaroslav Pelikan, *Credo: Historical and Theological Guide to Creeds and Confessions of Faith in the Christian Tradition* (New Haven, CT: Yale University Press, 2003).

23. See, for example, C. S. Lewis, *Mere Christianity* (New York: HarperCollins, 2001); N. T. Wright, *Simply Christian: Why Christianity Makes Sense* (San Francisco: HarperSanFrancisco, 2006); and Joseph Ratzinger (Pope Benedict XVI), *Introduction to Christianity* (Fort Collins, CO: Ignatius Press, 2004).

24. Alan Wolfe, *The Transformation of American Religion: How Americans Live Their Faith* (New York: Free Press, 2003). Also see, in particular, Luke Timothy Johnson, *The Creed: What Christians Believe and Why It Matters* (New York: Doubleday, 2003).

25. Robert Wuthnow, *After Heaven: Spirituality in America since the 1950s* (Berkeley: University of California Press, 1998), 1–18; Wayne Baker, *America's Crisis of Values* (Princeton, NJ: Princeton University Press, 2005), 57; Thomas Luckmann, "Shrinking Transcendence, Expanding Religion," *Sociological Analysis* 50 (1990): 126–28; Wolfe, *Transformation of American Religion*, 37–66. Overviews of the movement from doctrinal faith to self-expressive spirituality are in Wade Clark Roof, *Spiritual Marketplace: Baby Boomers and the Remaking of American Religion* (Princeton, NJ: Princeton University Press, 1999), and James A. Herrick, *The Making of the New Spirituality* (Downers Grove, IL: InterVarsity Press, 2003).

26. George Barna and Mark Hatch, *Boiling Point* (Ventura, CA: Regal Books, 2001), 190–93. On American views of human goodness as a denial of Christian doctrine, see the March 2000 poll results, "The Way We Live Now," discussed by Alan Wolfe in "The Pursuit of Autonomy," *New York Times Magazine*, May 7, 2000.

27. Wolfe, *Transformation of American Religion*.

28. See Seymour Martin Lipset, *American Exceptionalism* (New York: Norton, 1996).

29. See Andrew Walsh, "Church, Lies and Polling Data," *Religion in the News* 1 (Fall 1998): 1–8, and Penny Long Marier and C. Kirk Hadaway, "Testing the Attendance Gap in a Conservative Church," *Sociology of Religion* 60 (Summer 1999): 175–87.

30. See Randy Alcom, *Money, Possessions and Eternity* (Wheaton, IL: Tyndale House, 2003), and Barna, "Practical Outcomes."

31. Barna, *Index of Leading Spiritual Indicators*, 55.

32. Michael Horton quoted in a general review of the evidence presented by Ronald J. Sider in "The Scandal of the Evangelical Conscience," *Books and Culture* 11 (January–February 2005): 8–9, 39.

33. In Barna's research, those classified as evangelicals meet the born-again criteria and, in addition, affirm seven other beliefs (e.g., that one has a responsibility to share the gospel with non-Christians, that Satan exists, that eternal salvation is possible only through God's grace and not one's works, that Jesus lived a sinless life on earth, and that the Bible is accurate in all that it teaches). George Barna, "The State of the Church: 2006," accessed at Barna Research Online.

34. James Montgomery Boice, *Two Cities, Two Loves: Christian Responsibility in a Crumbling Culture* (Downers Grove, IL: InterVarsity Press, 1996), 28.

35. National Opinion Research Center, "Gambling Impact and Behavior Study" (report to the National Gambling Impact Study Commission, Washington, DC, April 1, 1999), 6.

36. American Gaming Association, *2004 State of the States: The AGA Survey of*

*Casino Entertainment* (Washington, DC: American Gaming Association, 2004), 17, 21, 23. See also http://www.americangaming.org/Industry/factsheets.

37. The statistics on "adult entertainment" and the difficulty of their calculation are discussed in Eric Schlosser, *Reefer Madness: Sex, Drugs, and Cheap Labor in the American Black Market* (New York: Houghton Mifflin, 2002), 113, 267–68. More detailed information is contained in Joseph W. Slade, *Pornography and Sexual Representation: A Reference Guide* (Westport, CT: Greenwood Press, 2000). On adult video releases, see charts from *Adult Video News*, accessed at http://www.pbs.org/wgbh/pages/frontline/shows/porn/business. On the extent and usage of pornography on the Internet, see Third Way Culture Project, *The Porn Standard: Children and Pornography on the Internet* (Washington, DC: Third Way Culture Project, 2005), 1–25.

38. These other relevant polls are cited in Schlosser, *Reefer Madness*, 179–80. Information on young consumers of Internet pornography is from Third Way Culture Project, *Porn Standard*, 3.

39. Peter Brown, *The Body and Society: Men, Women and Sexual Renunciation in Early Christianity* (New York: Columbia University Press, 1988).

40. Arguments in this section regarding political institutions and in the next section regarding the American political ethos are spelled out at much greater length in Hugh Heclo, *Christianity and American Democracy* (Cambridge, MA: Harvard University Press, 2007), 7–34.

41. Alexis de Tocqueville, *Democracy in America*, ed. J. P. Mayer and Max Lerner, trans. George Lawrence (New York: Harper and Row, 1966), 29, 30, 36–40.

42. In addition to John Noonan's work cited below, see Thomas E. Buckley, *Church and State in Revolutionary Virginia, 1776–1787* (Charlottesville: University Press of Virginia, 1977); William Lee Miller, *The First Liberty: Religion and the American Republic* (New York: Knopf, 1986); Leonard W. Levy, *The Establishment Clause: Religion and the First Amendment* (New York: Macmillan, 1986); and Michael McConnell, "The Origins and Historical Understanding of Free Exercise of Religion," *Harvard Law Review* 103 (May 1990): 1409–517.

43. Quoted in Frank Lambert, *The Founding Fathers and the Place of Religion in America* (Princeton, NJ: Princeton University Press, 2003), 239.

44. John T. Noonan Jr., *The Lustre of Our Country: The American Experience of Religious Freedom* (Berkeley: University of California Press, 1998).

45. On this score, it is worth repeating what Madison's 1785 petition, a promissory note on what would later appear in the Constitution's Bill of Rights, actually said. "We remonstrate against the said Bill, 1. Because we hold it for a fundamental and undeniable truth, that Religion or the duty which we owe to our Creator and the manner of discharging it, can be directed only by reason and conviction, not by force or violence. The Religion then of every man must

be left to the conviction and conscience of every man; and it is the right of every man to exercise it as these may dictate. This right is in its nature an unalienable right. It is unalienable, because the opinions of men depending only on the evidence contemplated by their own minds cannot follow the dictates of other men: It is unalienable also, because what is here a right towards men, is a duty toward the Creator. It is the duty of every man to render to the Creator such homage, and such only, as he believes to be acceptable to him. This duty is precedent both in order of time and degree of obligation, to the claims of Civil Society. Before any man can be considered as a member of Civil Society, he must be considered as a subject of the Governor of the Universe: And if a member of Civil Society, who enters into any subordinate Association, must always do it with a reservation of his duty to the general authority; much more must every man who becomes a member of any particular Civil Society, do it with a saving of his allegiance to the Universal Sovereign. We maintain therefore that in matters of Religion, no man's right is abridged by the institution of Civil Society, and that Religion is wholly exempt from its cognizance." James Madison, "A Memorial and Remonstrance" (June 1785), in *Religious Freedom: History, Cases, and Other Materials on the Interaction of Religion and Government,* ed. John T. Noonan Jr. and Edward McGlynn Gaffney Jr. (New York: Foundation Press, 2001), 173. See also, more generally, *The Virginia Statute for Religious Freedom: Its Evolution and Consequences in American History,* ed. Merrill D. Peterson and Robert C. Vaughan (New York: Cambridge University Press, 1988).

46. The anthropological contrast between a people's ethos and their worldview is drawn and illustrated in Clifford Geertz, *The Interpretation of Cultures* (New York: Basic Books, 1973).

47. Mark A. Noll, Nathan O. Hatch, and George M. Marsden, *The Search for Christian America* (Westchester, IL: Crossway, 1983). The varied but essentially Christian outlook of America's founding fathers is updated and documented in James H. Hutson, *The Founders on Religion: A Book of Quotations* (Princeton, NJ: Princeton University Press, 2005), and David L. Holmes, *The Faith of the Founding Fathers* (New York: Oxford University Press, 2006).

48. Many of the relevant provisions are catalogued in Brewer, *United States,* 14–29. The consensus and controversy surrounding such provisions are discussed in Noonan and Gaffney, *Religious Freedom,* 201–53.

49. John G. West Jr., *The Politics of Revelation and Reason: Religion and Civic Life in the New Nation* (Lawrence: University Press of Kansas, 1996); Mark A. Noll, *America's God: From Jonathan Edwards to Abraham Lincoln* (New York: Oxford University Press, 2000), 203.

50. Tocqueville, *Democracy in America,* 276, 269. While Tocqueville frequently uses the generic term "religion," he leaves no doubt that in relation

to American democracy, it is Christianity to which he is referring; see, for example, ibid., 40, 265–77, 396.

51. See James A. Marone, *Hellfire Nation: The Politics of Sin in American History* (New Haven, CT: Yale University Press, 2003); C. Howard Hopkins, *The Rise of the Social Gospel in American Protestantism, 1865–1915* (New Haven, CT: Yale University Press, 1940); and Michael Kazin, *A Godly Hero: The Life of William Jennings Bryan* (New York: Knopf, 2006).

52. For essential accounts, see Robert N. Bellah, "Civil Religion in America," in *Religion in America*, ed. William G. McLoughlin and Robert N. Bellah (Boston, MA: Beacon Press, 1968), and Jon Meacham, *American Gospel: God, the Founding Fathers, and the Making of a Nation* (New York: Random House, 2006).

53. For explorations of this theme in our history, see Ernest Lee Tuveson, *Redeemer Nation: The Idea of America's Millennial Role* (Chicago: University of Chicago Press, 1968); Conrad Cherry, *God's New Israel: Religious Interpretations of American Destiny* (Englewood Cliffs, NJ: Prentice-Hall, 1971); and Steven H. Webb, *American Providence: A Nation with a Mission* (New York: Continuum International, 2004).

54. Maurice Isserman and Michael Kazin, *America Divided: The Civil War in the 1960s* (New York: Oxford University Press, 2000), 300. On the 1960s as a "secular awakening," see Hugh Heclo, "The Sixties' False Dawn: Awakenings, Movements and Postmodern Policy-making," in *Integrating the Sixties*, ed. Brian Balogh (University Park: Pennsylvania State University Press, 1996), 34–63.

55. Pew Forum on Religion and Public Life, *Lift Every Voice: A Report on Religion in American Public Life* (Washington, DC: Pew Research Center, 2002); Steve Farkas, Jean Johnson, Tony Foleno, Ann Duffett, and Patrick Foley, *For Goodness' Sake: Why So Many Want Religion to Play a Greater Role in American Life* (New York: Public Agenda Foundation, 2001).

56. All biblical passages are from J. B. Phillips, *The Gospels Translated into Modern English* (New York: Macmillan, 1959).

57. Richard Niebuhr, "The Limitation of Power and Religious Liberty" (1939), *Religion and Values in Public Life* 3 (Winter 1995): 4.

58. Lambert, *Founding Fathers*.

59. These and similar findings are in Christian Smith, *Christian America? What Evangelicals Really Want* (Berkeley: University of California Press, 2000), and Greeley and Hout, *Truth about Conservative Christians*, 90.

# George Washington on Religion's Place in Public Life

## Daniel L. Dreisbach

George Washington, the father of our country, was a man of quiet, personal piety. Moreover, he was a man who gave serious thought to religion's public role in the American political system. His writings and public pronouncements frequently acknowledged God and divine interventions in the affairs of nations. Celebrations of the great American experiment in religious liberty are another familiar theme in his papers.

### Washington's Four Themes

These themes were not reserved for private musings or obscure missives; rather, they were central to his most important public addresses. A third of his first inaugural address, for example, is devoted to a "discussion of the 'providential agency' at work in the founding" of the American republic.[1] "These reflections, arising out of the present crisis," Washington opined, "have forced themselves too strongly on my mind to be suppressed."[2] In approximately two dozen missives written in the following months to diverse religious societies across the country, the new president grappled with the most fundamental and vexing church-state issues. These cordial and often eloquent communications encapsulated Washington's views on the definition and scope of religious liberty, the role of religious citizens in civil society, the prudential relationships between religious communities and the civil state, and religion's contributions to the political order.[3]

This essay considers several lessons we can learn from what George

Washington had to say in his celebrated farewell addresses about religion and the place of religion in American public life.

Note that I said "farewell address*es*."

## WASHINGTON'S FAREWELL ADDRESSES

Washington, in the course of a very public life, made two dramatic exits from the public stage, each accompanied by a valedictory address that captured the essence of his political thought and public philosophy.

First, in 1783 he resigned his commission as commander in chief of the Continental Army, preceded by his circular letter to the states (June 8, 1783), and returned to his beloved Mount Vernon after a nine-year absence. The circular letter, written to the governors of the thirteen newly independent states, was intended as a farewell to military command and public life.

Second, he gracefully declined a third term as president of the United States of America, leaving his final advice to the young republic in a celebrated farewell address (September 19, 1796). After eight years as president, he "bid a final adieu to the walks of public life," retiring in March 1797 to his home on the Potomac River, where he died two years and nine months later.[4]

Although the address of September 1796 is rightly thought of as *the* farewell address, Washington's circular letter of June 1783 deserves to be read alongside it. When read together, these two documents provide a more complete statement of Washington's core political beliefs concerning the new nation than does either piece individually. Washington himself paired the documents when he expressed a hope that the latter address might provoke the same "endulgent reception of my sentiments" that had been given "on a former and not dissimilar occasion."[5] Hence I speak of Washington's farewell address*es*.

In these two most important public statements of his career, Washington expressed not only his own deeply held views but also the prevailing sentiment of the day regarding the role of religion in public life. "Of all the dispositions and habits which lead to political prosperity," he famously declared in the latter message, "Religion and morality are indispensable supports."[6] This felicitous line, perhaps more than any other in American letters, has been used to justify an expansive role for religion in public life. It has become the locus classicus of the notion that religion has an indispensable public role in the American constitutional system. Given this vital role for religion, Washington was understandably attentive to the prudential relationship between religion and the polity in both of his farewell addresses.

## The Circular Letter to the States

Washington expected that his circular letter, written in anticipation of his resignation as commander in chief of the Continental Army, would be his "last official communication" before leaving the public stage for a much longed for "domestic retirement." In it he offered his disinterested political advice and "final blessing" to the country, promising, he said, not to take "any share in public business hereafter." The letter poignantly expressed his sentiments on important subjects respecting the political "tranquility of the United States" and their "mutual felicitation" or happiness.[7] One modern scholar has described the circular letter as the "centerpiece of [Washington's] statesmanship, carrying directly to his countrymen a coherent vision of the unfinished work which lay before them in the aftermath of peace."[8] It revealed much of Washington's mind on what was needed for Americans in 1783 "to establish or ruin their national Character forever"[9] and on the role of religion in establishing that character.

As was typical of Washington's public and private papers, the circular letter was liberally seasoned with expressions of thankfulness to an active Deity—three to "Heaven," and two each to "Providence" and to "God" (a formulation Washington rarely used).[10] Two passages in particular are striking for their unmistakable religious themes.

First, Washington described the propitious moment in human history at which the American "Empire" was founded:

The Citizens of America, placed in the most enviable condition, as the sole Lords and Proprietors of a vast Tract of Continent, comprehending all the various soils and climates of the World, and abounding with all the necessaries and conveniencies of life, are now by the late satisfactory pacification, acknowledged to be possessed of absolute freedom and Independency; They are, from this period, to be considered as the Actors on a most conspicuous Theatre, which seems to be peculiarly designated by Providence for the display of human greatness and felicity; Here, they are not only surrounded with every thing which can contribute to the completion of private and domestic enjoyment, but Heaven has crowned all its other blessings, by giving a fairer oppertunity for political happiness, than any other Nation has ever been favored with. Nothing can illustrate these observations more forcibly, than a recollection of the happy conjuncture of times and circumstances, under which our Republic assumed its rank among the Nations; The foundation of our Empire was not laid in the gloomy age of Ignorance and Superstition, but at an Epocha when the rights of mankind were better understood and more clearly defined, than at any former period, the researches of the human mind, after social happiness, have been carried to a great extent, the Treasures of knowledge, acquired by the labours of Philosophers, Sages and Legislatures, through a long succession of years, are laid open for our use, and their collected wisdom may be happily applied in the Establishment of our forms of Government; the free cultivation of Letters, the unbounded extension of Commerce, the progressive refinement of Manners, the growing liberality of sentiment, *and above all, the pure and benign light of Revelation,* have had a meliorating influence on mankind and increased the blessings of Society. At this auspicious period, the United States came into existence as a Nation, and if their Citizens should not be completely free and happy, the fault will be intirely their own.[11]

Washington reported, in other words, that the foundation of the American empire was laid at a nearly perfect moment in human history, not in some "gloomy age of Ignorance and Superstition" (one might expect this phrase, in the hands of a skeptic or unbeliever, to be the prelude to a jab at traditional, organized religion). Moreover, the cornerstone of that foundation, if you will, was revelation. Washington's audience could not have misunderstood that by "Revelation" he meant the Holy Bible. Significantly, he identified "the pure and benign light of Revelation" as the most important sustainer of American society. Again, he not only expressly mentioned the Bible but also singled it out as having "a meliorating influence on mankind" greater than an understanding of "the rights of mankind," the "researches of the human mind," knowledge and wisdom in the science of politics, an "extension of Commerce," or "liberality of sentiment."

In a second, even more remarkable, passage, Washington counseled his audience on how Americans could secure national happiness:

> I now make it my earnest prayer, that God would have you, and the State over which you preside, in his holy protection, that he would incline the hearts of the Citizens to cultivate a spirit of subordination and obedience to Government, to entertain a brotherly affection and love for one another, for their fellow Citizens of the United States at large, and particularly for their brethren who have served in the Field, and finally, that he would most graciously be pleased to dispose us all, to do Justice, to love mercy, and to demean ourselves with that Charity, humility and pacific temper of mind, which were the Characteristicks of the Divine Author of our blessed Religion, and without an humble imitation of whose example in these things, we can never hope to be a happy Nation.[12]

Washington borrowed a text from the Hebrew scriptures to communicate a vital political message for an American audience. The prophet Micah, more than two millennia before, had counseled the recalcitrant children of Israel on how to restore their covenant relationship with the Lord: "What doth the Lord require of thee, but to do justly, and to love mercy, and to walk humbly with thy God?" (Micah 6:8).[13] Significantly, Washington Christianized this Hebraic text, emphasizing the second element of the Trinity in the place of Micah's "God," to express his hope that God would help Americans in all the states to imitate Christ for the political reason that they should become a "happy Nation." Americans, Washington said, should not just be humble but should demonstrate the humility and charity of Christ. The prayer's placement in the final sentence of what he expected to be his "political last will and testament"[14] underscored the importance Washington placed on religion as an aid to civic virtue and to national happiness. The humble imitation of Christ, Washington counseled, is necessary for national happiness. To be sure, he did not say that belief in Christ is a necessary condition for national happiness, only the imitation of Christ; Christian practice, rather than

Christian faith, is required for that happiness. (In other words, we need not be Christians; rather, we need only act like Christians. This is the exact opposite of how most of us live: we call ourselves Christians, but we do not act like Christians.) And to be equally sure, Washington was speaking of political happiness, not the salvation of individual souls. Again, the stunning climax of what he wanted to be his final public utterance is that the imitation of Christ by American citizens is a necessary condition for their national happiness.

### The Farewell Address

Washington's second and more famous farewell address appeared in David C. Claypoole's *American Daily Advertiser* (Philadelphia) over his signature on September 19, 1796, less than six months before the end of his presidential term and little more than three years before his death.[15] The address's reputation as one of the quintessential statements of American political principle grew steadily from its publication onward until it came to be regarded as one of the nation's most important political documents, and it was often studied alongside the Declaration of Independence and the Constitution itself. Schoolchildren in the nineteenth century and well into the twentieth century studied, and even memorized major passages of, the address as part of a core curriculum in civic education.

The language of this pronouncement, especially two paragraphs on religion, quickly entered the American political vernacular. The phrases on religion were immediately singled out for special recognition. For example, in October 1796, just days after Washington published the address, its language on religion was quoted approvingly by William Loughton Smith in a pamphlet titled *The Pretensions of Thomas Jefferson to the Presidency Examined; and the Charges against John Adams Refuted*.[16] Smith, a staunch defender of Adams (and soon to be President Adams's ambassador to Portugal), used lines from the address to buttress his case against Adams's opponent, Thomas Jefferson, in the upcoming presidential election. Writing anonymously, Smith compared the "virtuous Washington" with the allegedly impious Jefferson. Smith's point of departure was Jefferson's infamous claim in the *Notes on the State of Virginia* that it did him "no injury" for his "neighbour to say there are twenty gods, or no god."[17] Smith retorted,

Which ought we to be the most shocked at, the *levity* or the *impiety* of these remarks? "it does me no injury, if my neighbour is AN ATHEIST, because it does not break my leg!" What? do I receive no injury, as a member of society, if I am surrounded with atheists, with whom I can have no social intercourse, on whom there are none of those religious and sacred ties, which restrain mankind from the perpetration of crimes, and without which ties civil society would soon degenerate into a wretched state of barbarism, and be stained with scenes of turpitude, and with every kind of atrocity? Good God! is this the man the *patriots* have cast their eyes on as successor to the *virtuous Washington,* who, in his farewell address, so warmly and affectionately recommends to his fellow-citizens, the *cultivation of religion.* Contrast with the above frivolous and impious passage [from Jefferson's *Notes on the State of Virginia*] the following dignified advice from that true patriot; "of all the dispositions and habits, which lead to political prosperity, *religion* and *morality* are indispensable supports. In vain would *that man* [he seems to point at Jefferson!] claim the tribute of patriotism, who should labor to subvert these great *pillars* of *human happiness,* these *firmest props* of the *duties of men and citizens.*"[18]

In early 1797, an ecumenical group of Philadelphia clergymen sent a message to the first president. Authored by Ashbel Green, the prominent Presbyterian minister and chaplain of the U.S. House of Representatives (and a future president of the College of New Jersey at Princeton), their statement noted approvingly Washington's lifelong acknowledgment of the aiding hand of divine providence and expressed special approbation for that passage in the farewell address affirming that "religion and morality" are "the firmest basis of social happiness." (Green copied out at length, with minor but revealing editorial revisions, the passage on religion from Washington's "affectionate parting address.")[19] In a reply to the Philadelphia clergymen, Washington reiterated his belief "that *Religion* and *Morality* are the essential pillars of Civil society," deviating only slightly from his formulation in the farewell address. The wording in this letter is, if anything, stronger than that in the farewell address. In the address, "religion and morality" (they invariably went together in the eighteenth century) are "indispensable supports" of "dispositions

and habits," which in turn hold up "political prosperity." In his reply
to the clergy, Washington eliminates the intermediary dispositions and
habits, and describes religion and morality themselves as essential pillars of civil society.[20]

In early January 1800, immediately following Washington's death in
December 1799, the *United States Oracle* newspaper in Portsmouth, New
Hampshire, began running already familiar language from the farewell
address in its masthead. "Of all the dispositions and habits which lead
to political prosperity," the masthead read, "religion and morality are
indispensable supports."

In the famous passage on religion, perhaps his most frequently
quoted, Washington wrote,

> Of all the dispositions and habits which lead to political pros-
> perity, Religion and morality are indispensable supports. In vain
> would that man claim the tribute of Patriotism, who should la-
> bour to subvert these great Pillars of human happiness, these
> firmest props of the duties of Men and citizens. The mere Politi-
> cian, equally with the pious man ought to respect and to cher-
> ish them. A volume could not trace all their connections with
> private and public felicity. Let it simply be asked where is the
> security for property, for reputation, for life, if the sense of reli-
> gious obligation *desert* the oaths, which are the instruments of
> investigation in Courts of Justice? And let us with caution in-
> dulge the supposition, that morality can be maintained without
> religion. Whatever may be conceded to the influence of refined
> education on minds of peculiar structure, reason and experi-
> ence both forbid us to expect that National morality can prevail
> in exclusion of religious principle.
>
> 'Tis substantially true, that virtue or morality is a necessary
> spring of popular government. The rule indeed extends with
> more or less force to every species of free Government. Who
> that is a sincere friend to it, can look with indifference upon at-
> tempts to shake the foundation of the fabric.[21]

Three points stand out to me in this extraordinarily rich passage,
each of which challenges the prevailing orthodoxies of our secular age.
First, and most obvious, is the bold statement that "Religion and mo-

rality are indispensable supports" to "political prosperity." This was a recurring theme in Washington's writings. Years earlier, in a letter to the Synod of the Dutch Reformed Church in North America, he had remarked, "True religion affords to government its surest support."[22] And, again, in his 1797 missive to the clergy of Philadelphia, he affirmed his belief "that *Religion* and *Morality* are the essential pillars of Civil society."[23]

In the farewell address, Washington illustrated religion and morality's expansive reach into civic life. Religion, he suggested, is the pillar of oaths, which are essential to the most basic transactions of a human society.[24] A few paragraphs later he said religion and morality should even shape our foreign affairs: "Observe good faith and justice towds. all Nations. Cultivate peace and harmony with all. Religion and morality enjoin this conduct."[25] Clearly, it was no exaggeration to describe religion and morality as indispensable supports for political prosperity.

Although no one made the argument more famously or succinctly than Washington in his farewell address, he was certainly not alone among the founders in advancing the notion that religion and morality are essential props for good civil government. The literature of the founding era is replete with this assertion. John Adams, for example, wrote in 1776, "Statesmen, my dear Sir, may plan and speculate for liberty, but it is religion and morality alone, which can establish the principles upon which freedom can securely stand. The only foundation of a free constitution is pure virtue."[26] Adams, again, in an 1811 letter to Benjamin Rush, said, "Religion and virtue are the only foundations, not only of republicanism and of all free government, but of social felicity under all governments and in all the combinations of human society."[27] Reverend Samuel Cooper, pastor of Boston's Brattle Street Church, similarly remarked in a sermon preached before Massachusetts's elected officials in October 1780,

> Our civil rulers will remember, that as piety and virtue support the honour and happiness of every community, they are peculiarly requisite in a free government. Virtue is the spirit of a Republic; for where all power is derived from the people, all depends on their good disposition. If they are impious, factious and selfish; if they are abandoned to idleness, dissipation, luxury, and extravagance; if they are lost to the fear of God, and the

love of their country, all is lost. Having got beyond the restraints of a divine authority, they will not brook the control of laws enacted by rulers of their own creating.[28]

On October 11, 1782, the Continental Congress issued a Thanksgiving Day proclamation, authored by the Presbyterian clergyman, president of the College of New Jersey at Princeton, and signer of the Declaration of Independence John Witherspoon, declaring that "the practice of true and undefiled religion . . . is the great foundation of public prosperity and national happiness."[29] Benjamin Rush, another venerated signer of the Declaration of Independence, opined in 1786, "The only foundation for a useful education in a republic is to be laid in RELIGION. Without this, there can be no virtue, and without virtue there can be no liberty, and liberty is the object and life of all republican governments."[30] David Ramsay, physician, delegate to the Continental Congress, and the first major historian of the American Revolution (and son-in-law of John Witherspoon), wrote in 1789, "Remember that there can be no political happiness without liberty; that there can be no liberty without morality, and that there can be no morality without religion."[31] Charles Carroll of Maryland, a Roman Catholic and signer of the Declaration of Independence, similarly remarked, "Without morals a republic cannot subsist any length of time; they therefore who are decrying the Christian religion, whose morality is so sublime & pure . . . are undermining the solid foundation of morals, the best security for the duration of free governments."[32] In an often cited 1799 case, the Maryland General Court opined, "Religion is of general and public concern, and on its support depend, in great measure, the peace and good order of government, the safety and happiness of the people."[33] The interdependence of religion, religious liberty, and political prosperity was acknowledged in the Northwest Ordinance of 1787, one of the organic laws of the United States of America, which declared, "Religion, Morality and knowledge being necessary to good government and the happiness of mankind," "no person" in the territories "demeaning himself in a peaceable and orderly manner shall ever be molested on account of his mode of worship or religious sentiments" (articles 3, 1).

The religious beliefs of the founding fathers ranged from orthodox Christianity to skepticism about Christianity's central transcendent claims. That said, there was a consensus among the founders that religion and morality were "indispensable supports" for civic virtue, social order, and political prosperity. Indeed, this was a virtually unchallenged assumption of the age. The challenge the founders confronted was how to nurture personal responsibility and social order in a political system of self-government. Tyrants used the whip and rod to compel subjects to behave as they desired, but this approach was unacceptable for a free, self-governing people. In response to this challenge, the founders looked to religion (and morality informed by religious values) to provide the internal moral compass that would prompt citizens to behave in a disciplined, controlled manner and, thereby, promote social order and political stability. They looked to religion to inform public ethics, guide the consciences of ordinary citizens and leaders alike, calm the passions, and soften popular prejudices. Thus religion was viewed as an essential component of the founders' system of self-government.

Few, if any, founders doubted that religion—for either genuinely spiritual or strictly utilitarian reasons—was vital to the regime of republican self-government they had created. The question was how best to encourage and promote religion. In this particular passage, Washington was somewhat vague, as were many of his contemporaries, about the affirmative steps he thought the civil state should take to promote the religion he believed was essential to social order and political prosperity. By the late eighteenth century, a declining number of Americans were agitating for the establishment of a state church, such as had existed in the former colonies and in the Old World. Some supported the idea of a general assessment collected by the civil state to sustain churches, clergy, and their ministries. There were many who thought oaths and religious tests for officeholders and voters would ensure that those who exercised political responsibilities embraced the requisite religious, and attendant moral, values. Very few opposed public acknowledgments of God and the community's reliance on the Deity in official state papers and public proclamations, such as proclamations setting aside days for public prayer, fasting, and thanksgiving. Most thought public leaders could and should promote religion through the example of their lives—by being models of moral rectitude, regular church attendance, and acknowledgment of God in their public pronouncements. A few, a very few, thought the civil state could take no action to promote religion and that religion must be encouraged through strictly private, nongovernmental means.

Virtually all the founders agreed that a regime of religious liberty was useful for unleashing religion and its beneficent contribution to society. (Interestingly, many Americans in the late eighteenth century did not view religious liberty as incompatible with what Americans would later regard as manifestations of religious establishment, such as religious oaths and general assessments.) Believing that religion and morality were indispensable to social order and political prosperity, the founders championed religious liberty to foster a vibrant religious culture in which a beneficent religious ethos would inform the public ethic and to promote an environment in which religious and moral spokesmen could speak out boldly, without restraint or inhibition, against corruption and immorality in civic life. Religious liberty was not merely a benevolent grant of the civil state; rather, it reflected the founders' awareness that the very survival of the civil state and a civil society was dependent on a vibrant religious culture, and religious liberty nurtured such a religious culture. In other words, the civil state's respect for religious liberty was an act of self-preservation.

This was not an argument in favor of an established church or compelled allegiance to a particular creed or bishop; rather, the argument advanced was that the political order must acknowledge and nurture basic religious values in order to prosper. Religious liberty created an environment in which religion and a religious culture could flourish and thereby nurture the values that give citizens a capacity for self-government.

Second, Washington discounted the notion, frequently voiced in our secular age, that morality can exist in the absence of religion. He contended, to the contrary, that religion is the wellspring of morality and virtue. He wrote, "Let us with caution indulge the supposition, that morality can be maintained without religion. Whatever may be conceded to the influence of refined education on minds of peculiar structure, reason and experience both forbid us to expect that National morality can prevail in exclusion of religious principle." (In the prevailing political philosophy of the late eighteenth century, reason and experience were widely accepted as two great sources of knowledge.) He seemed to concede that, for rare individuals (perhaps he had Jefferson in mind), "the influence of refined education on minds of peculiar structure" may account for a morality uninformed by religion;[34] however, he was adamant that "reason and experience" forbade us, especially in a large republic such as the United States, from relying on this as sufficient to sustain the popular morality essential to foster the civic virtue vital for social order and political prosperity.[35]

(What would Washington make of public education today that, when it professes any interest in nurturing morality, insists on imparting a vision of morality consciously stripped of religion's influences? Would he even acknowledge a morality uninformed by religious values? Based on these lines, I suspect he would doubt that such instruction would be effectual in sustaining social order and political prosperity.)

Third, once it is conceded that religion is indispensable to civic virtue, social order, and political prosperity, it then follows that the enemy of true religion (or one who would undermine the public role of religion) is a danger to society. In that vein, Washington audaciously challenged the patriotism of those in society who sought to undermine or destroy religion's public role. In the sentence immediately following his famous pronouncement that "Religion and morality are indispensable supports" to "political prosperity," he warned (in a sentence often omitted in modern quotations of this passage), "In vain would that man claim the tribute of Patriotism, who should labour to subvert these great Pillars of human happiness, these firmest props of the duties of Men and citizens." Washington came perilously close to calling someone who undermines or subverts religion and morality in our political society a traitor to the country. (Wags up and down the Atlantic seaboard soon wondered aloud whether the phrase "that man" was a generic reference or whether Washington had someone specific in mind. Among those concluding it was the latter, a consensus was soon reached that "that man" was a veiled reference to none other than Jefferson.[36] This conclusion is lent credence by the fact that the line was suggested to Washington by Alexander Hamilton, Jefferson's political foe.[37]) Washington returned to this theme in the next paragraph, albeit in somewhat muted terms. Having restated "that virtue or morality is a necessary spring of popular government," he warned, "Who that is a sincere friend to it [popular, free government], can look with indifference upon attempts to shake the foundation of the fabric." There is little doubt, given the context, that Washington regarded religion and morality to be "the foundation of the fabric" of free governments, and we are inattentive to their preservation at the peril of social order and political prosperity. (One easily imagines the scorn the mainstream media would heap on Washington if he were giving such speeches today.)

Washington was not alone in reaching this conclusion. John Witherspoon said, "That he is the best friend to American liberty, who is most sincere and active in promoting true and undefiled religion, and who sets himself with the greatest firmness to bear down profanity and immorality of every kind. Whoever is an avowed enemy to God, I scruple not to call him an enemy to his country."[38] These are strong words, indeed, that remind us of religion's vital place and role in the founders' design for our constitutional republic.

## REVISITING WASHINGTON'S REPUTATION

Although George Washington remains much loved in the hearts of his countrymen, there is an unfortunate tendency, especially among intellectual elites, to dismiss him as an intellectual lightweight. He is admired for his character and his heart, but not for his intellect and his head.

His farewell addresses, however, should put to rest false reports that he was not a serious thinker. His insightful analysis of religion's vital role in the polity, especially, demonstrates the mind of a trenchant thinker. His writings reveal a man acquainted with the Bible who had a theologically informed understanding of the nature of God, man, liberty, and political authority. He appropriately reminded Americans of religion's vital role in their constitutional system. We ignore at our peril the lessons he taught in his farewell addresses.

## NOTES

1. Richard Brookhiser, *Founding Father: Rediscovering George Washington* (New York: Free Press, 1996), 146. No inaugural address, until Lincoln's second in 1865, devoted as much to religious themes as Washington's first. Paul F. Boller Jr., *Presidential Inaugurations* (New York: Harcourt, 2001), 18.

2. "Final Version [of Washington's First Inaugural Address]" (April 30, 1789), in *The Papers of George Washington, Presidential Series*, ed. Dorothy Twohig (Charlottesville: University Press of Virginia, 1987–2007), 2:174.

3. See Daniel L. Dreisbach and Jeffry Hays Morrison, "George Washington and American Public Religion" (paper presented at the annual meeting of the American Political Science Association, Washington, DC, September 3, 2000).

4. George Washington to Marquis de Lafayette, October 8, 1797, in *The Writings of George Washington*, ed. John C. Fitzpatrick (Washington, DC: U.S. Government Printing Office, 1931–1940), 36:41.

5. George Washington, farewell address, September 19, 1796, in *Writings of George Washington*, 35:218.

6. Ibid., 229.

7. George Washington, circular letter to the states, June 8, 1783, in *Writings of George Washington*, 26:484, 483, 484, 486, 484.

8. *George Washington: A Collection*, ed. W. B. Allen (Indianapolis: Liberty Classics, 1988), 226.

9. Washington, circular letter, 486.

10. For the references to "Heaven," see ibid., 484, 485, 490; to "Providence," see ibid., 484, 485; and to "God," see ibid., 491, 496.

11. Ibid., 484–85 (emphasis added).

12. Ibid., 496.

13. This quotation is from the Authorized (King James) Version, the English translation most frequently used in the American founding era.

14. Brookhiser, *Founding Father*, 148.

15. See *Writings of George Washington*, 35:214–15n84.

16. See generally George C. Rogers Jr., *Evolution of a Federalist: William Loughton Smith of Charleston (1758–1812)* (Columbia: University of South Carolina Press, 1962), 292.

17. Thomas Jefferson, *Notes on the State of Virginia*, query 17, in *Thomas Jefferson: Writings*, ed. Merrill D. Peterson (New York: Library of America, 1984), 285.

18. [William Loughton Smith], *The Pretensions of Thomas Jefferson to the Presidency Examined; and the Charges against John Adams Refuted*, part 1 (Philadelphia, 1796), 37–38. Governor DeWitt Clinton of New York claimed four years later, during the presidential campaign of 1800, that the author of this pamphlet was the first to disseminate the calumny that "Mr. Jefferson is a *deist*, if not an *atheist*." Grotius [DeWitt Clinton], *A Vindication of Thomas Jefferson; against the Charges in a Pamphlet Entitled, "Serious Considerations," &c.* (New York: Denniston, 1800), 3–4n. In fact, the charge had been leveled against Jefferson in Virginia years earlier. See Thomas E. Buckley, "Reflections on a Wall," *William and Mary Quarterly*, 3rd ser., 56 (1999): 795.

19. [Ashbel Green], address of the clergy of different denominations residing in and near the city of Philadelphia (March 1797), in *Memoirs, Correspondence and Miscellanies, from the Papers of Thomas Jefferson*, edited by Thomas Jefferson Randolph; *Christian Advocate* (Philadelphia), June 1830, 305–6; *The Life of Ashbel Green*, ed. Joseph H. Jones (New York: Carter, 1849), 269, 614–15.

20. *Life of Ashbel Green*, 614–15; George Washington to the clergy of different denominations residing in and near the city of Philadelphia, March 3, 1797, in *Writings of George Washington*, 35:416.

21. Washington, farewell address, 229–30.

22. George Washington to the Synod of the Dutch Reformed Church in North America, October 1789, in *Writings of George Washington*, 30:432n33; *Papers of George Washington*, 4:264.

23. Washington to the clergy, 416.

24. Washington wrote, "Let it simply be asked where is the security for property, for reputation, for life, if the sense of religious obligation *desert* the oaths, which are the instruments of investigation in Courts of Justice?" His question reflected the then prevailing view that oath taking was an essentially religious act. The standard definition was repeated in the debates in the state ratifying conventions on Article VI of the U.S. Constitution. Judge James Iredell, for example, reminded fellow delegates in the North Carolina convention that "according to the modern definition of an oath, it is considered a 'solemn appeal to the Supreme Being, for the truth of what is said, by a person who believes in the existence of a Supreme Being and in a future state of rewards and punishments, according to that form which will bind his conscience most.'" Speech of James Iredell (July 30, 1788), in *The Debates in the Several State Conventions on the Adoption of the Federal Constitution*, 2nd ed., ed. Jonathan Elliot (Philadelphia: Lippincott, 1836), 4:196. John Witherspoon said, "An oath is an appeal to God, the searcher of hearts, for the truth of what we say, and always expresses or supposes an imprecation of his judgment upon us, if we prevaricate. An oath therefore implies a belief in God, and his Providence, and indeed is an act of worship, and so accounted in Scripture, as in that expression, *Thou shalt fear the Lord thy God, and shalt swear by his name* [Deuteronomy 6:13]." John Witherspoon, "Of Oaths and Vows," in *Lectures on Moral Philosophy*, ed. Varnum Lansing Collins (Princeton, NJ: Princeton University Press, 1912), 130. See also John Adams to the officers of the First Brigade of the Third Division of the Militia of Massachusetts, October 11, 1798, in *The Works of John Adams*, ed. Charles Francis Adams (Boston: Little, Brown, 1850–1856), 9:229. ("Oaths in this country are as yet universally considered as sacred obligations.")

Washington, like John Locke, feared that the oath of a man unleashed from a belief in and fear of God would be meaningless. In his *Letter Concerning Toleration*, Locke gave his reason for not tolerating atheists: "Lastly, those are not all to be tolerated who deny the being of God. Promises, covenants, and oaths, which are the bonds of human society, can have no hold upon an atheist. The taking away of God, though but even in thought, dissolves all; besides also, those that by their atheism undermine and destroy all religion, can have no pretence of religion whereupon to challenge the privilege of toleration." John Locke, *Treatise of Civil Government and A Letter Concerning Toleration*, ed. Charles L. Sherman (New York: Appleton-Century, 1937), 212–13. In short, there is no security (or trust) in the atheist's oath because the fear of divine sanction has no hold on the atheist. What good is an agreement if you cannot trust the word of the man with whom you are entering into it? How does a society survive if there is no trust in the basic agreements of social and economic transactions? Such agreements, contracts, and promises are essential to human society.

25. Washington, farewell address, 231.

26. John Adams to Zabdiel Adams, June 21, 1776, in *Works of John Adams*, 9:401.

27. John Adams to Benjamin Rush, August 28, 1811, in *Works of John Adams*, 9:636.

28. Samuel Cooper, *A Sermon Preached before His Excellency John Hancock, Esq; Governour, the Honourable the Senate, and House of Representatives of the Commonwealth of Massachusetts, October 25, 1780; Being the Day of the Commencement of the Constitution, and Inauguration of the New Government* (Boston: Fleet and Gill, 1780), 37.

29. Thanksgiving Day proclamation (October 11, 1782), in *Journals of the Continental Congress, 1774–1789*, ed. Worthington C. Ford et al. (Washington, DC: U.S. Government Printing Office, 1904–1937), 23:647. See also Jeffry H. Morrison, *John Witherspoon and the Founding of the American Republic* (Notre Dame, IN: University of Notre Dame Press, 2005), 21.

30. Benjamin Rush, "Thoughts upon the Mode of Education Proper in a Republic" (1786), in *American Political Writing during the Founding Era, 1760–1805*, ed. Charles S. Hyneman and Donald S. Lutz (Indianapolis: Liberty Press, 1983), 1:681.

31. David Ramsay, *The History of the American Revolution* (London, 1790), 2:356.

32. Charles Carroll to James McHenry, November 4, 1800, in Bernard C. Steiner, *The Life and Correspondence of James McHenry* (Cleveland: Burrows, 1907), 475.

33. *Runkel v. Winemiller*, 4 Harris and McHenry, 429, 450 (Gen. Ct. Oct. Term 1799).

34. Michael and Jana Novak describe the clause as a "disguised dig at Jefferson" for his presumed belief that God is not the essential foundation for a moral life. Michael Novak and Jana Novak, *Washington's God: Religion, Liberty, and the Father of Our Country* (New York: Basic Books, 2006), 43.

35. See Peter R. Henriques, *Realistic Visionary: A Portrait of George Washington* (Charlottesville: University of Virginia Press, 2006), 182–83. ("Interestingly, Washington refused in his Address to place secular humanists beyond the pale of the moral life. He acknowledged that the 'influence of refined education on minds of peculiar structure' might make a moral life unsupported by religion possible for select individuals, but a nation as a whole needed religion.")

36. In *The Pretensions of Thomas Jefferson to the Presidency Examined*, for

example, Smith strongly implied that Washington accused Jefferson of being "that man" who tried to subvert the great pillar of religion.

37. See "Hamilton's Original Major Draft for an Address Called 'Copy Considerably Amended,'" in *Washington's Farewell Address*, ed. Victor Hugo Paltsits (New York: New York Public Library, 1935), 192.

38. John Witherspoon, "The Dominion of Providence over the Passions of Men: A Sermon Preached at Princeton, on the 17th of May, 1776," in *Political Sermons of the American Founding Era, 1730–1805*, ed. Ellis Sandoz (Indianapolis: Liberty Press, 1991), 554.

# VIRGINIA AND THE ORIGINS OF RELIGIOUS LIBERTY

## Michael Novak

Just before his twenty-fifth birthday, James Madison heard troubling news about an event that occurred not far from where he lived in central Virginia. A group of Baptists had gathered on a hillside—like a natural stadium—when a posse of Anglicans rode up, pulled the minister from the pulpit, strung him up and had him lashed.

### ANGLICANS VERSUS BAPTISTS

There were during this period somewhere between thirty-four and fifty Baptist ministers in jail for preaching the gospel without a license from the state. But their argument was, "We don't need a license from the state. Our license comes from God."

Touched by these stories, Madison came to the defense of the Baptists and eagerly added his contribution to the Declaration of Rights of 1776, particularly the part on religious liberty that Thomas Jefferson said is a prominent part of that declaration.

It happened this way. Patrick Henry, the governor of Virginia, reassigned Madison to a district he didn't know very well, where between one-half and one-third of the 2,500 voters were Baptists. These Baptists came to Madison and said, "We want a Bill of Rights; otherwise no votes from us." Madison responded, "You don't need a Bill of Rights. All your rights are maintained in the Constitution. If you start writing them down, people will think that the only rights you have are the ones written down and the others belong to the states." They replied, in essence, "You understand that. We understand that. But we don't trust the Anglicans to understand that. We want it written down."

And this is why when Madison went back to the Congress, the first order of business politically for him was to argue through the Bill of Rights. The role of the Baptists of Virginia in bringing about the Bill of Rights is woefully overlooked in American history. Virginia led the way in articulating the grounds of religious liberty, as revealed by a couple of Virginia's founding documents.

## THE DECLARATION OF RIGHTS OF 1776

Article 16 of the Declaration of Rights of 1776 (George Mason's document, with some help from James Madison) mentions "that religion, or the duty which we owe to our Creator." That definition of religion is used repeatedly in the founding period, persisting even in Daniel Webster's 1828 dictionary.

"Religion," the declaration says, "that is the duty which we owe to our Creator and the manner of discharging it, can be directed only by reason and conviction, not by force or violence." Now understand the power of that in the contemporary world, and understand the peculiar God it is who cares about what happens in our conscience—not what we do externally only but what goes on in our hearts. And it's not our hearts, exactly; it's our minds, because we're moved to recognize these duties by reason and conviction.

What kind of a God is this, present in everything and in every act of reason? As Thomas Aquinas said, "You cannot *not* know God." Once you begin to reason, you are invoking not only the source of that reason but also its power to grasp the intelligibility of things around you. This notion of God that was held in Virginia and, as Daniel Webster shows, universally in the founding period is not the God of will—this is what William of Ockham implied to change the direction of Western philosophy, but it's also what the Muslim philosophers held: that God is primarily will, that he can will whatever he wants with no regard to reason. It's the power of the will that matters.

Not so this God. It's the power of reason that matters. I'm not a student of all the world religions, except amateurishly, but this is not, I think, the god of Hinduism and not the god of Buddhism, and there's some doubt as to whether one needs to believe in a god to be a Buddhist. I don't think there's any god known to human beings except the Jewish-Christian God who fulfills the requirements of this definition.

Now I hasten to say that this is a universal God. He's the Creator of all. And it happened that, not in this debate but a few years later, with Jefferson's statute for religious liberty, pushed through by Madison while Jefferson was abroad, reference was made to the divine Author of our religion and there was a motion in the Virginia assembly to specify "Jesus Christ, the Divine Author of our Religion" because it talks immediately about meekness, charity, humility, and so forth. That was voted down, as Jefferson said, to mark the fact that this reference to the divine Author of our religion is meant to include within its sweep Hindus, "Mohammedans," and "infidels" of every stripe.

This is a conscious reflection of the people of Virginia, at least through their representatives. In essence, they are saying, "We know who the divine Author of our religion is, but it is not necessary to recognize him to enjoy the rights. The rights that we are about to declare do not belong to us only, but belong to all human beings." It is a wonderfully self-denying ordinance. It is a product of Christian philosophy, but its reach is universal, and nothing in it applies only to Christians if you follow the logic of these documents.

But let me go on. "And therefore all men are equally entitled to the free exercise of religion, according to the dictates of conscience." There it is again. Conscience. "And it is the mutual duty of all to practise Christian forbearance, love, and charity toward each other."

## MADISON'S MEMORIAL REMONSTRANCE OF 1785

Let me jump ahead to Madison's memorial remonstrance of 1785. This was what irritated Patrick Henry. I am not going to give the whole story, but let me go to his words. Madison was opposing with this circular letter a move by Henry to tax everybody in Virginia to pay the salaries of clergymen. This was of practical importance because the clergymen were most of the teachers in the early commonwealth, not just Virginia, and you need to maintain the teachers.

Now if you didn't believe in paying taxes, you could exempt yourself. Churches that didn't believe in it—the Quakers and others who didn't want any federal support—they didn't need to pay. Henry tried to have opt-outs.

Madison thought this was not good enough. His memorial remonstrance illustrates how he came to his notion of rights: "Because we hold it for a fundamental and undeniable truth, 'that religion or the duty which we owe to our creator and the manner of discharging it, can be directed only by reason and conviction, not by force or violence.' [We've heard that before, and he cites it in the text. So the same definition of religion as religion of conscience is at the background of this.] The Religion then of every man must be left to the conviction and conscience of every man, and it is the right of every man to exercise it as these may dictate." Now he wanted to back up that last sentence. How do you get the right? And he proceeded, "This right is in its nature an unalienable right. It is unalienable, because the opinions of men, depending only on the evidence contemplated by their own minds cannot follow the dictates of other men." It's the root of our equality and the root of our independence—personal independence. We go by the evidence of our own mind. And by the way, we need to respect this; this comes up in other places. People come, even to the recognition of God, at different times of their lives, and you must wait until the evidence prompts their minds: nothing else will do. And please notice this reverence for conscience and conviction, reason, and evidence.

"It is unalienable also, because what is here a right towards men is a duty to the Creator." See how he's arguing? Religion, or the duty that creatures owe to their Creator. Right back to duty. "It is the duty of every man to render to the Creator such homage and such only as he deems to be acceptable to him." We have a duty, and "this duty is precedent both in order of time and in degree of obligation to the claims of Civil Society." Before there's a civil society, we have this duty. It is precedent even to the family: neither mother, nor father, nor brother, nor sister can take over your responsibility for your own decision.

"Before any man can be considered a member of Civil Society, he must be considered as a subject of the Gouvernor of Universe." Religion is a duty to the Creator. Now if you have the duty, you must also have the right. There's no sense in your having a duty to the Creator unless you have the right to exercise it, according to conscience. And this is how the founders came to rights.

## INALIENABLE RIGHTS

Now, I've mentioned to you why these rights are inalienable: First, they are dependent on evidence only, of your own mind and nobody else's.

Second, they are inalienable because they are rooted in a duty to the Creator. Nobody can get in the way of your duty to your Creator. No one has the authority to do that. This right is inalienable. It is between you and God. Now this doesn't mean that we are all individuals. This can be always the same, in a community, going through the same thing. But it's a peculiar community in that it recognizes the rights of the person and it has a notion of a person that a person is not fulfilled until he or she also serves the common good, the public good. So it's a most beautiful and intricate relationship between the person and the community. And if I may, that's another point where the doctrine of the Trinity has enormous political significance. The notion of the person and the notion of community of the person. That is not made explicit. These people are not theologians. They are practical statesmen and lawyers. I conclude with this story.

## THOMAS JEFFERSON AND THE CHRISTIAN FAITH

Thomas Jefferson, with a red prayer book under his arm, was walking from the White House to the Capitol one day to attend the church service that was held there. A man along the way asked him, "Mr. Jefferson, where are you going?" "To church, sir!" "But Mr. Jefferson, you don't believe a word of it!" Now Jefferson didn't deny that. But his response was, and I'm paraphrasing, "Sir! The Christian religion is the most important and precious support of republican government and I mean to bring to it the full force of the magistracy as long as I am president."

That vignette is particularly acute for the two points we've been making: On the one hand, some persons may or may not need religion. But on the other hand, Jefferson argued that religion—he thought particularly the Christian religion, meaning Christian and Jewish—is peculiarly the religion of freedom and the support of republican government. And you should bring the support of government, not the oppressions of government, not the infringements on liberty of government, but the support of government to the strengthening of this fundamental pillar.

# Evangelical Political Models

## James Fenimore Cooper or William Wilberforce?

*Marvin Olasky*

The future of American politics clearly includes religion. The real question is, Which religion? A religion that describes the reality of the human condition, or a religion based on utopian hopes and claims?

I can say confidently that the future of American politics includes religion because the past is prologue: American politics always has included religion. I'd like, first, to address briefly that past; second, to spotlight a politician who did immense good by bringing to bear his religious beliefs on a crucial issue; third, to show how he contrasted reality and utopia, and how we should do the same; and fourth, how we should react to the new respect that religion is receiving.

### RELIGION'S IMPACT ON AMERICAN POLITICS

Without the Great Awakening in the 1730s and the political thinking it generated, we would have had no American Revolution a generation later. Without the Second Awakening of the early nineteenth century and the abolitionist movement that it spawned, we would not have seen the end of slavery a generation later. Without the courage of many pastors and of groups like the Southern Christian Leadership Conference, we would not have seen the civil rights movement of the 1950s and the 1960s. Without the pro-life movement that began in the 1970s, we would not have seen many Democrats vote for Ronald Reagan in the 1980s, and the resultant victorious conclusion of the cold war. Without the massive evangelical vote in his favor, George W. Bush would not have been elected and reelected. Without some neutralization of that vote, the Democrats would not have gained a Congressional majority in 2006 and will not be able to win the presidency in 2008.

This next campaign will force us to address the question not of whether religion has a future in American politics, but which religion: a religion of reality or a religion of panaceas? This is a subject so serious that I need to approach it through a joke, one involving a debate among three engineers as to the occupation of the Creator.

The first says, "God is a mechanical engineer. Look at the beauty with which our joints are constructed. Only a mechanical engineer could put together our bodies with such flair."

The second counters, "No, God is clearly an electrical engineer. Consider the elegant use of electrical charges by the millions of neurons in our brains. This is the handiwork of an electrical engineer."

The third says, "You're both wrong. God is obviously a civil engineer. Who else would put a toxic waste pipeline right through a recreational area?"

Recreational areas are always next to toxic waste pipelines. The heavens, as well as tender mercies such as marriage, declare the glory of God, but the streets declare the sinfulness of man. In both domestic and foreign policy, Americans have debated for decades whether to adhere to the religion of panaceas or the religion of reality.

For example, regarding poverty fighting, believers in the religion of panaceas state that poor people everywhere want to do the right thing, so solving the poverty problem is like solving a math problem: move dollars from $x$ to $y$ and the job is done. Believers in the religion of reality, though, see poverty as a complex tangle of spiritual, psychological, political, social, historical, institutional, and technological factors.

Regarding foreign policy, those who subscribe to the religion of panaceas believe that leaders and nations essentially want peace, so if only we clear up misunderstandings and sign treaties or arms control agreements, all will be well. Adherents to the religion of reality, though, understand that leaders and people generally often covet their neighbors' homes, industries, and wealth, and if they can grab such by force they often will. Those who want peace need to stop aggression and terrorism, by force if necessary.

Those with faith in panaceas seem to me much like the group of incompetent Indians described in the novels of James Fenimore Cooper two centuries ago. Mark Twain wonderfully pointed out their problems in his essay "Fenimore Cooper's Literary Offenses": a Cooper Indian plans to jump onto a slow-moving barge and waits so long that he lands in the water. The next Indian ponders the miss and then jumps, landing even farther behind the boat. The next Indian waits, jumps, and of course misses by even more.

That's the history of political panaceas. They don't work, and panacea adherents—perhaps we could call them Cooper liberals—don't learn. They always want to take something complicated and say they've found the solution. They don't take into account the sewage pipes.

## WILLIAM WILBERFORCE AND RELIGION'S POSITIVE IMPACT

Contrast that religion with the religion of reality. William Wilberforce, the great British parliamentarian who lived at the same time as Cooper, criticized those who keep jumping for the barge as it gets farther away. Wilberforce wrote of those who "either overlook or deny the corruption and weakness of human nature. They acknowledge there is, and always had been, a great deal of vice and wickedness, [but they] talk of frailty and infirmity, of petty transgressions, of occasional failings, and of accidental incidents. [They] speak of man as a being who is naturally pure. He is inclined to virtue."

Wilberforce contrasted that view with "the humiliating language of true Christianity. From it we learn that man is an apostate creature. He has fallen from his high, original state. . . . He is indisposed toward the good, and disposed towards evil. . . . He is tainted with sin, not slightly and superficially, but radically, and to the very core of his being. Even though it may be humiliating to acknowledge these things, still this is the biblical account of man."

You've probably guessed by now that Wilberforce is the political leader I want to spotlight. That's because Cooper liberals keep jumping into the river, but Wilberforce kept running along the bank of the river for two decades—his fight to end the British slave trade lasted that long. He lost and lost and lost again, but on February 23, 1807, the debate in the House of Commons went in his favor. One member of Parliament contrasted Napoleon and Wilberforce, one who brought bloodshed and one who had "preserved so many millions of his fellow creatures." The other MPs stood and gave three hurrahs while Wilberforce bowed his head and wept at the culmination of so many years of struggle. The Commons then voted 283 to 16 to abolish the trade.

You may have heard about this in 2007, when two hundredth anniversary memories kicked in. In a BBC New Year's Day broadcast, Archbishop of Canterbury Rowan Williams praised Wilberforce and his colleagues. Washington DC now has a Wilberforce Forum, under Chuck Colson's auspices, and that organization, with the Trinity Forum, has cosponsored Wilberforce Weekends. The British Labour Party planned to spend £20 million for two hundredth anniversary celebrations.

Furthermore, a major film biography of Wilberforce, *Amazing Grace*, ran in theaters across the United States in 2007; a documentary titled *The Better Hour: William Wilberforce, a Man of Character Who Changed the World* was broadcast in the United States and the United Kingdom; and John Templeton funded a U.S. national essay contest for school kids.

## REALISTIC AND UTOPIAN RELIGION

A century and a half ago, Frederick Douglass praised Wilberforce's effort "that finally thawed the British heart into sympathy for the slave, and moved the strong arm of government in mercy to put an end to this bondage. Let no American, especially no colored American, withhold generous recognition of this stupendous achievement—a triumph of right over wrong, of good over evil, and a victory for the whole human race." Abraham Lincoln in 1858 called Wilberforce a person whom "every school boy knew." That's clearly not the case today. I hope the movie, documentary, and essay contest will restore Wilberforce to his rightful place in history, because he has much to teach everyone, including modern conservatives, about the intersection of religion and politics.

First, when Wilberforce went through a spiritual crisis that led to his becoming a Christian in 1785, at age twenty-six, his first impulse was to drop out of politics and abandon his non-Christian acquaintances. Providentially, John Newton, the former slave ship captain and author of the hymn "Amazing Grace," advised him to stay in Parliament and keep up his connections. Another counselor, minister Thomas Scott, gave the same advice, and later speculated that had Wilberforce dropped out, "the slave trade might have been continued to future generations."

But Wilberforce did not drop out. He told his mother that it "would merit no better name than desertion . . . if I were thus to fly from the post where Providence has placed me. . . . I am serving God best when from proper motives I am most actively engaged" in public life.

Second, Wilberforce—like other Christian politicians and writers—dealt throughout his career with those who believed that Christians in politics should stay away from dirty business and engage only in high-minded talk. Newton understood that critique and wrote to Wilberforce,

> You meet with many things which weary and disgust you [but] they are inseparably connected with your path of duty. . . . [Your calling] exposes you to many impertinences from which you would gladly be exempted, but if, upon the whole, you are thereby instrumental in promoting the cause of God and the public good, you will have no reason [for] regret. . . .
>
> You are not only a representative for Yorkshire, you have the far greater honour of being a representative for the Lord, in a place where many know Him not, and an opportunity of showing them what are the genuine fruits of that religion which you are known to profess. . . . The great point for our comfort in life is to have a well-grounded persuasion that we are where, all things considered, we ought to be. Then it is no great matter whether we are in public or in private life, in a city or a village, in a palace or a cottage.

Third, Wilberforce had to deal with many kinds of disappointment—including the agonizing one that many of his initially reform-minded colleagues gave in to political lures. Biographer Kevin Belmonte writes that Wilberforce was initially one of forty MPs called "the independents" who covenanted "not to accept a plum appointment to political office, a government pension, or the offer of hereditary peerage." And yet as years went by, only Wilberforce and one other stuck to that resolution. (Sounds like the Republican revolutionaries of 1994.)

Wilberforce also had to face sharp attacks. James Boswell, famed now for his biography of Samuel Johnson, wrote of Wilberforce,

> I hate your little wittling sneer,
> Your pert and self-sufficient leer,
>
> . . . . . . . . . . . . . . . . .
>
> . . . begone, for shame,
> Thou dwarf, with a big-sounding name.

Other famous writers—Lord Byron, William Cobbett, Henry Hazlitt—also wrote hit pieces. Early in his career Wilberforce responded in kind, but after he became a Christian he struggled with his temper and finally buried it, along with invective.

Fourth, many observers concentrated on Wilberforce's humility. Joseph Gurney, who visited the aged leader in 1833, noted that he did not speak of his own accomplishments but stated with "feeling and emphasis" that his only hope was in the message of the prayer "God be merciful to me a sinner." Gurney later wrote, "If Wilberforce, who had been labouring for these fifty years in the cause of virtue, religion, and humanity, could feel himself to be a poor criminal, with no hope of happiness, except through the pardoning love of God in Christ Jesus, surely we all ought to be bowed down and broken under similar feelings."

That humility helped Wilberforce to retain his composure when under attack. Once he received a letter with only three words on it, "Thou vile hypocrite," and reflected that "I should have been thirty or forty years in public life to little purpose, if this discomposed me."

Fifth, he was a compassionate conservative. Thomas Jefferson had emphasized "the pursuit of happiness" on an individual basis, but Wilberforce proposed that Christians promote the happiness of others (and in that way also promote their own). He emphasized voluntarism rather than government fiat, and even his use of government to abolish first the slave trade and then slavery itself in the British Empire reflected a willingness to trade rather than demand.

The British abolition of slavery, unlike the American one, came with some compensation for slaveholders. Wilberforce died in 1833 soon after receiving word that the House of Commons would surely pass a bill to abolish slavery throughout the British empire—and to do it peacefully, by setting aside funds to purchase the freedom of about eight hundred thousand slaves in the British colonies. Wilberforce said, "Thank God that I should have lived to witness a day in which England is willing to give 20 million pounds for the Abolition of Slavery."

Sixth, he showed that the messenger doesn't have to be a matinee idol if his message is strong. Wilberforce's appearance may have been like that of Jesus and Paul: He was only five feet tall, and none of his features were handsome, according to biographer Robert Furneaux, "but they had a liveliness which was attractive. His movements were very fast and he was seldom still. His conversation followed the same pattern. He would pick up an idea very quickly, play with it, and turn to another . . . with a speed and pleasure which entranced his listeners. . . . His mind was so quick that his contemporaries found it difficult to gauge his intellectual powers."

Crucially, Wilberforce reasoned with opponents, and did not rant at them.

He emphasized teaching about Christianity but not imposing it—he wanted to commend, not command. And that sensibility worked: soon after Wilberforce's death, one of his contemporaries, James Mackintosh, said that he had conferred on the world "the encouraging example that the exertions of virtue may be crowned by such splendid success."

But that was then; this is now. Will today's evangelical exertions—to help the people of Darfur, to help the victims of the new international slave trade, to help the domestic poor, to save the lives of unborn children—be crowned with success? We can hope, pray, and work together.

Mutual exhortation and encouragement can be useful in this regard. For example, members and staffers of the state legislature in Alaska have a Clapham Fellowship, named after the British group Wilberforce headed. One fellowship member, Wes Keller, wrote me that the group's fundamental intent "is captured in Hebrews 3:13 . . . 'so that we might not be hardened by the deceitfulness of sin.' Typically we have between 25 and 30 Christians gather each week and spend a bit of time identifying the evidences of Jesus' action and authority in our midst, prayer, and Bible study. Fellowship gives us comfort as we see others who are primarily focused on a personal relationship with our Friend and King, Jesus. . . . It is somehow easier to believe and remember when we have the encouragement of our brothers and sisters."

## A NEW GREAT RESPECTING

Is there an awakening in America? Maybe, yet overall I suspect that we are in not a new Great Awakening but a new Great Respecting. Awakenings are dramatic changes in religious belief. Respectings are appreciations of the power of religious belief. When George Whitefield, John Wesley, and others preached in the 1730s and tens of thousands turned to Christ, that was a Great Awakening. When politicians in the 1950s told constituents to attend "the church or synagogue of your choice" because "the family that prays together stays together," that was a Great Respecting.

Today, when Democratic presidential candidates and legislative leaders hire religious outreach advisers and take less extreme positions on abortion, that is also a Great Respecting. I'm not knocking the change: Many problems have arisen from disrespecting the power of religion. Not only politicians but foreign policy planners and Supreme Court justices have erred in that way.

But, as a Christian, I cannot be satisfied with a Great Respecting. William Wilberforce was not. What is the future of the Christian religion in American politics? Only God knows, but Christians can be all they can be by following Wilberforce's example. It's easy for evangelicals, sinners as are we all, to blame others when things go wrong. Wilberforce, though, wrote that the emphasis should be how "true Christians, with becoming earnestness, [should strive] to silence the vain scorn of ignorant objections. Let them boldly assert the cause of Christ in an age when so many who bear the name of Christian are ashamed of Him."

He continued, "Let them be active, useful, and generous toward others. Let them show moderation and self-denial themselves. Let them be ashamed of idleness. When blessed with wealth, let them withdraw from the competition of vanity and be modest, retiring from ostentation, and not be the slaves of fashion." At a time when Britain faced the Terror of Napoleon, Wilberforce concluded that "my own solid hopes for the well-being of my country depend, not so much on her navies and armies . . . as on the persuasion that she still contains many who love and obey the Gospel of Christ. I believe that their prayers may yet prevail."

And so do I.

# LEFT TURN?

## Evangelicals and the Future of
## the Religious Right

### *D. G. Hart*

Imagine yourself at a small academic seminar, listening to the presentation of two political scientists on the influence of faith on American electoral politics. Each man happens to teach at a different evangelical college and is genuinely excited by their project's findings, though how they manifest excitement differs according to the shades of northern European ethnicity. Their argument—no, their evidence—proves that religion was decisive in the most recent presidential contest. By now this sort of analysis of exit polls that divides Americans into red and blue has become commonplace. But a decade ago, when these evangelical political scientists were presenting their findings, the argument about the importance of religion for deciding elections was still in search of widespread acceptance, especially since the womanizing and truth-trimming Bill Clinton was able surprisingly to garner a sizeable part of the God vote.

After listening to the presentation and looking at the charts and graphs, one participant in this seminar questioned the validity of the findings. He knew both political scientists well enough to be familiar with their political party affiliations. The one with Scandinavian American roots was a staunch Democrat; the other, of German American descent, was firmly Republican. So, he wondered, if religion was so important to electoral politics and if each of these academics was a professing evangelical Protestant, why did they vote for different candidates in national elections? After all, members of the seminar had just listened

129

to lots of evidence, sorted by the most sophisticated form of regression analysis, indicating that born-again Protestants generally voted as a bloc for candidates of religious and moral character. Of course, the statistics allowed for some diversity. But one would have thought that the two evangelical Protestant political scientists arguing for the importance of religion in American elections would resemble the American evangelical citizens they studied. When asked about their own voting record, each man still insisted that his faith had informed his evaluation and selection of candidates. Their data were still sound. But the reason for voting Democrat or Republican depended on which part of the Bible each man read—a response that suggested a red-state edition of the Bible might sell as well as the red-letter variety. But the question persisted—if the Bible can be read so differently, how dependable a variable is faith for understanding the results of elections? In other words, if like a wax nose scripture can be shaped to conform to each reader's political convictions, then perhaps religion is not as decisive in electoral outcomes as, say, the old trinity of race, class, and gender.[1]

This not so imaginary scenario raises an interesting question of where a Bible-thumping Republican Christian would go in scripture for support of conservative politics. One could well imagine finding a basis for law-and-order policies in the Old Testament. But what about free markets, limited government, federalism, or strong national defense? If the answers are not immediately obvious, the reason may have to do with the steadily voluble chorus of evangelical Protestant writers who are reading the Bible for liberal rather than for conservative ends. Some reactions to the 2006 midterm elections suggested that the religious Right might be faltering in its hold on born-again Protestants. But even before the unceremonious dumping of Donald Rumsfeld, evangelicals indicated in a variety of ways that the Bible the religious Right reads for political guidance could just as easily be turned against conservatives in support of liberal policies and candidates. In which case, the religious Right's insistence that faith matters for the life of a nation may have given credence ironically to political convictions very different from theirs, even unleashing a left turn by baby boomer evangelicals. What follows is a three-part exploration of the emerging evangelical Left. The first part describes the leftward drift of the sons and daughters of evangelicalism's Greatest Generation; the second examines the historical precedents for liberal politics among evangelicals; and the concluding section critiques and attempts to resolve an approach to Bible-based politics that abuses scripture for the sake of political gain. In the process, this essay may show evangelicals a way to accept the idea that the duties and interests of citizens and nations are more important than faith for thinking about public life, and that without seeing the importance of prior political questions, believers may let their politics determine their reading of scripture.

## The Greatest Generation's Not So Great Children

As unthinkable as it was fifty years ago that a prospective nominee from one of the major political parties would consider Bob Jones University a significant campaign stop—which Ronald Reagan and George W. Bush did during the 1980 and 2000 South Carolina primaries—almost as unlikely a half century ago was the idea that born-again Protestants would consider the Democrats, the party of big government, ethnic diversity, and social engineering, a political option.[2]

Of course, evangelical Protestants have never been an easy fit within the post–World War II conservative movement. The arguments and convictions of libertarians like Friedrich Hayek, anti-Communists like Whittaker Chambers, and traditionalists like Russell Kirk and Richard Weaver did not figure prominently in periodicals like *Christianity Today*, where editors and writers used the Bible regularly to oppose the welfare state and communism. Even so, evangelical leaders during the 1950s and 1960s shared enough of the concerns of the emerging conservative wing of American politics that they constituted a natural piece of the quilt Ronald Reagan patched together to secure the conservative revolution of 1980.[3]

During the 1950s and 1960s, before Republican strategists and pollsters discovered the electoral potential of born-again Protestants, evangelical ideas on politics were predictably right of center. For instance, in a study of born-again Protestants during the twenty-five years after World War II, the University of Wisconsin political scientist Robert Booth Fowler concluded that evangelicals invariably spoke and wrote in defense of free markets, balanced budgets, and common standards of public decency, and conversely opposed communism as well as domestic policies that might increase the centralization of America's federal government. Their defense of freedom was so strong that many evangelical leaders believed labor unions were incompatible with a liberal society because they impeded free markets. This did not mean that evangelicals endorsed the American way completely. America's God-blessed status meant that the United States needed to conform to a higher standard. As such, evangelical leaders regularly complained about the nation's materialism, secularism, and hedonism. At the same time, evangelical leaders were also suspicious of church-based social action for two reasons. First, they objected that progressive reforms threatened to increase the size and power of government. Second, religiously inspired political activism tempted the church to forget that the fundamental human problem was sin and that it could be remedied only through faith in Christ. For this reason, mainstream evangelical leaders insisted that the church should not become embroiled in politics, an entanglement that would distract the church from its primary spiritual mission of evangelism.[4]

This generally conservative set of political convictions was widespread among many evangelicals during the 1960s and 1970s, but some did dissent at particular points in hope of making born-again Protestantism more responsive to the needs of the nation. For instance, Carl Henry contended that social involvement was not antagonistic to soul winning but a vital part of it. This did not mean that churches or pastors should pursue social reform. Henry simply advised that evangelicals needed to adopt a positive attitude to the state and its necessary work of preserving order and implementing a just society. Even so, Henry maintained that the state's work was fundamentally different from the church's. Whereas the former pursued order and justice, the latter's aims were love and mercy. Consequently, Henry faulted the liberal mainline denominations for having abandoned preaching and evangelism for a social gospel of political action. The evangelical alternative was to place the primary responsibility for Christian political involvement on individual Christians. Above all, Henry insisted that evangelical social involvement should "give no quarter to the illusion that Christianity is primarily an ethical idealism engaged in denouncing political and social injustice."[5]

Billy Graham provided another form of minor dissent from the mainstream of post–World War II evangelical politics. Like most Protestants during the middle decades of the twentieth century, Graham advocated liberty, democracy, and small government and viewed communism as the great threat to American ideals. Even so, his conservatism did not prevent his challenging evangelicals on race relations. In 1953, in Chattanooga, Tennessee, Graham held his first integrated evangelistic crusade, which became the norm for subsequent revivals. A decade later he also supported civil rights legislation, at a time when many evangelicals objected that the proposed reforms would increase unhealthily the size of the federal government. Graham also cautiously spoke out on behalf of the poor and offered muted support for Lyndon Johnson's War on Poverty. Graham's not so cogent logic was that conversion inevitably leads to the love of one's neighbor and a concern for the well-being of society. Still, he insisted that the fleeting concerns of politics needed to be kept in perspective against the eternal realities of heaven and hell. As he told one evangelical audience, "Let us rejoice in social action, and yet insist that it alone is not evangelism, and cannot be substituted for evangelism."[6]

From the perspective of earlier evangelical attitudes, the religious Right that emerged in the late 1970s was repeating the previous generation's approach to American public life, not instigating a form of fundamentalism, as many scholars have argued.[7] In addition to the perennial concerns of limited government, free markets, and strong national defense, leaders like Jerry Falwell and Pat Robertson identified a number of cultural issues that involved the ability of families to retain a measure of autonomy and authority without being swept up in vast federal programs designed to overturn traditional hierarchies in favor of individualistic equality. Prior to the 1970s, American society was not overly threatening to evangelical ways of life. It was generally a family-friendly and WASP-dominated culture. To be sure, evangelicals were not part of the so-called Protestant establishment. But they did benefit ironically from the social gospel that the mainline churches adopted to Christianize the United States. Public schools included prayer and Bible reading; abortion was illegal; federal officials were not threatening to bus Johnny and Susie to a school in another neighborhood; and domesticity was still a laudable and desirable outlet for most women. All in all, an American society dominated by the Protestant establishment maintained exactly what the religious Right would eventually promote as the best for the United States' well-being—religiously informed standards of public decency. But the feminist movement, the sexual revolution, civil rights legislation, and the Supreme Court's rulings on contraceptives and abortion fundamentally challenged the plausibility structures that undergirded the Christian home. At that point—roughly in 1975—the theological division between conservative and liberal Protestants that had surfaced in the 1920s during the so-called fundamentalist controversy finally played out politically; the religious Right basically adopted the old Protestant establishment's efforts to preserve the United States as a God-fearing land, and the collective leadership of the mainline churches in contrast abandoned their old social agenda because it seemed racist, bourgeois, and patriarchal.

Yet ironically the addition of family-values activism to the premises of cold war conservatism did not strengthen American conservatism. On the one hand, the effort to harness the federal government, especially in presidential contests, to do battle in the emerging culture wars was an invitation to the sort of big government and political centralization that post–World War II conservatives had always opposed. This is, of course, the point made recently and at times tendentiously by the likes of Andrew Sullivan in *The Conservative Soul: How We Lost It, How to Get It Back*. And it is not clear that religious and political conservatives necessarily had lots of options in the culture wars, since the trend of recent Supreme Court rulings had been to forget the sort of local option for legislation in the realm of morality that federalism originally encouraged. Even so, the desire to force the government in Washington DC to adopt a religiously inspired conservative agenda that would restore the nation's moral integrity was at odds with a conservatism that had historically feared big government. On the other hand, the religious Right inserted Christianity into American politics in a way that forced evangelicals to flip-flop on the separation of church and state. Prior to the late 1970s, the eventual leaders of the religious Right, such as Falwell and Robertson, had been forceful critics of the mainline churches for politicizing the faith. Like Graham and Henry, they insisted that the church's mission was not political but spiritual. But once faith-based electioneering and policy making became more attractive, those older expressions of the church's inherently religious character turned mum. In fact, along with the temptation of big government came the seduction of the big, politically active church. In which case, the religious Right facilitated ironically the rise of the evangelical Left.[8]

The rise of evangelical dissent from conservatism did not owe simply to the missteps of the religious Right's leadership, however. As early as 1973 a group of young evangelical academics convened in Chicago to propose an alternative to the conservatism of their evangelical parents and professors, who seemed woefully stolid as members of the silent majority. For this generation of evangelicals, growing up in the 1960s and experiencing many of the social protest movements of the era, either as participants or observers, the cautious adjustments to conservatism by Graham and Henry were insufficient to respond appropriately to women, blacks, and the poor. The fifty evangelicals who gathered in the Windy City produced a statement that indicated their frustration with the status quo. "The Chicago Declaration of Evangelical Social Concern" was an explicit call for social righteousness, a phrase that hearkened back to the social gospel sentiments of liberal Protestantism between the Civil War and World War I. The statement's policy prescriptions were thin; the Chicago declaration was shorter than five hundred words. But it did provide the opportunity to confess evangelical complicity in the United States' domestic and foreign policy sins. The heart of the Chicago declaration was its affirmation of the social justice that God requires of righteous nations: "Although the Lord calls us to defend the social and economic rights of the poor and oppressed, we have mostly remained silent. We deplore the historic involvement of the church in America with racism and the conspicuous responsibility of the evangelical community for perpetuating the personal attitudes and institutional structures that have divided the body of Christ along color lines. Further, we have failed to condemn the exploitation of racism at home and abroad by our economic system."[9] The importance of this statement is not lost on historian Joel Carpenter, who argues that this statement signaled a "radical shift" within the evangelical movement. What was considered political meddling by the church during the 1960s, today, according to Carpenter, has become axiomatic for evangelicals, namely, that "social justice is one of the central callings of all Christians."[10] The Chicago declaration is an indication then that evangelicals need not necessarily line up on the right.

Of course, the Chicago Declaration was not the only sign of evangelical movement on the left.[11] One of the statement's signers was Ron Sider, then a religion professor at Messiah College, an evangelical Anabaptist school in Pennsylvania, who achieved a measure of fame with his book *Rich Christians in an Age of Hunger* (1977). As the title suggests, Sider was pointing out what the Chicago declaration had noted, namely that evangelicals were invariably middle class and indifferent to pressing social needs. Like most reform-minded evangelicals, he tried for a middle course by arguing that individuals needed to change behaviors that contributed to poverty and that social structures were also in need of reform. But the larger message of the book was that fighting such social ills as hunger and poverty was a duty the Bible demanded of the church.

At roughly the same time that Sider was trying to steer evangelicals on a more progressive tack, Jim Wallis, having recently graduated from Trinity Evangelical Divinity School in suburban Chicago, was challenging the evangelical status quo with *Sojourners* magazine (originally the *Post-American*) and the formation of a Christian community in inner-city Washington DC. Wallis's intent was to break down walls that divided blacks and whites, poor and middle class, cities and suburbs. For him it was insufficient to provide simply for the poor and hungry. Christians also needed to identify with people in need because God himself exalted the humble over the proud. Wallis also created a stir with his 1976 book *Agenda for a Biblical People*, which was as far from Billy Graham as it was from Jimmy Carter. Unlike the moderate Sider, Wallis intentionally adopted a radical pose and held up Anabaptists as a worthy model for evangelical political activism.

Both Sider and Wallis appealed to the Bible as a means to call evangelicals to repent of their conservative ways. The proof of such repentance would be found not in correct doctrine or disciplined churches but in the daily realities of the believer's life in the world. Unlike the evangelicals of Henry and Graham's generation, who always placed evangelism as a priority before social engagement, Sider and Wallis put proclamation on a par with deeds of mercy, if not elevating the latter in reaction to middle-class evangelicals' erroneous understanding of Christianity.

Wallis has remained something of an acquired taste among evangelicals. After his first book, in which he drew a line between mere supporters of "establishment Christianity" and practitioners of biblical faith, Wallis added vitriol against the religious Right to his plea for social justice. In 1996 he came out with *Who Speaks for God? An Alternative to the Religious Right* and reiterated the desirability of a biblically based politics. He also echoed the Chicago declaration by asserting that evangelicalism had turned a deaf ear to scripture's prophetic voice and been turned by political conservatives into an ideology. Most recently, in *God's Politics: Why the Right Gets It Wrong and the Left Doesn't Get It* (2005), Wallis tried to triangulate between the religious Right and the secular Left by insisting that evangelicals add to the conservative issues of the family, sexual integrity, and personal responsibility the "progressive" or "even radical" issues of race, poverty, and war.

As President George W. Bush has become less popular, Wallis's brand of politics has produced more buyers.[12] That several authors have come out recently with books that express a Wallisian form of exasperation with the religious Right may be coincidental, but it may also be an indication that the editor of *Sojourners* is gaining a following, at least from the lectern and pulpit. Randall Balmer, an evangelical religious historian at Columbia University, hammered the religious Right by accusing evangelicals of "grasping for power" in a very un-Christian way—"an expansion of tax cuts for the wealthiest Americans, the continued prosecution of a war in the Middle East that enraged our longtime allies and would not meet even the barest of just-war criteria, and a re-jiggering of Social Security, the effect of which, most observers agree, would be to fray the social-safety net for the poorest among us."[13] Gregory Boyd, an evangelical pastor and theologian, echoed Balmer's critique, though not so abrasively, by questioning the basic assumptions of the religious Right about freedom, national defense, and participation in the military. Boyd invoked Christ's instruction about turning the other cheek, while ignoring the apostle Paul's teaching that the magistrate legitimately wields the sword, to argue that Christians may not resort to violence of any kind to repay evil.[14]

In this growing evangelical chorus of the religious Left, Sider's influence has been more significant than Wallis's, perhaps because of Sider's generally cautious approach to social justice. One important instance of Sider's longevity was the recent policy statement adopted by the National Association of Evangelicals (NAE) titled "For the Health of the Nation: An Evangelical Call to Civic Responsibility." This white paper drew on the social justice ideals evident in the earlier Chicago declaration. One important reason for the similarities was that Sider played a role in developing both documents.[15]

Prior to this statement, the NAE was predictably right of center.[16] Since its founding in 1942, the association has maintained a Washington DC office, which initially coordinated relations with the federal government for member denominations when seeking the proper documentation for foreign missionaries, military chaplains, and religious broadcasting, for instance. Over time the Washington office assumed minor responsibilities for lobbying the federal government on issues and measures important to the NAE's membership. During the first three decades, the NAE issued statements that were generally designed to preserve Protestant hegemony in the United States, though often by opposing encroachments on the separation of church and state through state funding of Roman Catholic institutions such as schools and hospitals. By the 1970s the NAE became more critical of the United States' domestic and international policies, but with Reagan's victory in 1980 the organization resumed a posture more in step with the Republican ascendancy. In the 1990s the NAE found sufficient room in the pursuit of religious freedom and human rights to work with the Clinton administration. Once George W. Bush articulated the ideal of compassionate conservatism, the NAE picked up the older agenda of the evangelical Left.

But with "For the Health of the Nation," the NAE occupied territory to the left of its founders. It combined conservative favorites such as religious liberty, families, the sanctity of human life, and human rights with humanitarian initiatives generally associated with liberal politics—economic justice, the environment, and opposition to violence that bordered on pacifism. By no means radical in its goals, the NAE's embrace of liberal concerns was decisively out of step with the laissez-faire, anti-Communist strain of Republicanism that appealed to evangelicals as part of the silent majority or the religious Right. Sider's influence looked particularly strong in the statement's stress on justice: "Because we have been called to do justice to our neighbors, we foster a free press, participate in open debate, vote, and hold public office," the statement affirmed. "When Christians do justice, it speaks loudly about God" and demonstrates to nonbelievers "how the Christian vision can contribute to the common good and help alleviate the ills of society." The execution of justice was especially important for the NAE's consideration of poverty. According to the statement, economic justice requires a restoration of wholeness in community. The statement urged Christians to become involved in politics to "shape wise laws pertaining to the creation of wealth, wages, education, taxation, immigration, health care, and social welfare that will protect those trapped in poverty and empower the poor to improve their circumstances."

The NAE's openness to liberal policy was by no means radical. Following Wallis and Sider, it included family values and so attempted to bridge the divide between religious conservatives and secular liberals. Even so, the NAE's declaration was not very different from the social gospel reforms proposed a century earlier when the Federal Council of Churches also tried to harmonize evangelism and social reform. According to "For the Health of the Nation," evangelical policies need to include individuals as well as institutions. "While individuals transformed by the gospel change surrounding society, social institutions also shape individuals," and although "good laws encourage good behavior, bad laws and systems foster destructive action." Consequently, significant social change requires "personal conversion and institutional renewal and reform." Arguably the closest resemblance between evangelical activism and the old liberal Protestant social gospel was a redefinition of the church's social responsibility. Moving away from the post–World War II conviction that placed the eternal destiny of persons before their physical conditions, the NAE had come around to an older liberal Protestant conception of the kingdom of God that called on the church to improve this world as the embodiment of the world to come. The NAE declaration concluded, "We know that we must wait for God to bring about the fullness of the kingdom at Christ's return. But in this interim, the Lord calls the church to speak prophetically to society and work for the renewal and reform of its structures."

There are limits on how far left the NAE may veer. In 2005, when the Evangelical Climate Initiative released its statement "Climate Change: An Evangelical Call to Action," the NAE declined to add its formal support.[17] Chuck Colson, Richard Land of the Southern Baptist Convention, and Focus on the Family's James Dobson urged the evangelical interdenominational agency to "stay on the sidelines." "There should be room for Bible-believing evangelicals," these evangelical heavyweights advised, "to disagree about the cause, severity, and solutions to the global warming issue." But that did not deter the head of the NAE's lobbying efforts in Washington, Richard Cizik, from advocating that evangelicals embrace the cause of "creation care." According to Cizik, "There are people who disagree with what I'm doing . . . within the evangelical community of America." But, he said, he does not understand why it is controversial to stand up and say, "Climate change is real, the science is solid, we have to care about this issue because of the impact on the poor." Cizik's position prompted a number of evangelical leaders, including Land and Dobson, to call for his resignation from the NAE.[18]

The controversy surrounding the Evangelical Climate Initiative stems from its obvious departure from the sorts of political convictions that defined American conservatism during the last half of the twentieth century—limited government, free markets and the culture of enterprise that sustains them, and a strong national defense. In fact, whatever the merits of contemporary considerations about the environment and the harmful consequences of an economy dependent on fossil fuels, the greening of evangelicals could very well indicate that values voters will be more inclined to give their support to the Democratic Party than to the GOP. The Evangelical Climate Initiative's support for the Democrat-sponsored Domenici-Bingaman resolution on global warming only confirms this impression, not to mention the signatures attached to the statement, which include such usual suspects as Wallis and Sider but also such evangelical figures as Wheaton College president A. Duane Litfin, megachurch pastor extraordinaire Bill Hybels, and the Emergent Church's very own Brian McLaren.

Arguably, the best indication of the leftward political drift of evangelicalism is the pastor in the Hawaiian shirt, purpose-driven Rick Warren. Fast on the heels of his enormously popular book, Warren has shifted his attention from cultivating committed Christians to solving the world's problems. His recently launched PEACE initiative may not have the official status of the NAE's declaration, but given the Southern California pastor's popularity, it may be more indicative of evangelicalism's political soul. Rather than using the profits from *Purpose Driven Life* (2002) to add to his Tommy Bahama collection, Warren formed an organization to mobilize 1 billion Christians around the world in an "outreach effort to attack the five global, evil giants of our day . . . spiritual emptiness, corrupt leadership, poverty, disease, and illiteracy." According to Warren, no government "can effectively eradicate" these afflictions.[19] That leaves the church to do it. His implicit distrust of the state suggests that contemporary evangelicals' sentimental left-of-center humanitarianism may not find a ready home in the big government programs typically favored by Democrats. But by assigning to the church tasks typically reserved for the modern state, Warren's initiative will likely prompt American evangelicals to demand that the United States follow the church's lead in fixing the world's problems. Whatever the effects of Warren's efforts, to embrace social justice, the environment, and AIDS as the next evangelical political causes is to take more cues from Jim Wallis than Jerry Falwell. After all, Wallis has been arguing for almost three decades that born-again Protestants need to move beyond the social issues of abortion and gay marriage to the structural ones of poverty, the environment, and war.

This is clearly the impression with which Jeffery Sheler leaves readers in *Believers: A Journey into Evangelical America* (2006). His last chapter features interviews with two seminary presidents, Al Mohler of the Southern Baptist Theological Seminary and Richard Mouw of Fuller Theological Seminary. Both men addressed the subject of politics, and, unsurprisingly, they proposed markedly different accounts. According to Sheler, Mouw's agenda of social justice and Mohler's of limited government and the defense of the family are "miles apart." Significantly, Sheler let Mouw have the last word. On the question of evangelical identity and the fragmentation of the movement, Mouw, who was one of the signers of the 1973 Chicago declaration, remarked that the future of evangelicalism might be an encouraging one. "How we as evangelicals respond to the AIDS crisis in Africa, how we deal with children and orphans, how we deal with poverty-related issues," Mouw said, "could bring a new sense of mission and unity to the movement." He added, "That's something I can begin to feel very optimistic about."[20] Sheler tried to finesse the difference between Mohler and Mouw by asserting that underlying each man's agenda was the redemptive message of the gospel. But in point of fact, Mohler's understanding distinguishes between efforts to improve this world and those that prepare men and women for the world to come. Such a distinction is less clear in the agenda of folks like Mouw, Warren, Wallis, and Cizik. In which case, just as the social gospel of the mainline churches set into motion theological liberalization, so too the social justice advocacy of contemporary evangelicals may reveal more fundamental changes at play not just in political party preferences but also in theological convictions.

## The Return of Evangelical Biblicism

The $64,000 question (and those are 1956 dollars) is whether the recent shift among evangelicals from a conservative to a liberal political agenda is indicative of a future of evangelical political reflection or simply a momentary aberration. One way to consider the future is to look for trends in the past. Here it is worth considering what evangelical politics looked like prior to the rise of post–World War II conservatism. Could it be that the evangelical Left has more historical precedents than the religious Right, thus making evangelicals' alliance with conservatism the exception rather than the rule?

To generalize about evangelical Protestants prior to World War II is tricky because of regional differences, especially between the North and the South, and because religiously motivated partisans could as easily find a home in the Republican Party as in the Democratic. Equally difficult is trying to extract an evangelical brand of political activism prior to the 1940s that was identifiably distinct from that of mainline Protestantism. For instance, in Mark Noll's periodization of Protestant politics, the time before 1925 revealed a version of political reflection that appealed to Protestants on both sides of the fundamentalist-modernist divide. It was characterized by the following:

> Protestants in the progressive era relied instinctively on the Bible to provide their ideals of justice. They believed in the power of Christ to expand the Kingdom of God through the efforts of faithful believers. They were reformists at home and missionaries abroad who felt that cooperation among Protestants signaled the advance of civilization. They were thoroughly and uncritically patriotic. On more specific issues, they continued to suspect Catholics as being anti-American, they promoted the public schools as agents of a broad form of Christianization, and they were overwhelmingly united behind prohibition as the key step toward a renewed society.[21]

Although the Republican Party possessed a legacy of social reform thanks to its antislavery origins and Abraham Lincoln's policies to end slavery, by the early twentieth century Democrats were as much a home for evangelicals as the GOP. One reason for this was Woodrow Wilson, who George Marsden has said was "as Puritan as any New Englander" who ever was president.[22]

Another reason was William Jennings Bryan. The Great Commoner gained the Democratic nomination for the presidency three times but lost in each general contest. He also played a leading role in arguably the most important religious episode in American history, as the chief prosecuting attorney in the Scopes trial. Furthermore, Bryan was active in the fundamentalist controversy in the northern Presbyterian Church, thus showing that he was as concerned with the health of his communion as he was with that of civil society. Bryan was also significant because, according to Noll, the Nebraskan's political instincts were typically evangelical. Bryan was no political philosopher. Like most evangelicals, his populism implied support for the sovereignty of the people in ways that made him suspicious of political and economic elites. Bryan was also intuitive in his approach to politics. From a straightforward reading of the Bible and a sanctified common sense, he cut through complex issues to arrive at a position that he believed was morally unambiguous.

As congenial as Bryan's approach might be to evangelical activists today, the specifics of his policies would likely give the Chuck Colsons, Jerry Falwells, and Pat Robertsons of the religious Right fits. For instance, Bryan was no advocate of small government but in fact championed such measures as a federal income tax and Prohibition. Economically, he favored silver coinage in a way that would have increased inflation, an outcome that was beneficial to his beloved farmers and harmful to the bankers whom he berated famously for crucifying the working poor on a "cross of gold." Bryan's opposition to the United States' entrance into World War I could sound pacifist and hardly in keeping with a view of the United States as the global umpire. Furthermore, Bryan was a member of the Democratic Party, which has historically been less uniform and less Protestant than the GOP that the religious Right found so congenial. These positions prompt Mark Noll to remark that if Bryan were alive today he "might have been with Jimmy Carter and Mark Hatfield on the [first] Gulf War, with pro-lifers on abortion, with Democratic rhetoric and Republican practice on the budget deficit, with the fence-straddlers on an Equal Rights Amendment, and with those who appeal for massive federal action against drugs and for inexpensive housing." Much more certain for Noll is that Bryan would have been "a dedicated opponent of Reaganonomics and would have gone into orbit over the savings-and-loan catastrophe."[23]

Bryan's alternative to evangelical politics has encouraged his recent biographer, Michael Kazin, to suggest that the Christian liberalism, or social gospel, that the Great Commoner defended has real potential for the future of American politics. On the one hand, Bryan showed that liberalism does not play well with the American electorate if its leaders appeal solely to economic self-interest. Millions of Americans, Kazin writes, "derive their political views from their faith and prefer that others do the same." On the other hand, Bryan was also indicative of a better political culture than the current diet of "nonstop satire and twenty-four-hour commerce." He stood for a "society run by and for ordinary people who lead virtuous lives."[24] Kazin's sympathetic rendering of Bryan leads Jackson Lears, in his review for the *New Republic*, to write that no matter how much Bryan may not be a prophet for our times, he does allow for a reimagination of Christianity's role in politics. With Bryan, Lears concludes, we have a candidate who took Christianity seriously, "as something more than a source of self-satisfaction, who finds the waste of war appalling and the persistence of poverty outrageous." Indeed, Bryan was someone who actually believed, "against all the odds, that the meek should have a shot at inheriting the earth."[25]

With such favorable interpretations from liberal academics in mind, the suggestion that the future of evangelical politics is William Jennings Bryan holding forth in an oversize Hawaiian shirt is not so far fetched. Jim Wallis and other leaders within the evangelical Left do not seem to be aware of Bryan's potential, resorting mainly to the abolitionists of the nineteenth century as models for contemporary Christian activism. But if Bryan's politics do gain some credibility among the evangelical Left, faith-based politics in the United States might be much less Republican in the future than it is now.

In fact, the similarities between the emerging evangelical Left and Bryan's progressive populism suggest that the religious Right is actually an aberration within the history of evangelical politics. The reasons that a generation of evangelicals who were reared during a depression and lived through a world war supported a political party more friendly to elites and corporations are many. But the one that stands out is the cold war.

Arguably the most important consideration for understanding boomer evangelicals' distaste for conservatism is the defeat of communism. During the cold war, not only did the Soviet Union stand for an ideology at odds with America's unique blend of liberal democracy and Christianity, but it also convinced born-again Protestants of the necessity and virtues of free institutions, market capitalism, and a strong military. Just as anticommunism held together the post–World War II patchwork of libertarians and traditionalists, it also allowed born-again Protestants to merge relatively seamlessly into the conservative movement. But with the destruction of the Berlin Wall, the barrier to sentiments like those of the Chicago declaration also came down. Which means that the generation of conservative Protestants led by such figures as Jerry Falwell, Pat Robertson, and James Dobson is giving way to Jim Wallis, Rick Warren, and Ron Sider.

## BEYOND BIBLICAL POLITICS

The original Republican strategists Richard Viguerie and Paul Weyrich may have thought that born-again Protestants would turn out to be a reliable constituency for the GOP. In the 1970s concerns about declining standards of social morality and decency made evangelicals appear to be worth courting. But biblical standards of morality have a way of nurturing an interest in biblical standards of justice. Consequently, whereas the older generation of evangelicals read the Bible for its application to sex and family relations, younger evangelicals turn to holy writ for guidance on war, hunger, and poverty. To be sure, baby boomers' interpretations of scripture and its applications to American politics are just as debatable as their parents' biblical politics. Nevertheless, the irony is that, once the religious Right let the genie of faith-based politics out of the bottle of American conservatism, it may have unleashed a Protestant force that Republicans will find impossible to harness.

For conservatives who would like to continue to see baby boomer evangelicals as part of the Right's constituency, one way to convince contemporary evangelicals to follow their parents and reject Bryan's progressivism is to show boomers that the Bible is not a sufficient guide to public life and that political circumstances may be evaluated apart from the high stakes of a cosmic struggle between the forces of heaven and hell. No matter what their party affiliation, the one constant in evangelicals' political reflection has been biblicism. But rather than being an asset to political engagement, as it surely is for theological reflection, the Bible has been evangelicals' Achilles' heel. As Mark Noll has concluded, "Evangelical political reflection is nurtured by a commonsensical Biblicism for the same reasons that a 'Bible only' mentality has flourished among evangelicals."[26] Whether for populist or conservative politics, the Bible has been the wax nose evangelicals have used to find support for their policies and votes.

One obvious problem for American evangelicals is that their appeal to scripture in public life can be a serious challenge to building a consensus because the Bible is not an authoritative standard for all of the nation's citizens.[27] Richard John Neuhaus spotted this problem only five years into the religious Right's ascendancy when he noted that making the Bible a standard for public morality while also protecting religious liberty was an impossible feat. According to Neuhaus,

> The religious new right . . . wants to enter the political arena making claims on the basis of private truths. The integrity of politics itself requires that such a proposal be resisted. Public decisions must be made by arguments that are public in character. . . . Fundamentalist morality, which is derived from beliefs that cannot be submitted to examination by public reason, is essentially a private morality. If enough people who share that morality are mobilized, it can score victories in the public arena. But every such victory is a setback in the search for a public ethic.[28]

Steve Bruce, a sociologist of religion who has spent several decades exploring religious-based politics in the English-speaking world, adds to Neuhaus's observation a point about the essentially secular character of modern politics. As much as contemporary societies in the West undermine the authoritative claims made on behalf of religion, they also facilitate a remarkable degree of social harmony within a culturally heterogeneous setting. As such, Bruce explains,

> Our societies permit (and in some places even encourage) the maintenance of distinctive religious world-views and thus encourage socio-moral contests, but they also create a structure (the division of the life world into public and private spheres) and a culture (universalism and tolerance) which of necessity restrain such contests and require that they be fought on general universalistic ethical and public-policy principles. In modern democratic culturally plural societies, no socio-moral interest group can plausibly promote its case on the grounds that "the Bible (or the Koran or the Book of Mormon) says so." Instead it must argue that equity or reason or the public good says so.[29]

Bruce's point is not that Christian believers are prohibited from appealing to the Bible. It is instead that such arguments are not plausible in a religiously mixed society. In other words, the evangelical appeal to the Bible in a post-Protestant era of American history is unwise even if permissible. It is, after all, a free country, and people entering the public realm may appeal to any number of arguments to try to persuade others to join them in a common enterprise. But for such an appeal to be effective, it may need to remove barriers that prevent others from finding it plausible.

The difficulty facing scriptural reasoning in public life may account for Noll's suggestion that evangelicals need to find another approach to politics. He has argued that born-again Protestantism's biblicist instinct about society and government "holds out only mixed prospects for the future." To continue to think that public life needs to conform to the same standards as those governing the community of faith, whether on the right or the left, may allow evangelicals to "contribute sporadically to political action" but will not produce serious "political reflection." What evangelicals need, according to Noll, is "some kind of dual vision" that provides the vantage from which "to speak at the same time with a common vocabulary both inside and outside the community of faith."[30] Clearly, constant appeals to the Bible as the basis by which to judge elected officials, domestic policies, and international relations will not achieve this "dual vision."

Where can evangelicals turn for an approach to public life that yields such a hyphenated perspective? One figure from evangelicals' past is J. Gresham Machen, a lifelong Democrat and Presbyterian fundamentalist who maintained a dual vision by insisting on the separateness of state and church. As a courageous defender of historical Christianity against liberal Protestant errors, Machen almost single-handedly fought modernism within the northern Presbyterian Church in the 1920s until he was suspended from the ministry and had to start a new Presbyterian denomination.[31] What is more, he was particularly active in fighting legislation that undermined, in his view, family life and the legitimate authority of parents and local government. In other words, Machen would appear to meet the religious Right's theological and political litmus tests. But he was keenly aware that religious liberty in the United States restricted appeals to the Bible as a norm for public life. Machen even ridiculed the hypocrisy of liberal Protestant churches that took pride in theological openness within the church while supporting legislation aimed at promoting biblical standards of decency and justice. One such instance was the Presbyterian Church's support throughout the 1920s for Prohibition. Machen's dissent from the chorus of liberal and conservative Presbyterians who believed the Eighteenth Amendment and Volstead Act would preserve a Christian America cost him a promotion at Princeton Theological Seminary and enabled his denominational foes to depict him as a libertarian who was soft on crime. But as he tried to explain to his critics, the constitution of the Presbyterian Church may have condemned drunkenness but had nothing to say about the methods of dealing with it. On such policy questions, he believed the church should have room for those who opposed and those who supported Prohibition. Where the constitution of the Presbyterian Church was clear, however, was on the mission of the church, which, in Machen's estimation, was to bring to bear "upon human souls the sweet and gracious influences of the gospel." Yet, by supporting legislation and forms of enforcement, the church was "in danger of abdicating its proper function," which was to proclaim the forgiveness of sins through the life, death, and resurrection of Christ.[32]

As his reasoning on Prohibition implies, Machen was especially concerned about the effects of a politicized church on Christian witness. To make religion relevant to public life, he argued, Protestants had turned to the Bible only for its ethics while ignoring almost completely its ultimate message about sin and grace. This was one of the reasons for Machen's opposition to prayer and Bible reading in public schools. Aside from constitutional questions surrounding the state's establishment of religion, even more significant for Machen was what invoking faith for political ends did to Christianity. "What could be more terrible," he asked, "from the Christian point of view, than the reading of the Lord's Prayer to non-Christian children as though they could use it without becoming Christians?" In effect, a politicized Christianity ends up being little more than moralism. "When any hope is held out to lost humanity from the so-called ethical portions of the Bible apart from its great redemptive core," Machen concluded, "the Bible is represented as saying the direct opposite of what it really says."[33] If Machen provides any lesson for politically engaged evangelicals, it is that efforts to bring faith to bear on public life invariably lead to a distortion of religious truth for political ends.

By recognizing the difference between the politics of this world and those of the world to come, Machen was in effect following the insights of St. Augustine, who at a time of greater discouragement to Christians saw that God's ways transcended earthly efforts. In *The City of God*, the Bishop of Hippo established the dual vision that has informed Roman Catholic, Lutheran, and older Reformed understandings of religion and politics. Augustine distinguished clearly between cult and culture, between religious and secular affairs. In the cultic realm, the sphere of worship, the relationship between Christians and non-Christians would be characterized by varying degrees of antagonism. But in civil society Christians had no inherent scruples against "diversities in the manners, laws, and institutions whereby earthly peace is secured and maintained, . . . recognizing that, however various these are, they all tend to one and the same end of earthly peace." Other than opposing laws that injured "faith and godliness," believers were free to be good citizens of the earthly city by desiring and maintaining "a common agreement among men regarding the acquisition of the necessaries of life."[34]

From an Augustinian perspective, then, the earthly city is a temporary arrangement ordained by God to restrain evil and promote proximate ideals of justice until the dawn of the heavenly city at the return of Christ. By recovering this older Christian perspective, evangelicals could find a way around the impasse of biblical politics. This involves the recognition that the Bible is the church's standard for carrying out its mission of evangelism and edification. Because the state has a different jurisdiction and mission, its norm cannot be the Bible but must come from truths revealed in the created order. This recognition of the different aims and means of church and state might force evangelicals to abandon the notion of an explicitly Christian or Bible-based politics. That would certainly be an uncomfortable position for born-again Protestants who are widely known as people of *the* book. But if this change in outlook allowed evangelicals to preserve the integrity of the Bible they revere as well as the message it reveals, such a transformation might turn out for them to be entirely agreeable.

## Notes

1. The identities of the seminar participants have been withheld to protect the innocent. But this incident is not fictional.

2. The identification of evangelicals with the Republican Party is complicated by the South, a decidedly evangelical region, and its overwhelming historical allegiance to the Democratic Party. For the southern wrinkle on the Republican membership of evangelicals, see Lyman A. Kellstedt and Mark A. Noll, "Religion, Voting for President, and Party Identification," in *Religion and American Politics: From the Colonial Period to the 1980s*, ed. Mark A. Noll (New York: Oxford University Press, 1990).

3. See George M. Marsden, "Religion, Politics, and the Search for an American Consensus," in Noll, *Religion and American Politics*.

4. See Robert Booth Fowler, *A New Engagement: Evangelical Political Thought, 1966–1976* (Grand Rapids, MI: Eerdmans, 1982).

5. Carl Henry, *Aspects of Christian Social Ethics* (1964), in *Readings in Christian Ethics: A Historical Sourcebook*, ed. John Philip Wogaman and Douglas M. Strong (Louisville, KY: Westminster John Knox, 1996), 371.

6. Graham quoted in Fowler, *New Engagement*, 48.

7. This paragraph is slightly adapted from D. G. Hart, "Mainstream Protestantism, Conservative Religion, and Civil Society," in *Religion Returns to the Public Square: Faith and Policy in America*, ed. Hugh Heclo and Wilfred M. McClay (Baltimore: Johns Hopkins University Press, 2003), 202.

8. On the political shifts among twentieth-century evangelicals, see, for instance, Michael Lienesch, *Redeeming America: Piety and Politics in the New Christian Right* (Chapel Hill: University of North Carolina Press, 1993), 1–4, and George M. Marsden, "Preachers of Paradox: Fundamentalist Politics in Historical Perspective," in *Understanding Fundamentalism and Evangelicalism* (Grand Rapids, MI: Eerdmans, 1991), 104–9.

9. Evangelicals for Social Action, "The Chicago Declaration of Evangelical Social Concern," available at http://www.esa-online.org/Display.asp?Page=HistDocs.

10. Joel A. Carpenter, "Compassionate Evangelicalism," *Christianity Today*, December 1, 2003, http://www.christianitytoday.com/ct/2003/december/2.40.html.

11. This and the following paragraphs are slightly adapted from D. G. Hart, "Leftward Christian Soldiers," *American Conservative*, January 29, 2007, 24–25.

12. Not to be discounted are a series of books by evangelical academics whose influence has been less visible but still substantial. See, for instance, Richard V. Pierard, *The Unequal Yoke: Evangelical Christianity and Political Conservatism* (Philadelphia: Lippincott, 1970); David O. Moberg, *The Great Reversal: Evangelism versus Social Concern* (Philadelphia: Lippincott, 1972); and Richard Mouw, *Politics and the Biblical Drama* (Grand Rapids, MI: Eerdmans, 1976).

13. Randall Balmer, "Jesus Is Not a Republican," *Chronicle of Higher Education*, June 23, 2006, B6. This piece is an excerpt from Randall Balmer, *Thy King-*

*dom Come: How the Religious Right Distorts the Faith and Threatens America; An Evangelical's Lament* (New York: Basic Books, 2006).

14. Gregory A. Boyd, *The Myth of a Christian Nation: How the Quest for Power Is Destroying the Church* (Grand Rapids, MI: Zondervan, 2006), chap. 9.

15. This statement is published in an appendix to *Toward an Evangelical Public Policy: Political Strategies for the Health of the Nation*, ed. Ronald J. Sider and Diane Knippers (Grand Rapids, MI: Baker Books, 2005).

16. This paragraph and the next two are slightly adapted from Hart, "Leftward Christian Soldiers," 25–26.

17. Evangelical Climate Initiative, "Climate Change: An Evangelical Call to Action," available at http://christiansandclimate.org/learn/call-to-action/.

18. Stephanie Simon, "Evangelicals Battle over Agenda, Environment," *Los Angeles Times*, March 10, 2007.

19. See "Saddleback Missions: Bringing P.E.A.C.E. to the World," http://www.saddlebackfamily.com/peace/.

20. Richard Mouw, interview by Jeffery L. Sheler, in *Believers: A Journey into Evangelical America* (New York: Viking, 2006), 286.

21. Mark A. Noll, "The Scandal of Evangelical Political Reflection," in *Being Christian Today: An American Conversation*, ed. Richard John Neuhaus and George Weigel (Washington, DC: Ethics and Public Policy, 1992), 73.

22. Marsden, "Religion, Politics," 385.

23. Noll, "Scandal," 72.

24. Michael Kazin, *A Godly Hero: The Life of William Jennings Bryan* (New York: Knopf, 2006), 303, 304.

25. Jackson Lears, "When Jesus Was a Democrat," *New Republic*, April 10, 2006, 28.

26. Noll, "Scandal," 70.

27. This and the following paragraphs are slightly adapted from Hart, "Mainstream Protestantism," 214–15.

28. Richard John Neuhaus, *The Naked Public Square: Religion and Democracy in America* (Grand Rapids, MI: Eerdmans, 1984), 36–37, quoted in José Casanova, *Public Religions in the Modern World* (Chicago: University of Chicago Press, 1994), 165.

29. Steve Bruce, *Conservative Protestant Politics* (New York: Oxford University Press, 1998), 185, 188, 189.

30. Noll, "Scandal," 90, 91.

31. On Machen, see D. G. Hart, *Defending the Faith: J. Gresham Machen and the Crisis of Conservative Protestantism in Modern America* (Baltimore: Johns Hopkins University Press, 1994).

32. J. Gresham Machen, "Statement on the Eighteenth Amendment," in

*J. Gresham Machen: Selected Shorter Writings*, ed. D. G. Hart (Phillipsburg, NJ: P and R, 2004), 395.

33. J. Gresham Machen, "The Necessity of the Christian School," in *What Is Christianity? and Other Essays*, ed. Ned B. Stonehouse (Grand Rapids, MI: Eerdmans, 1951), 299.

34. Augustine, *The City of God*, in *The Essential Augustine*, ed. Vernon J. Bourke (Indianapolis: Hackett, 1974), 203.

# THE DECLINING ROLE OF RELIGION IN POLITICS?

## Michael Barone

Religion has played a role in our politics since the beginning of the republic, and even before—one of the grievances of our founding fathers was that they thought King George III was going to send an Anglican bishop to Virginia. Our tradition of religion in politics is equivocal. The Glorious Revolution of 1688–1689 in England resulted in an uneasy compromise. Churches were established—Episcopal in England and Ireland, Presbyterian in Scotland—but they were not given a spiritual monopoly. They were favored—in England you had to take communion in the established church to hold public office or be graduated from university—but not hugely favored; you usually qualified if you took communion just once a year. At the same time the bishops of the Church of England refused to water down their doctrine to become a "comprehensive" church, including Presbyterians and other Protestant Dissenters in their ranks. Instead there was a proliferation of Dissenting churches. Catholics, seen as subversive of the Protestant regime (as they were), were positively barred from public office and from the throne but were allowed to worship (though the Catholic bishops were expelled from majority-Catholic Ireland). Jews, expelled from England in 1290, were readmitted by the Cromwell regime in 1656 and were left free to worship and go their way by the restored monarchy. After all, the Jews of Amsterdam helped to finance William of Orange's invasion of England, which led to the ouster of the Catholic King James II.

We Americans with our English traditions fail to understand that this was a unique settlement. Diarmaid MacCulloch, the great contemporary chronicler of the Reformation, wrote that the Glorious Revolution settlement "produced a very different texture in the Protestantism of the

English-speaking world to that of overwhelmingly Lutheran or Calvinist states in mainland Europe.... The several different faces of British Protestantism were each destined to give rise to worldwide families of Churches. Moreover, the centre of gravity in these bodies other than Anglicanism was destined to move from the Atlantic [i.e., British] Isles to the western seaboard of the ocean, to the new English-speaking colonies of America."

Differences over religion had resulted in a civil war and military dictatorship in England in the 1640s and 1650s. The Glorious Revolution produced a tradition of tolerance, greater in practice than at first in theory, which led to a profusion of Protestant sects and to toleration, grudging at first, of Catholics and Jews. The founding fathers built on this tradition by establishing a regime of entire tolerance but refrained from wiping out religious establishments in the states. Lurking behind these decisions, I think, was a realization that religion had the potential of splitting the nation and that it was dangerous for religion to become intermeshed with politics.

Of course religion and religious beliefs play an important part in determining political beliefs and political allegiances. The antislavery movement, first in England and then here, was the work of men and women motivated by religious conviction. And those of different religious beliefs responded very differently to it. Congregationalists and other northerners embraced it; southerners split away from northern-dominated denominations in response. Politicians as different as Abraham Lincoln and William Jennings Bryan used religious language and evoked religious fervor. In different states, politics split people primarily along religious lines—Protestants versus Catholics in New England, with Jews a wild card in New York, for example. And of course the nation was split very deeply when Roman Catholics were nominated for president. In 1928 Al Smith lost usually Democratic southern and border states. But he made great gains in the immigrant neighborhoods of big cities. In 1960, Gallup tells us, 78 percent of Catholics voted for John Kennedy and 63 percent of white Protestants voted for Richard Nixon—candidates descended from southern Irish Catholics and northern Irish Protestants.

## RELIGION IN POLITICS AFTER 1960

After 1960, religion seemed to disappear from politics. But it returned later, in response to the rebellions of the 1960s. Issues that split tradition-minded Americans from liberation-minded Americans became increasingly prominent in the Vietnam War period and after. In 1976 Jimmy Carter made much of being a born-again Christian and carried white evangelical Protestants. But in 1980 those voters reacted against policies of his administration and moved in large numbers to Ronald Reagan. Reagan delivered his "evil empire" speech before the National Association of Evangelicals and spoke to an evangelical group at the Republican National Convention in Dallas. The issue of abortion became increasingly prominent, and although it once split the constituencies of both parties, in time voters on both sides switched, to the point that by 1984 the Republican Party was a largely antiabortion party and the Democratic Party a largely pro–abortion rights party. So much so that the antiabortion governor of Pennsylvania was not allowed to speak at the 1992 Democratic National Convention.

In the last fifteen to twenty years, religious convictions, or lack of them, have been central to American politics. Starting in the early 1990s, the demographic factor that has been correlated most highly with voting behavior, other than race, is religion, and especially degree of religious observance. The divisions are by now familiar. White evangelical Protestants and Mormons have been heavily Republican, white mainline Protestants somewhat less so, and Catholics split, with the more observant tending to the Republicans and the less observant to the Democrats. Seculars, Jews, and black Christians have been overwhelmingly Democratic. Much attention has been given, rightly, to the white evangelical Christian bloc, which by some estimates amounts to one-quarter of the electorate (and which, by the way, did not stay home in 2006). But attention should be given as well to the secular bloc, which is substantially larger than it was a generation ago, large enough that it has become a visible and visibly important part of the Democratic base. In his Senate primary in Connecticut in August 2006, Joseph Lieberman carried Catholics and Jews. That would have been enough, in the years when he started in politics, to be assured of victory. But he lost the seculars by a wide margin and lost the Democratic nomination.

Why has religious belief played such an important part in our recent politics? Why, particularly since I think most of us share the founders' sense that there are dangers in intermeshing religion and politics? One reason is the issues, especially abortion, but also gay rights (including same-sex marriage), embryonic stem cell research—the list could go on.

In an affluent country that, at least until September 11, did not seem threatened from abroad, voters on all sides of these issues feel free to concentrate on their moral concerns. They seem more important than economics and foreign policy. Another reason is the character of our two most recent presidents. Both were born in 1946, the year usually considered the first year of the baby boom; both graduated from high school in 1964, the year of the peak SAT scores; and both happen to have personal characteristics that people on the other side of the cultural divide absolutely loathe.

## RELIGION'S DECLINING ROLE IN POLITICS?

My sense is that this period of close correlation between religious belief and voting behavior is coming to an end and that we are entering a period when religion and religious belief, or lack thereof, will be less relevant in our politics. For the first time in eighty years, it is clear that the incumbent president and vice president are not running for president. The parties will have new leaders, and the images of the parties are shaped greatly by the identities of their leaders. Interestingly, the candidates who competed for the two parties' nominations are in opposition to, or in tension with, the party base on different issues. For example, Rudy Giuliani is out of line with religious conservatives on cultural issues, while John McCain is out of line with the base on partisan issues and, though he takes conservative stands on cultural issues, seems little interested in them. Hillary Rodham Clinton is out of line with the antiwar Left on the Iraq war and other foreign policy issues, while Barack Obama is out of line with the angry bloggers in degree of partisanship. But McCain and Obama seem unlikely to foment the kind of polarization along religious lines that Bill Clinton and George W. Bush have.

Also, I think the cultural issues that split people along religious lines are fading in importance. Abortion in particular. I think it's becoming obvious even to the strongest pro-life people that abortion is not going to be criminalized again any time soon, even in the unlikely event that *Roe v. Wade* is overturned. The referendum vote against South Dakota's antiabortion law should make that plain. At the same time, I think it's becoming, or will soon become, obvious even to the strongest prochoice people that abortion is going to be allowed but disfavored, as it is in our medical schools, rather than set in a place of honor. It was not surprising to me that the new Supreme Court upheld the partial-birth abortion bans that Sandra Day O'Connor's vote overturned. The number of abortions will continue to decline, as it has since the early 1990s.

Other cultural issues seem to be of smaller magnitude. The Democrats have been pushing embryonic stem cell research, but I think it's not a major voting issue—and the Missouri referendum on the issue only barely passed in 2006. And the unpopularity of Congress's action on Terri Schiavo—which surprised and dismayed me—makes it unlikely that we will see other such political interventions. Gay issues will still be around. But antidiscrimination laws against gays are not especially unpopular; indeed they're quite popular in many states. The issue of gays in the military doesn't seem likely to be raised soon. Same-sex marriage has been imposed in Massachusetts by a 4–3 vote of its supreme court, but opposition seems less widespread than when the court decision came down. In any case, there's not a solid national majority against same-sex civil unions, such as that imposed by the supreme court of New Jersey. And it's not clear whether the current balance of opinion will obtain in the future. Young voters are about equally split on same-sex marriage. If they continue to feel that way as they grow older (as they did on the issue of abortion), that will mean in time an electorate less strongly or not opposed. If they change their minds and grow more conservative as they grow older (as they did on the issue of marijuana legalization), then the current balance of opinion will continue. I'm not at all certain which will be the case.

I think already these issues are overshadowed by issues of foreign policy. We are divided between those who see the United States threatened by attack by Islamic fascists and those, currently more vocal, who believe the United States is threatened by its own actions and the military action in Iraq. True, opinion on these issues does tend to run along the same partisan and religious lines with which we have become familiar. But not completely, as suggested by the fact that the cultural liberal Rudy Giuliani takes a firm line against the Islamic fascists while the religious conservative Sam Brownback wants us to withdraw from Iraq.

There is the possibility as well that cultural issues could be overshadowed by economic issues. The imminent tax rise that will occur in 2010 if Democrats win in 2008 could convince some cultural liberals to vote Republican. Or the perception that jobs are increasingly insecure and that economic outcomes are increasingly unequal could persuade some cultural conservatives—Thomas Frank's Kansans—to vote Democratic. I'm not so sure that these economic issues will rise in importance, but it's possible.

In fact I think just about anything is possible. I think we have moved from being a 49 percent nation, divided just about evenly and particularly along lines of religion, into a nation with open-field politics, in which events that have not yet happened, decisions that have not yet been made, and issues that have not yet been raised could make a critical difference—and move us in the direction of either party, or conceivably toward a third-party candidate. I think it's going to be like the period between 1990 and 1995, when all the old rules didn't seem to apply anymore. In that period we had the rise of actual and putative third-party candidates like Ross Perot and Colin Powell, the election of the untested Bill Clinton in 1992, and Newt Gingrich's Republican sweep in 1994. No one I know predicted all three of those developments. So I'm not ready to make any firm predictions about the next few years now.

# RED GOD, BLUE GOD

## Is There a God Gap between the Parties?

*Michael Cromartie*

The importance of religion in American politics cannot be overstated: except for race, since 1992 religion has become the most important determining variable in predicting voting behavior in the electorate. Religious belief and religious behavior have become almost as consistent as race in predicting voting behavior.

### WHAT IS THE GOD GAP?

I became particularly interested in this topic when it was being widely discussed in the run-up to the 2004 presidential election. In late August 2004, during the Republican National Convention, Wesley Theological Seminary hosted a panel in New York City titled "The God Gap in Presidential Politics: Is It Real?" The panel was moderated by Michael McCurry, Bill Clinton's former press secretary, and included John Podesta, President Clinton's former chief of staff; Shaun Casey, a professor of Christian ethics at Wesley Seminary; and me. The questions McCurry put to me were these: What lies behind the headlines of recent research that appears to show that the more religious a person is, the more likely he or she is to vote Republican? What causes Republicans to get this "religion thing" right more often than Democrats? Why, he wanted to know, are Republicans better at this than Democrats?

Perhaps he had read the editorial in the liberal Protestant magazine the *Christian Century*, which, in July 2004, pointed out that a recent *Time* magazine poll had found that 59 percent of those who consider themselves "very religious" would support President Bush, while only 35 percent said they would favor Senator Kerry. The *Time* poll also found that, among those who are not religious, 69 percent favored Senator Kerry, compared to only 22 percent for President Bush. "The Democrats have a religion problem. . . . Democrats are in danger of becoming the party of the nonreligious. In a country where religion is part of the mainstream, this is clearly a political liability. . . . Candidates and party operatives appear skittish about religion."[1]

It has been common among political reporters and editorial writers to take notice of what has been called the "God gap" in American politics. Michael Barone wrote after the 2000 election that the "single greatest divide in American politics is that the Bush coalition consists of people who are religious and respect traditional morality while the Gore coalition consists of people who are not traditionally religious and favor a more relativistic morality."[2] Several important surveys and polls support his contention. They show that those who attend worship services at least once a week tend to vote Republican, while those who seldom enter churches tend to vote Democratic. Often it appears that one party talks about moral values, God, Providence, and the obligations we owe our Creator while the other party talks about progress, science, reason, tolerance, and free choice.

A substantial number of Americans claim to attend worship services frequently. Michael Novak has observed that more people attend church on Sunday than attend football games over the weekend, and that includes high school, college, and pro football games. And not only do numerous surveys indicate that an overwhelming majority of Americans claim to believe in God, but a poll conducted by the Pew Forum on Religion and Public Life found that over 70 percent of Americans desire their president to hold a similar belief in God.[3] This would clearly seem to put the Democratic Party at a disadvantage.

## Redefining the God Gap

But this may be changing. In December 2006, Senator Hillary Clinton hired what the press called a "faith guru" to help her win over evangelicals and other so-called moral values voters as she began her 2008 presidential campaign. The early appeal of Senator Barack Obama included his professed Christian faith and a speaking style that is impressively comfortable when explaining how his policy positions are tied to his religious convictions. He also hired a full-time "religious outreach" person for his staff.

That the two top contenders for the Democratic nomination for president hired aides who specialized in religious outreach is a dramatic change from 2004, when the only candidate who employed a religious outreach consultant was Howard Dean, a man who could not locate the book of Job in the right testament.

And candidates on the statewide level are getting the message also. In August 2005, an aspiring Democratic politician for governor in an important midwestern state said,

> The next time some politician, including me, starts preaching to you a sermon on values, look us in the eye and ask us point-blank: Do your values include doing everything in your power to make sure that my hard work translates into a decent living for my family, that we have access to affordable health care, that I can offer my kids a solid, affordable education as far as their abilities will take them? . . . It's necessary to say this, because it seems, as far as the general culture and the press is concerned, one side of the political spectrum is deeply religious and deeply affected by moral values and the other side is not. [4]

That was then Democratic candidate, now governor of Ohio Ted Strickland, speaking before the Columbus Metropolitan Club. Reporters who were there said many people in attendance were moved to tears by his words.

What is going on here? Are some Democratic candidates learning to use religious language to appeal to religious believers in their campaigns for office? In light of the results of the November 2006 elections, have the Democrats closed the God gap between the parties? Or does the gap still exist?

Just over a decade ago, something new began to happen: polling data began to indicate that if people attended church services on a regular basis, they were more likely to vote Republican by a two-to-one margin. And if they never attended church, they were more likely to vote Democratic by a two-to-one margin. Put simply, frequency of worship attendance has begun to become a reliable predictor of how one will vote. In fact, what has come to be known as the "religion gap" or the "God gap" in American politics is best understood as differences in frequency in worship attendance (or in attendance at all). The general point from recent research is that the more often a person goes to church, the more likely he or she is to vote Republican.

The speculation about a God gap between our two major parties has created much controversy, not least because it suggests that the Republican Party has become the party of "religious believers" and the Democratic Party the party of "nonbelievers."

## THE CULTURE WARS GAP

However, I want to put forward a different thesis: There is a God gap, but it is not a gap between entirely religious people in one party and totally secular people in the other party. It is a fundamental disagreement over different views of the nature of faith and what that faith demands of us concerning the proper direction of our public policies.

Polls do show that the Republican Party is seen by the American public as the more religion-friendly party. How do we account for that? And why (despite the work of countless new organizations and the relentless efforts of people like Jim Wallis, Amy Sullivan, and Mara Vanderslice[5]) is the Democratic Party deemed to be less religion friendly?

I want to posit two possible explanations.

First, instead of wondering why so many devoted religious believers have become Republicans, we should wonder why so many secular nonbelievers want to be Democrats.

The Democratic pollster Stanley Greenberg has described secular voters as "the true loyalists" of the Democratic Party, estimating that they are up to 15 percent of the party's base. In an important essay from 2002, two political scientists from Baruch College in New York, Louis Bolce and Gerald DeMaio, argue that the Democratic Party has become the political home to nonbelievers and, more than that, the political home to many who are actively hostile toward religious conservatives. They argue that Republicans have become the traditionalist party "by default more than by overt action."[6]

The authors argue that "although considerable attention has been devoted to religious and cultural conflict in American political life, few in the mainstream media have acknowledged the true origins of the conflict—namely, the increased prominence of secularists within the Democratic party, and the party's resulting antagonism toward traditional values." They point out that a dramatic shift occurred at the Democratic National Convention in 1972. "Prior to the late 1960s," they argue, "there was something of a tacit commitment among elites in both parties to the traditional Judeo-Christian teachings regarding authority, sexual mores, and the family." But the nomination of George McGovern as their candidate for president shattered that consensus on the Democratic side, when the party was "captured by a faction whose cultural reform agenda was perceived by many (both inside and outside the convention) as antagonistic to traditional religious values."[7] At the convention, over a third of the white delegates fit the definition of secularist, compared with only about 5 percent of the general population. ("Secularist" in this study meant those who reject scriptural authority, have no religious affiliation, never attend religious services or pray, and say religion provides no guidance in their life. I might add the observation of the historian Wilfred McClay, who argues that there are two kinds of secularists in our society: those who are simply indifferent to religion and those who are actively hostile to religion and see it as a dangerous, socially damaging phenomenon that stands in the way of all forms of progress.[8])

Bolce and DeMaio note that as secularists have become more numerous in our society, they have also become an important Democratic voting bloc. They observe, "The religious gap among white voters in the 1992, 1996, and 2000 presidential elections was more important than other demographic and social cleavages in the electorate; it was much larger than the gender gap and more significant than any combination of differences in education, income, occupation, age, marital status, and regional groupings." Again, with the sole exception of race, the religion gap has become the most significant division in the current electorate. Bolce and DeMaio also observe that secularists are as large and loyal a Democratic constituency as organized labor. They point out that in the 2000 election, both composed "about 16% of the white electorate and both backed Al Gore with two-thirds of their votes."[9]

More important, they highlight the rise of what they call a new type of voter—the "anti-fundamentalist voter" (and by this term I believe they mean to include evangelical voters). They wrote this in 2002, and it is all the more relevant now. They write, "The results indicate that over the past decade persons who intensely dislike fundamentalist Christians have found a partisan home in the Democratic Party. President Clinton captured 80% of these voters in his victories over President Bush in 1992 and over Senator Dole four years later; Al Gore picked up 70% of the anti-fundamentalist vote in the 2000 election. One has to reach back to pre-New Deal America . . . to find a period when voting behavior was influenced by this degree of antipathy toward a religious group."[10]

How did this animosity come into existence? DeMaio says elsewhere that "the subculture of the evangelicals was a pretty safe place to live until the 1960s. Then everything started changing. They have been fighting a rear-guard operation ever since. Once they mobilized, there was this huge counter-mobilization on the left, which only built on the counter-cultural trends that affected the Democratic Party so much in the 1970s."[11] Or as Harvard's Nathan Glazer has argued, the mobilization of evangelicals and fundamentalists into politics was a "defensive offensive" against the moral and cultural values that grew out of the counterculture of the 1960s.[12] Thus, according to Bolce and DeMaio, the Democratic Party faces a challenge: "Gaining solid support from anti-fundamentalist voters has become crucial to achieving victories at the national level. . . . Just as Republicans need to win the evangelical-fundamentalist vote without scaring off religious moderates, so too must Democrats mobilize secularists and anti-fundamentalists without becoming too identified in public discourse as the party hostile to religion."[13]

It is, therefore, a huge challenge for the Democratic Party, and recent polls indicate the challenge continues. In July 2005, the Pew Forum on Religion and Public Life conducted a poll that asked if people "feel the Democratic Party is generally friendly toward religion, neutral toward religion, or unfriendly toward religion." Only 29 percent of the respondents indicated that the Democratic Party was religion friendly, as opposed to 55 percent who felt that Republicans were friendly toward religion.[14] So this is precisely the problem for Democrats: an important segment of the party has become identified as unfriendly toward religion and religious values. As a result, they are perceived as indifferent or even hostile to what most Americans see as a positive force in our society, namely, the influence of religion and religious believers.

While it is true that many religious people are Democrats, it is also true that many of the secular elites who have considerable control and power in the party are the same people who have worked long and hard to marginalize religion in America and to banish its influence in the public arena.

Second, an explanation that can help us understand the causes of this religion gap and the reasons for this hostility toward religion among many Democrats can be found by revisiting the "culture wars" thesis put forth by several important sociologists and political scientists.

Much has been made of the red and blue maps in the 2000 and 2004 presidential elections. In the two-color versions, big blocks of red denoting states that went for President Bush stretched across the heartland, while the blue states that went for Vice President Gore and Senator Kerry were concentrated along the East and West coasts. This polarity, however, extends far beyond the political map. The heartlanders and the coastalites appear to inhabit divergent social and religious worlds as well. Hardly a day goes by without our being reminded by scholars and pundits that our society is divided and fractured—and that we are involved in a values war between two very different worldviews. We are, according to the historian Gertrude Himmelfarb, "one nation, two cultures." Or as my fellow panelist Michael Barone describes us, we are either "hard America" or we are "soft America." According to sociologist James Davison Hunter, we are engaged in a culture war between religious traditionalists and liberal progressives. Or as New York Times columnist David Brooks describes us, we are either bourgeois bohemians or patio men, living in latte towns or sprinkler towns; we reside on the left coast but also reside in flyover country. We are Red America and we are Blue America.[15]

People in Blue America, according to the lyrics of the singer-songwriter Chuck Brodsky, like to "watch ducks and feed 'em," while people in Red America like to "shoot ducks and eat 'em." Writing in the Atlantic Monthly about the two-colored map used to describe our voting patterns, David Brooks observed that people in Blue America sip lattes and drink champagne while people in Red America down sodas and drink brewskies. But most important, Brooks argues that the divide is best understood as one between completely divergent mental, intellectual, and religious sensibilities. Here is his very perceptive observation:

> Those of us in the coastal metro Blue areas read more books and attend more plays than the people in the Red heartland . . . but

don't ask us, *please*, what life in Red America is like. We don't *know*. We don't *know* who Tim LaHaye and Jerry Jenkins are, even though the novels they have co-written have sold about 40 million copies over the past few years. We don't *know* what James Dobson says on his radio program, which is listened to by millions.... We don't *know* what happens in mega-churches on Wednesday evenings, and some of us couldn't tell you the difference between a fundamentalist and an evangelical, let alone describe what it means to be a Pentecostal.[16]

## CAUSES OF THE CULTURE WARS

Why is this? Peter Berger of Boston University has made the following observation about America: He says that the most religious country in the world, qua religion, is India. Empirically, the most secular country in the world is Sweden. And "America is a country of Indians ruled by Swedes."

Berger is suggesting that the messages conveyed by those who are the "gatekeepers" of our society—many who work and live in Blue America; those who command our educational and cultural leadership positions in our society, what some political scientists have called the new class elites: the editors and publishers of our major newspapers and newsmagazines, the heads of almost all of the major television networks, the leaders and academics at our major universities, the Hollywood movie producers, many of those at the cultural street corners of our society and the major transmission centers of information in our society—are simply not recognized by millions and millions of Americans who call themselves religious believers. This explains why four prominent political scientists have concluded that "evangelicals have become the religious mainstay of the GOP," while Democrats have "established a strong link to the growing coterie of unaffiliated voters, perhaps building a large constituency of 'secular warriors.'"[17]

The emergence of the religion gap in our national elections was in many ways foreshadowed in the academic work of three scholars I would like to highlight: James Davison Hunter, Gertrude Himmelfarb, and Christopher Lasch.

James Davison Hunter, in his book *Culture Wars*, notes that in America today we are in the midst of a culture war. On one side of this war are progressives and secular people. On the other side are people who hold to traditional Judeo-Christian moral values. Hunter argues that there is a battle raging between the orthodox, committed to "an external, definable and transcendent authority," and the progressives, "defined by the spirit of the modern age, a spirit of rationalism and subjectivism." Hunter suggests that just below all of our political disputes is a cultural battle going on between two totally different views of morality. What we are seeing is the public expression of different "moralities-in-conflict" between people who, Hunter says, hold totally different "conceptions of moral authority, with two fundamentally different conceptions of reality."[18] It is a struggle between competing truth claims—between people who are living in almost two separate worlds, people who are quite simply "worlds apart" in their views.

Hunter was writing before the Internet, talk radio, and cable television became the strong forces they are in our current public debates. But the insights in his book are prescient for our discussion on the religion gap between our political parties. Along with Robert Wuthnow of Princeton, Hunter also observed, as Father Andrew Greeley points out in his review of *Culture Wars* in the *New York Times Book Review*, that our "differences across denominational lines are now less important than differences within denominations." Regarding the new religious coalitions and alignments that Hunter describes, Greeley notes, "the orthodox within each tradition are more likely to share values and causes with the orthodox from other traditions than with the progressives within their own traditions."[19] As the results of recent elections have indicated, this is why conservative Protestants tend to vote with conservative Catholics and Orthodox Jews, while liberal Catholics, liberal Protestants, and liberal Jews are more likely to vote with one another.

Similar observations are made by the eminent historian Gertrude Himmelfarb in her book *One Nation, Two Cultures*. She observes that we are quite simply a nation divided into two cultures. One side of the culture originated in our conservative, Puritan heritage, and the other grew out of the counterculture of the late 1960s. This later culture generated what is dominant today, as represented in the media and at the major universities of America. The more conservative, traditionalist culture, which she calls the "dissident culture," continues to promote the values of family, religion, and sexual morality. (Interestingly, she argues that this "dissident culture" is today's new counterculture.) She further observes,

As a minority, the traditionalist culture labors under the disadvantage of being perennially on the defensive. Its elite—gospel preachers, radio talk show hosts, some prominent columnists, and organizational leaders—cannot begin to match, in numbers or influence, those who occupy the commanding heights of the dominant culture: professors presiding over the multitude of young people who attend their lectures, read their books, and have to pass their exams; journalists who determine what information, and what "spins" on that information, come to the public; television and movie producers who provide the images and values that shape the popular culture; cultural entrepreneurs who are ingenious in creating and marketing ever more sensational and provocative products. An occasional boycott by religious conservatives (of the Disney enterprises, for example) can hardly counteract the cumulative, pervasive effect of the dominant culture.[20]

The late social historian Christopher Lasch had similar concerns about our progressive establishment in his last book, *The Revolt of the Elites and the Betrayal of Democracy*. He writes, "Our public life is thoroughly secularized. The separation of church and state, nowadays interpreted as prohibiting any public recognition of religion at all, is more deeply entrenched in America than anywhere else. . . . Among elites, religion is held in low esteem—something useful for weddings and funerals but otherwise dispensable. A skeptical, iconoclastic state of mind is one of the distinguishing characteristics of the knowledge classes. Their commitment to the culture of criticism is understood to rule out religious commitments. The elites' attitude to religion ranges from indifference to active hostility."[21]

This perspective may be present in parts of the Republican Party but is far more prominent, by many degrees of magnitude, in today's Democratic Party. Rightly or wrongly, in the recent past, there has been an impression that the most important political operatives in the Democratic Party, along with the financial donors who support them, are committed to secular values and are more than a little wary of religion and its believers.

Let me be clear: both parties have strong religious constituencies that support them. It just so happens that an important growing edge in

American religion is religious conservatism. These conservative constituents overwhelmingly vote for the GOP. As a result, some Democratic candidates and political operatives have realized that this is not a healthy approach for their party. But in light of the elections of 2006, has this dilemma for the Democratic Party been resolved or at least diminished?

The results of the November 2006 elections were striking. Exit polls indicated that the Republican Party held on to voters who attend religious services more than once a week and those who attend church at least once a week. But a survey by the Pew Forum on Religion and Public Life found that "less frequent churchgoers were much more supportive of Democrats than they were four years ago. Among those who attend church a few times a year, for instance, 60% voted Democratic . . . and among those who never go to church, 67% voted Democratic. . . . As a result, the gap in Democratic support between those who attend church more than once a week and those who never attend church has grown from 18 percentage points in 2002 to 29 points today."[22] In other words, these polls showed that the gains Democrats made in 2006 were in large part from secular and non-Christian voters. This is especially interesting given the hard work by many well-intentioned people in the Democratic Party to bring in more religious voters. But it also poses questions for the Republican Party: How can it appeal to less religious voters? Are there ways Republicans can make appeals to them?

In light of all of this, what should we expect in the 2008 presidential campaign? I conclude with two challenges and two comments. But first: Democrats and Republicans must both realize that the culture war I described earlier that is taking place in our wider culture is now taking place within each of the two parties.

The challenge for Democrats is this: they must find ways to calm the passions of the "secular warriors" in their midst, so that the party will not continue to be perceived as hostile to religious believers. The challenge for the Republicans, on the other hand, is this: they must find ways for the libertarians and nonbelievers in the party to continue to feel at home there. (See the constructive dialogue of Michael Novak, Ramesh Ponnuru, and Heather McDonald at *National Review Online* for an example of how this dialogue ought to proceed.)

Finally, two comments. First, a prediction: Any candidate who attempts to contrive an inauthentic religious sensibility will be seen for what for he or she is, namely, as insincere and politically calculating.

However, any candidate who is tone-deaf to religious language and who is uncomfortable speaking publicly about religious themes in even the most general way will not be nominated by his or her party, much less have a chance to win the presidency.

Second, there are sincere and devout religious believers who will run for president in both parties. But the point to remember is not whether candidates are sincere in their religious beliefs but instead whether they are right on the public policy issues that are so urgently in dispute. Being a sincere and devout religious person is not a guarantee of wisdom, especially of political wisdom. Ultimately, a candidate's position on decisive policy issues will be the most important test—not whether a candidate can speak eloquently on matters of religion to his or her constituents.

## NOTES

1. "Getting Religion," *Christian Century*, July 13, 2004, 5.

2. Barone quoted in *Is There a Culture War? A Dialogue on Values and American Public Life*, ed. James Davison Hunter and Alan Wolfe (Washington, DC: Pew Research Center), 2006, 63.

3. Pew Forum on Religion and Public Life, "GOP the Religion-Friendly Party, but Stem Cell Issue May Help Democrats," August 24, 2004, http://pew-forum.org/docs/?DocID=51.

4. Strickland quoted in "Closing the God Gap," *Atlantic Monthly*, January–February 2007, 39.

5. For an overview of the key activists, strategists, and organizations that have spent the past several years trying to help Democrats "get religion," see Daniel Burke, Kevin Eckstrom, and Peter Sachs, "With the Help of a Dozen, Democrats Learn to 'Get Religion,'" *Religion News Service*, October 20, 2006.

6. Louis Bolce and Gerald DeMaio, "Our Secularist Democratic Party," *Public Interest*, Fall 2002, 8.

7. Ibid, 7.

8. Wilfred McClay, "Two Concepts of Secularism," *Wilson Quarterly*, Summer 2000.

9. Bolce and DeMaio, "Our Secularist Democratic Party," 12.

10. Ibid, 13.

11. DeMaio quoted in Terry Mattingly, "Stalking the Anti-Fundamentalist Voter," *Scripps Howard News Service*, May 5, 2004.

12. Nathan Glazer, "Toward a New Concordat?" *This World*, Summer 1982.

13. Bolce and DeMaio, "Our Secularist Democratic Party," 14.

14. Cited in Gregory A. Smith, "Do the Democrats Have a 'God Problem'?" Pew Research Center, July 6, 2006.

15. Gertrude Himmelfarb, *One Nation, Two Cultures* (New York: Knopf, 1999); Michael Barone, *Hard America, Soft America: Competition vs. Coddling and the Battle for the Nation's Future* (New York: Crown Forum, 2004); James Davison Hunter, *Culture Wars: The Struggle to Define America* (New York: Basic Books, 1991); David Brooks, *Bobos in Paradise: The New Upper Class and How They Got There* (New York: Simon and Schuster, 2000).

16. David Brooks, "One Nation, Slightly Divisible," *Atlantic Monthly*, December 2001.

17. John Green, James Guth, Lyman Kellstedt, and Corwin Smidt quoted in Smith, "Do the Democrats."

18. Hunter, *Culture Wars*, 128.

19. Greeley quoted in Hunter and Wolfe, *Is There a Culture War*, 3.

20. Himmelfarb, *One Nation*, 125.

21. Christopher Lasch, *The Revolt of the Elites and the Betrayal of Democracy* (New York: Norton, 1995), 215.

22. Pew Forum on Religion and Public Life, "The God Gap Widens: Religion and the 2006 Elections," January 3, 2007.

# RELIGION, CIVIC ENGAGEMENT, AND POLITICAL PARTICIPATION

## Corwin E. Smidt

Public life itself is essential to human flourishing (Cochran 1990, 84). To participate in, share responsibility for, and develop affective ties to some social entity outside oneself, whether a voluntary association, a church, a neighborhood, or a workplace, adds a dimension to human life beyond that present in the private realm. And such participation serves to balance the limitations of private life and moderate its negative tendencies.[1]

Religion plays an important role related to public life in that it fosters both civic and political engagement (e.g., Verba, Schlozman, and Brady 1995; Wuthnow 1996; Putnam 2000). Yet, while there is a rich tradition that links religion to public engagement, it is also true that the nature of the relationship between religion and public engagement is complex and not fully understood (Miller 2003, 51).[2]

Studies analyzing the role of religion in fostering civic and political activity have generally assessed religion's role in a rather unsystematic fashion. Some have focused on church membership, others on church attendance, some on the salience of religion in one's life, and still others on the religious tradition of one's religious affiliation. It is unclear, therefore, just how these different facets of religion relate to the shaping of both civic and political engagement. In other words, what is it specifically about religion that contributes to such engagement? Is it religious beliefs, religious commitment, religious networks, or some combination of such factors? Are certain religious traditions or certain types of people within a religious tradition more likely to manifest high levels of civic engagement?

This chapter examines the nature of the relationship between religion and public life. However, rather than examining the full range of ways in which religion might be related to civic and political engagement (something not possible anyway within the confines of one chapter), it assesses one particular analytical approach to religion as a means to do so. Broadly speaking, the chapter examines whether the way in which Americans express their religiosity has become more private over the past several decades and whether the privatization of religious faith may be linked to diminished patterns of engagement in public life. A relatively simple, yet revealing, measure of different forms of religious expression is constructed and applied across a variety of publicly available data files to address three basic questions about religion and public life: (1) Have the ways in which the American people manifest their religious faith changed over time? (2) Are the ways in which people are religious related to the ways in which they engage in public life? (3) Is religion similarly or differentially related to civic and political activity, and has this relationship changed over time?

## THE DIMENSIONS OF RELIGIOUS, POLITICAL, AND PUBLIC LIFE

Advocates of public life tend, all too often, to equate public life with political activity. Just as it is important to recognize that participation in religious organizational life does not encompass all of religious life, neither is public life limited to political life. If politics is far more than elections, so too public life entails more than electoral and pressure politics. The means by which such citizens choose to address collective problems need not be through governmental institutions. Whereas political life seeks to influence "the selection of governmental personnel and/or the actions they take," civic life reflects "publicly spirited collective action," nonremunerative in nature, that is not directly guided "by some desire to shape public policy" (Campbell 2004, 7).

In recent years, there has been a growing discussion among political scientists about the relationship between civic and political life. While some argue that civic engagement is essentially apolitical and distinctive in nature (e.g., Theiss-Morse and Hibbing 2005), others argue that civic engagement and political participation are related, as "a vibrant politics depends on a vibrant civil society" (Macedo et al. 2005, 6–7;

see also Zukin et al. 2006). Nevertheless, while this debate regarding the extent to which civic activity is political in nature is ongoing, it appears that political scientists are "increasingly accepting the notion that civic behavior is politically relevant" (Jenkins et al. 2003, 3).

## The Changing Nature of American Public Life

Historically, one important characteristic of American public life has been the relatively high level of civic engagement displayed by the American people. But, today, there is growing concern over what appears to be a declining willingness of Americans to be so engaged. Evidence documenting this decline comes from a number of different vantage points. Perhaps most noted has been a decline in most levels of political participation over the past several decades. Whether measured in terms of attending a political rally or speech, attending a meeting to address some civic concern, or working for a political party or election campaign, there has been a marked decline (roughly between one-third and one-half, depending on the particular indicator examined) in such reported activities (Putnam 2000, 45). And, generally speaking, there has been a slow erosion of voter turnout rates in American presidential elections over the past four decades, dropping from approximately 60 percent turnout to 50 percent turnout.[3]

But this decline in public engagement is not limited to the political sphere—it also appears to have extended to civic life as well. The records of many longstanding, but diverse, organizations (e.g., the PTA, the Elks, the League of Women Voters) reveal that there has been a decline in their levels of membership over the past three decades (Putnam 2000, chap. 3). Likewise, the amount of time Americans report engaging in informal socializing and visiting with others has declined as well (Putnam 2000, chap. 6).

Not all scholars necessarily share this perspective that America is witnessing a decline in civic engagement (e.g., Ladd 1996; Skocpol and Fiorina 1999; Becker and Dhingra 2001).[4] Still, despite these counterarguments, it would appear that, at a minimum, Americans are less socially connected through face-to-face interaction with others outside their family than was true several decades ago. This decline in social interaction among individuals, within families, and within voluntary associations raises concerns that America's "social capital" is in decline

(Putnam 1995, 2000), as any diminution in social ties is likely to lead to a subsequent decline in civic engagement. And, little, if any, countervailing data have been generated to demonstrate that there has not been a decline in political participation over the past several decades.[5] As a result, "a consistent theme of social and political analysis over the past four decades has been the gradual disengagement of the American citizenry from public life, and especially from traditional political participation" (Zukin et al. 2006, 3).[6]

## The Changing Nature of American Religious Life

The religious character of the American people has important consequences for public life, as it can shape the way people interact socially, how they relate to those outside the boundaries of their religious group, and the particular ends for which they engage in public life. In addition, religion may shape the ways in which individuals view the role of the state and their responsibilities related to public life. Thus religion may well shape the motivations for civic and political engagement and the goals of such engagement, as well as the means by which to accomplish such ends.

However, according to secularization theory, religion is largely a vestige of premodern culture and constitutes a human expression that is destined to decline in importance and, perhaps, disappear altogether in an age of science and reason (Hadden 1989, 3). Within this perspective, as societies modernize, they secularize; religion disappears—or, at the very least, its expression becomes highly private.[7] Thus, according to secularization theory, any "impact" that religion may have in contemporary American civic and political life is simply a remnant of some outmoded, and disappearing, facet of social life.

Although the countervailing evidence to secularization theory could be examined in great detail, perhaps it is sufficient here simply to note several prominent features of contemporary life that serve to undermine the contentions of the secularization thesis. For example, even though the United States might be considered among the most modern of societies, religious life continues to be among the most vibrant of civic activities in which Americans engage, as virtually half of all associational memberships in America are church related (Putnam 2000, 66). Moreover, despite the passage of time, this relative vibrancy has not necessarily diminished, as a variety of religious behaviors have remained relatively stable within the United States over the past fifty years (Smidt et al. 2003, 34).[8]

Religious life in America has hardly disappeared, and it continues to exhibit certain patterns of stability. Nevertheless, important changes may be taking place within American religious life. A variety of analysts have contended that a more "fluid and flexible" religious situation has emerged in American religious life, one that has been labeled the "new volunteerism" (Roof and McKinney 1987). As a result, religious faith today in America is thought to be shaped less by the social characteristics of its people and more by the personal preferences and values of the believers themselves. In this sense, contemporary religion in America is viewed to be less bound today than even several decades ago by custom or social bonds, being anchored more fully in the private and subjective spheres of life (i.e., less rooted in the web of cultural heritage and childhood socialization and more a personal matter).

Thus one important challenge to religious associational life is the growing individualism within American religious life, as denominational and congregational life has been influenced by the individualistic, subjective, and anti-institutional spirit of contemporary American culture. Although these changes are not likely to lead to the disappearance of religion or the demise of organized religious life, they certainly serve to redefine its public expression. Even now we are seeing a shift from "the religious" to "the spiritual," as many Americans willingly define themselves as spiritual while rejecting ties to "organized religion."

With such changes, it may be that, at least among some segments of American society, there has been a growth in what might be labeled a "privatized faith," reflecting those who are "believers but not belongers" (Davie 1994). Such religionists are those for whom the presence of religious belief within their lives is more individual than institutional, more private than public. With the severance of individual spirituality from institutional religion and its collective authority, it is likely that believers will increasingly exhibit personal autonomy from religious institutions, as individuals become more and more idiosyncratic and eclectic in forging their religious faith. Thus "private religion," as it is used here, indicates that one's religious faith is practiced primarily within a personal, rather than an organizational, locus.

## Private Religion and the Decline of Public Life

Are the broad changes in American public life discussed earlier possibly linked to changes in American religious life? Has there been a growth in the extent to which Americans express a private faith? And are those who express a private religious faith more inclined also to withdraw from public life? Some analysts may hold that, given the separation of church and state, it is desirable that religious beliefs and values remain private in nature and not be permitted to be expressed within the public square. Yet it may well be that private religion leads to lower levels of public engagement as well; in other words, private religion may work at cross-purposes with the normative value of high levels of public engagement.

Thus, when considering the link between religion and civic or political engagement, what may be important about religion is not so much one's particular religious beliefs or membership in some particular religious tradition but the way in which one is religious (Ammerman 1997). In fact, Jean Bethke Elshtain (2002, 24) has suggested that participation in public religious life and participation in political life are related in that "contemporary distrust of organized politics and organized religion goes hand in hand." She notes in support of her contention that both organized religion and organized politics are public expressions, involving groups of people engaging in a shared enterprise, operating under particular rules, and expressing particular convictions. Accordingly, she contends, religious believers who disvalue organizational life within the religious sphere of life may well express diminished enthusiasm for organizational endeavors within the civic and political spheres of life as well.

### CATEGORIES OF PRIVATE AND PUBLIC RELIGIOUS BEHAVIOR

To what extent, if at all, has the way in which Americans express their religiosity changed over time? Is there any evidence that religious expression within American life has become more private in nature? And, if so, can such changes help to account for any decline in participating in civic and political life?

The data in table 1 begin to address these questions, as the table presents the levels of church attendance and frequency of prayer reported by

Americans over the past thirty-five years. Data presented in the second column of table 1 are drawn from Roper surveys collected between 1973 and 1994 (made available as the Roper Social and Political Trends Data, 1973–1994). More than 400,000 respondents are contained in this data file, as a number of surveys were conducted within each of the years over that period of time. In many of the surveys conducted throughout these years, respondents were asked whether or not they had attended church in the past seven days, and the resulting percentages obtained in the various surveys for nineteen years[9] are presented in the second column of table 1.[10]

In examining responses to this question over time, several tentative inferences can be drawn from the data. First, there do not appear to be any dramatic shifts in reported levels of church attendance over the two-decade period analyzed. Of course, there is some shifting, sometimes increasing and sometimes decreasing, in the percentages from one year to the next. Yet, overall, there is no evidence of any dramatic downturn in reported levels of church attendance across this span of time.

Second, over this two-decade period, there does appear to have been a slight, though not dramatic, erosion of weekly church attendance. A cursory examination reveals that during the first seven years (1974–1980), the percentage reporting that they had attended religious services in the last seven days never dipped below 40 percent. During the next seven years (1981–1987, with no data for 1983 and 1986), however, the percentage dipped below 40 percent twice. And, during the last seven years (1988–1994), the percentage reporting attendance at church in the past seven days dipped below 40 percent four times. In fact, if one combines the data collected for the five years from 1974 through 1978, the percentage of respondents reporting attendance at a worship service in the last seven days was 43.5 percent, whereas the corresponding percentage for the last five years of data collected (1990–1994) was 37.9 percent.

Third, despite this small decline in reported levels of attendance at services of public worship, a substantial proportion of the American people continued to engage in such activity. When asked in this particular question format, roughly 40 percent of the American people responded each year over the course of these two decades that they had been at a religious service in the last seven days. In 1974, the first year for which such data are available, 41.2 percent of the respondents so re-

Table 1. Reported Religious Behavior of Americans over Time

| | Roper | General Social Surveys | | |
|---|---|---|---|---|
| Year | Attended church in last week (%) | Attend church weekly (%) | Pray daily (%) | Attend church monthly (%) |
| 1972 | — | 35 | — | 56 |
| 1973 | — | 28 | — | 50 |
| 1974 | 41 | 30 | — | 53 |
| 1975 | 44 | 29 | — | 52 |
| 1976 | 46 | 29 | — | 49 |
| 1977 | 43 | 30 | — | 52 |
| 1978 | 42 | 28 | — | 51 |
| 1979 | 44 | — | — | — |
| 1980 | 40 | 29 | — | 50 |
| 1981 | 44 | — | — | — |
| 1982 | 39 | 29 | — | 49 |
| 1983 | — | 32 | 55 | 53 |
| 1984 | 43 | 33 | 57 | 53 |
| 1985 | 43 | 33 | 58 | 51 |
| 1986 | — | 32 | 58 | 56 |
| 1987 | 39 | 29 | 57 | 52 |
| 1988 | 40 | 26 | 54 | 51 |
| 1989 | 41 | 30 | 53 | 51 |
| 1990 | 39 | 30 | 52 | 51 |
| 1991 | 40 | 29 | 42 | 52 |
| 1992 | 36 | — | — | — |
| 1993 | 37 | 29 | 56 | 50 |
| 1994 | 39 | 27 | 56 | 48 |
| 1996 | — | 25 | 58 | 45 |
| 1998 | — | 25 | 55 | 48 |
| 2000 | — | 25 | 56 | 44 |
| 2002 | — | 24 | 57 | 47 |
| 2004 | — | 28 | 59 | 50 |

*Source:* Roper Social and Political Trends Data, 1973–1994; General Social Surveys, 1972–2004.

ported, and in 1994, the last year for which such data are available, 38.7 percent of the respondents did so.

Of course, different survey organizations utilizing different survey questions may obtain somewhat different results. Consequently, the remaining columns of table 1 present data drawn from each General Social Survey (GSS) since its inception in 1972. The third column of table 1 examines levels of reported weekly church attendance, this time using a different question format and extending the analysis by another decade. The GSS results reveal a somewhat lower percentage of weekly church attendance than that found through the Roper surveys. Nevertheless, despite the different question format and sampling frame employed, there are important parallels between the Roper and GSS religious attendance patterns. Just as was evident with the Roper data, the GSS data do not reveal any dramatic declines in the weekly attendance at religious services, though as was evident with the Roper data, there appears to have been a slight decline in reported levels of weekly church attendance. Prior to 1986, the percentages of those who reported weekly attendance were in the high 20s and low 30s; beginning in 1991, the results never again attain a level of 30 percent, and have remained around 25 percent for the past decade. Again, if one pools the data collected from the first five surveys (1972–1976) and compares it to the data collected from the last five surveys (1996–2004), one finds a decline of about 5 percentage points, from 30.3 percent to 25.0 percent, in reported weekly church attendance over the past three decades.

Thus there does appear to have been a gradual decline in attendance at public worship services over the past three decades. However, it is unclear whether such a decline in attendance at public worship services is a function of a decline in the salience of religion among the American people over time or a function of religion's becoming more private in nature. Even if there has been a slight decline in the level of attendance at public worship services, there may not be any similar decline in reported levels of private devotional activity.

The fourth column of table 1 addresses this matter. The GSS did not ask respondents how frequently they prayed until 1983, but that question has been asked in each of its subsequent surveys (though sometimes only of one-half or one-quarter of the respondents). As evident in table 1, the percentage of Americans who report engaging in prayer on a daily basis exhibits far greater aggregate stability than that related to church attendance (though it is unclear why the 1991 percentage related to daily prayer is so atypical). Moreover, the data reveal that the frequency with which Americans report praying on a daily basis may have increased over the past two decades. Again, if one combines the data from the 1983–1987 surveys (the first five years for which we have data) and compares it to the data from the 1996–2004 surveys (the last five surveys conducted), the percentage of Americans reporting that they pray on a daily basis has increased slightly, from 56.3 percent to 56.9 percent.

Thus it may well be that there has been a growth in a private form of religious expression, as the decline in attendance at public worship services is not associated with any decline in prayer as a religious practice. However, such aggregate patterns do not necessarily reveal how widespread such private religious behavior is in the mass public. Consequently, it is necessary to discuss briefly the scheme employed to classify respondents in terms of the particular form in which their religious life is expressed and to explain how a measure was constructed to examine these forms of religious expression across the various surveys employed in this analysis.

### Categories of Private and Public Religious Behavior

To categorize the American people broadly in terms of the way in which they are religious, respondents were initially classified along two dimensions: (1) the extent to which they engaged in private religious practice and (2) the extent to which they engaged in public religious practice. To ensure comparability of measures across various studies and to be able to use the widest array of data possible, a minimal number of questions were used to make such assignments. Given that most surveys ask a limited number of religious questions, the two most common measures related to each dimension were employed—namely, level of reported attendance at religious services and the extent to which the respondent reported engaging in a personal prayer life.

The particular cut point utilized in classifying respondents along the public dimension of religiosity was whether or not the respondent reported attending church on a monthly basis or more often, while the cut point for the private dimension was whether or not the respondent reported praying on a daily basis. These particular points were used because they marked roughly the point at which approximately one-half of the respondents fell on either side at the turn of the millennium (see the last two columns of table 1).

By dichotomizing respondents along each dimension (in terms of low and high levels of practice), four broad categories were created to reflect the forms by which people express their religiosity. First, there are those whose religious expression is relatively low along both dimensions; these respondents exhibited what might be labeled a "diminished" form of religious life. Those who fall in this category may be atheists, agnostics, or even private theists. But while such respondents may vary in terms of their religious beliefs, they share a similarity in terms of how they express their religious faith: it is not particularly important to them, as they report relatively low levels of public worship attendance as well as relatively low levels of private prayer.

Second, some exhibit a "private" religious faith. In terms of their religious activities, private religionists exhibit high levels of private, but low levels of public, expressions of their religious faith. Such individuals are likely to report that their religious faith is salient to them but that their personal beliefs and practices are more important to them than what is taught by any religious body with which they may or may not be affiliated. While they may engage in public worship occasionally, they do not do so with any frequency. Nevertheless, they remain relatively religious—at least in terms of their reported frequency of private prayer.

Third, some Americans exhibit their religious faith primarily in a "public" fashion. These respondents report high levels of religious attendance but relatively low levels of private religious activity. Some who fall in this category may be associated with religious faiths in which public participation at religious services is more highly emphasized than personal devotional activity, but others in this category may be religiously involved for self-oriented reasons (Edgell 2006, 71). And for yet others in this category, religious attendance may be a function of "extrinsic" motives (Allport and Ross 1967), in that they may choose to attend religious services simply for utilitarian ends, for example, as a means to promote their particular business or professional practice or for purposes of socializing with fellow worshippers. For such individuals, if spiritual growth is a priority at all, it is secondary.

Finally, there are those who exhibit high levels of both private and public religious activity, labeled here as an "integrated" form of religious expression. Clearly, for such respondents, religion is highly salient in their lives. It is likely, therefore, that such respondents are those who "find their master motive in religion" (Allport and Ross 1967, 434), desiring to internalize their faith and to subordinate all other aspects of life to their religious commitment (Allport and Ross 1967, 441). For such individuals, spiritual growth is a priority, but such growth is seen to be intertwined with active participation in the worship life of a religious community.

Does such a classification system, based on such relatively crude measures, have any validity in reflecting the religious expressions of the American people? Fortunately, two surveys, the God and Society in North America survey (1996) and the Arts and Religion Survey (1999), contain a number of questions that permit an initial validation of this classification system. The analysis, presented in table 2, supports the conclusion that this relatively simple classification scheme captures important differences in religious orientations that are anticipated theoretically.

First, those who are classified as exhibiting a diminished form of religious expression are, by far, the most likely to report that religion is not important in their lives (57 percent), while relatively few (19 percent) report that religion serves to provide them any significant level of guidance in their lives. Likewise, two-thirds of those who fall in this category strongly agree (and nearly all, 91 percent, agree) that one does not need to attend religious services to be a good Christian, while one-half strongly agree and an overwhelming majority (76 percent) agree that their personal beliefs are more important than what is taught by any religious institution.

Since those exhibiting a private form of religious expression are relatively high in their level of reported prayer life, they are much more likely than those who exhibit a diminished form of religious expression to indicate that religion does provide guidance in their lives; in fact, a majority (57 percent) of those who fall within the category report that religion provides either quite a bit or a great deal of guidance in their lives. Moreover, in accordance with theoretical expectations, those who exhibit a private expression of their religious faith also overwhelming agree that one does not need to attend religious services to be a good Christian, and they overwhelming insist that their personal beliefs are much more important than what is taught by any religious institution. In fact, those who exhibit a private form of religious behavior are the most likely of all the groups examined to strongly agree with these two statements.

## Table 2. Validation of Form of Religious Expression Variable

| | Form of religious expression | | | |
|---|---|---|---|---|
| | Diminished (%) | Private (%) | Public (%) | Integrated (%) |
| **God and Society 1996** | | | | |
| *Salience of religion* | | | | |
| Not important | 57 | 24 | 11 | 3 |
| Some guidance | 24 | 18 | 37 | 10 |
| Quite a bit of guidance | 9 | 22 | 25 | 24 |
| A great deal of guidance | 10 | 35 | 27 | 64 |
| *Don't need to go to church to be a good Christian* | | | | |
| Strongly disagree | 4 | 5 | 16 | 32 |
| Strongly agree | 67 | 71 | 34 | 23 |
| *My personal beliefs are more important than what is taught by any church* | | | | |
| Strongly disagree | 9 | 8 | 10 | 16 |
| Strong agree | 50 | 61 | 39 | 43 |
| **Arts and Religion 1999** | | | | |
| *My spirituality does not depend on being involved in a religious organization* | | | | |
| Agree | 88 | 82 | 57 | 51 |
| *It doesn't matter what you believe, as long as you are a good person* | | | | |
| Disagree | 18 | 34 | 38 | 61 |
| *How important has attending services at your place of worship been in your efforts to grow spiritually or develop a closer relationship with God?* | | | | |
| Very important | 12 | 34 | 58 | 84 |

*Source:* God and Society in North America, 1996; Arts and Religion Survey, 1999.

It is likely that those whose religious form is characterized by relatively higher levels of public, but lower levels of private, religious behavior would also be inclined to report that religion provides a good deal of guidance in their lives. But what is likely to distinguish such religionists from those who fall in the private category is that the former are likely to value public worship and religious institutions more fully than those who exhibit a more private faith (as well as those who exhibit a diminished form of religious life). Still, given the earlier noted influence of religious individualism within American religious life, such expectations should be viewed in a more relative than absolute fashion.

These expectations are also fulfilled in the patterns revealed in table 2. First, a majority (52 percent) of those who exhibit a primarily public form of religious expression report that religion provides either a quite a bit or a great deal of guidance in their lives. Second, while somewhat less than a third (30 percent) of those who fall in this category disagree with the contention that one need not go to church to be a good Christian, they are three times more likely to do so than those who exhibit a private faith and nearly four times more likely to do so than those who exhibit a diminished form of religious expression. And, while only a little more than one-quarter (27 percent) of those who fall in this category express disagreement with the contention that their personal beliefs are more important than what is taught by any church, the proportion of those who do express such disagreement exceeds the proportion found among those whose faith is more private in nature according to the classification scheme employed.

Finally, those who exhibit high levels of both public and private religious behavior (an integrated religious form) are the most likely to report that religion has a great deal of salience in their personal lives (64 percent report it provides a great deal of guidance). And they are the most likely (32 percent) to disagree with the contention that one does not need to attend worship services to be a good Christian and the most likely (43 percent) to agree with the contention that their personal religious beliefs are more important than what is taught by any church.

Wuthnow's 1999 Arts and Religion Survey also contains several items that permit a further assessment of the validity of these categories. First, respondents in the survey were asked to express agreement or disagreement with the following statement: "My spirituality does not depend on being involved in a religious organization." If the different forms of religious expression have any validity empirically, then one would anticipate that those who exhibit either a diminished or a private form of religious life should differ in their responses to this question from those who exhibit either a public or integrated form of religious expression. Specifically, since regular attendance at worship services of some religious congregation characterizes those who exhibit a public or integrated form of religious expression, one would expect that those with a diminished or private form of religious expression would be much more likely to agree with the statement than those who exhibit a public or integrated form of religious expression. And clearly this is the case: whereas more than four of five of those with diminished or private forms agreed with the statement, only a little more than one of two of those with public or integrated forms did so.

On the other hand, these analytical categories suggest that there are also important differences among those who attend church on a regular basis. Clearly the public and integrated forms of religiosity part ways on the basis of their devotional lives, but what does this suggest about the nature of their religious faith? It may reflect, in part, differences in perspectives about the desire to grow spiritually, but it may also be related to their assessments concerning the certainty of religious truth. What concerns those who exhibit public forms of religious expression is the public aspect of that religious expression, but this public expression is not sufficient for those who exhibit an integrated form of religious expression.

Thus one might anticipate that those exhibiting these forms of religious expression would differ in their level of agreement or disagreement with the statement "It doesn't matter what you believe, as long as you are a good person." Since those who exhibit an integrated form of religious expression see participation in the worship life of a particular religious community as linked to their personal spiritual growth, one might anticipate that such individuals are less likely to be "relativists" religiously; for them, adherence to, or the failure to hold, particular religious beliefs is likely to have important consequences. This expectation is also evident in table 2, as those who exhibit an integrated form of religious expression tend to stand alone in their disagreement with the statement "It doesn't matter what you believe, as long as you are a good person." More than 60 percent of those who exhibit an integrated form of religious expression disagreed with the statement, while only 38 percent of those exhibiting a public form of religious expression did so and only 34 percent of those exhibiting a private form did so.

Finally, respondents were asked, "How important has attending services at your place of worship been in your efforts to grow spiritually or develop a closer relationship with God?" Here one might anticipate a gradual increase in the percentage of those responding "very important" as one moves from diminished to private, from private to public, and from public to integrated forms of expression. Certainly, those exhibiting a diminished religious expression are the least likely to be concerned about growing spiritually, while those with a private expression may seek spiritual growth, but largely outside regular attendance at places of worship. On the other hand, those who exhibit a public form of religious expression attend church regularly, but spiritual growth may or may not be a consideration as a basis for such regular attendance. Hence, because they attend church regularly, they are more likely than those in the private category to indicate that attending worship services is important in their efforts to grow spiritually. Finally, those who exhibit an integrated form of religious expression are more likely than those who exhibit a public expression to be motivated by a desire for spiritual growth (given their active devotional life). Thus one would anticipate that the former would be more likely than the latter to indicate that attending worship is important in their efforts to grow spiritually.

And, once again, this expectation is reflected in the data presented in table 2, as there is a monotonic pattern in the percentage of respondents reporting that church attendance is very important in terms of their spiritual growth and desire to develop a closer relationship with God. A little more than one in ten (12 percent) of those in the diminished category responded "very important" to the inquiry, while a little more than one in three (34 percent) did so among those with a private form of religious expression. On the other hand, nearly three of five (58 percent) of those exhibiting a public form of religious expression stated attending worship services was very important in their efforts to grow spiritually, while more than four of five (84 percent) of those with an integrated religious form did so.

Overall, therefore, the measurement strategy does capture empirically the theoretical distinctions advanced. Having now provided a foundation for proceeding with this measurement scheme, the remainder of the paper focuses on the theoretical questions at hand.

## Changing Religious Forms

Have the ways in which the American people manifest their religious faith changed? Table 3 addresses this question by examining changes in the forms of religious expression among the American people over time. The table presents the distributions found based on the responses given by the American people over the past two decades in the GSS, the National Election Studies (NES), and other national surveys.

Three important inferences can be drawn from table 3. First, despite that different entities conducted these surveys and employed somewhat different questions, the resulting distributions are roughly similar in that the largest percentages of Americans fall in the diminished and the integrated religious categories. Together, such respondents constitute about two-thirds to three-quarters of the American people, with about one-third of the respondents in the various surveys falling in the diminished religious category and about one-third to two-fifths of the respondents

**Table 3. Distribution of Forms of Religion over Time**

| | Form of religious expression | | | | | |
|---|---|---|---|---|---|---|
| | Diminished (%) | Private (%) | Public (%) | Integrated (%) | Total (%) | N |
| General Social Surveys | | | | | | |
| 1984 | 29 | 17 | 13 | 41 | 100 | 1447 |
| 1988 | 32 | 17 | 14 | 37 | 100 | 1468 |
| 1996 | 31 | 21 | 12 | 37 | 101 | 948 |
| 2000 | 35 | 22 | 9 | 34 | 100 | 778 |
| 2004 | 30 | 21 | 11 | 38 | 100 | 1335 |
| National Election Studies | | | | | | |
| 1988 | 36 | 14 | 17 | 33 | 100 | 2040 |
| 1996 | 34 | 14 | 15 | 38 | 101 | 1714 |
| 2000 | 34 | 15 | 13 | 38 | 100 | 1807 |
| 2004 | 35 | 14 | 12 | 39 | 100 | 1212 |
| Verba 1990 | 37 | 13 | 11 | 38 | 99 | 2517 |
| God and Society 1996 | 27 | 13 | 16 | 43 | 99 | 3000 |
| Saguaro 2000 | 31 | 12 | 16 | 41 | 100 | 3003 |

*Note:* Total percentages may not equal 100 because of rounding.

exhibiting an integrated level of religiosity. Thus only about one-quarter to one-third of the respondents reflect either a private or a public form of religiosity.

Second, the GSS data examined in table 3 do suggest that there may have been some growth in the private expression of religious life among the American people over time. Whereas 17 percent of GSS respondents could be classified as exhibiting a private religious life in 1984 and in 1988, the percentage so classified in GSS studies jumped to 21 percent in 1996 and remained at a similar level in 2000 and 2004. However, the presidential election surveys conducted by NES (as well as the other national surveys examined in the table) do not reveal such a growth in private religion. Thus, if there has been any increase among the American people in choosing to express their religious faith in a more private fashion, such a growth has been, at most, somewhat modest.

## Changing Patterns of Religion and Civic and Political Engagement

Given that any changes in the forms by which Americans express themselves religiously have been modest, they cannot account fully for any dramatic drop in levels of public engagement among the American people. Nevertheless, the question remains whether or not such private expressions of religious faith are linked to lower levels of public engagement more generally. Therefore, the fundamental question that this section of the chapter seeks to address is whether the ways in which people are religious are related to the ways in which they engage more broadly in public life and, if so, whether such differences in forms of religious expression are similarly or differently related to civic and political activity.

To address these questions, one can employ only those data files that contain both a number of variables related to civic participation and a number of variables related to political participation, along with the requisite questions related to the religion of the respondents. In addition, the questions related to civic participation need to be asked of respondents generally, and not simply respondents who report membership in voluntary associations.[11] We utilized three national surveys that contain the required component measures: the NES of 1996, the Saguaro Social Capital Community Benchmark Survey of 2000, and the NES of 2004.[12]

Each study contains four questions that assess civic participation and four questions that tap political participation. Fortunately, for each variable, the four component questions are relatively similar in nature. With regard to civic participation, each of the three studies contains a question regarding whether the respondent was a member of some voluntary association, had volunteered in the past year, or had made a charitable contribution in the past year. The fourth component measure of civic participation, however, varies somewhat by study.[13]

Likewise, each study contains four questions that assess level of political participation. The items employed in the 1996 and 2004 NES tap the same specific types of political activity.[14] The items used for the 2000 national random Saguaro survey include some that are similar to those used in the NES and some that are not.

## Frequency of Participation

Civic and political participation are somewhat different forms of engagement in public life. Given that voting in the last presidential election is one common measure of political participation, one might anticipate that a significant proportion of the American people would exhibit some level of participation in political life. Participation in major elections generally is viewed as the cultural norm, since most Americans hold that citizens should vote when given the opportunity to cast their ballots on important matters. However, political involvement at the mass level tends to be episodic, geared toward the election cycle, and Americans historically have also exhibited what some have labeled an "antiparty" bias. Consequently, one might anticipate that relatively few Americans engage in political activity beyond the common act of voting in presidential elections.

On the other hand, cultural norms related to civic participation are more nebulous. Historically, America has been viewed as "a nation of joiners" (Tocqueville 1969; Schlesinger 1944), and much of civic life, in terms of both demands and outcomes, can be characterized as more immediate and direct than political life. Consequently, one might anticipate that Americans are more likely to engage in civic than political activity and that a larger percentage of Americans are likely to exhibit more extensive levels of civic than political engagement as well.

Table 4 examines the frequency distribution of related levels of civic and political participation across the three studies in which multiple measures of both variables are available. Since voting in the last presidential election was utilized as a component measure of political participation, most respondents reported at least some level of political activity. Nevertheless, both anticipated patterns are evident. First, there is a consistent pattern across all three studies that more Americans report engaging in some form of civic participation than in some form

Table 4. The Distribution of Civic Participation and Political Participation

| | Civic participation[a] (%) | Political participation[b] (%) |
|---|---|---|
| National Election Study 1996 (N = 1521) | | |
| No acts | 8 | 21 |
| One act | 15 | 63 |
| Two acts | 33 | 11 |
| Three or four acts | 44 | 4 |
| Total | 101 | 99 |
| Saguaro 2000 (N = 3003) | | |
| No acts | 8 | 23 |
| One act | 17 | 39 |
| Two acts | 24 | 26 |
| Three or four acts | 52 | 12 |
| Total | 101 | 100 |
| National Election Study 2004 (N = 1066) | | |
| No acts | 14 | 20 |
| One act | 28 | 54 |
| Two acts | 26 | 19 |
| Three or four acts | 32 | 7 |
| Total | 100 | 100 |

Note: Total percentages may not equal 100 because of rounding.
[a] Component measures of civic participation
NES 1996: (a) was a member of some voluntary association, (b) volunteered within the past year, (c) made a charitable contribution in the past year, (d) worked on a committee to address some community problem
Saguaro 2000: (a) was a member of some voluntary association, (b) volunteered within the past year, (c) made a charitable contribution in the past year, (d) worked on a project related to some community problem
NES 2004: (a) was a member of some voluntary association, (b) volunteered within the past year, (c) made a charitable contribution in the past year, (d) attended a community meeting about some issue
[b] Component measures of political participation
NES 1996: (a) voted in 1996, (b) wore a campaign button or had a yard sign, (c) attended a political meeting of some kind, (d) contributed to a political candidate or party
Suguaro 2000: (a) voted in 1996, (b) had a yard sign, (c) attended a political rally, (d) marched in a political demonstration
NES 2004: (a) voted in 2004, (b) wore a campaign button or had a yard sign, (c) worked for a political candidate or party, (d) contributed money to either a political candidate or party

of political participation. Second, a far higher percentage of Americans report engaging in three or more acts of civic engagement than in three or more acts of political engagement.

## The Nature of the Relationship

Civic and political participation are analytically distinct, but one might anticipate that they are empirically related. What is unclear is the extent to which the two are related, and whether religious factors are similarly or differentially related to each form of participation.

Table 5 begins to address this issue by examining the relationship

**Table 5. The Relationship between Political Participation and Civic Participation**

| Index of political participation | Index of civic participation | | | |
|---|---|---|---|---|
| | 0 | 1 | 2 | 3+ |
| National Election Study 1996 | | | | |
| 0 (%) | 62 | 39 | 21 | 10 |
| 1 (%) | 36 | 55 | 68 | 67 |
| 2 (%) | 3 | 6 | 9 | 15 |
| 3+ (%) | 0 | 0 | 2 | 8 |
| Total (%) | 101 | 100 | 100 | 100 |
| N | 117 | 226 | 504 | 666 |
| | | | $r = .35^*$ | |
| Saguaro 2000 | | | | |
| 0 (%) | 61 | 36 | 27 | 11 |
| 1 (%) | 30 | 45 | 48 | 35 |
| 2 (%) | 8 | 16 | 20 | 34 |
| 3+ (%) | 1 | 3 | 6 | 20 |
| Total (%) | 100 | 100 | 101 | 100 |
| N | 213 | 478 | 673 | 1473 |
| | | | $r = .41^*$ | |
| National Election Study 2004 | | | | |
| 0 (%) | 42 | 27 | 15 | 7 |
| 1 (%) | 49 | 55 | 56 | 54 |
| 2 (%) | 8 | 14 | 22 | 26 |
| 3+ (%) | 1 | 4 | 7 | 14 |
| Total (%) | 100 | 100 | 100 | 101 |
| N | 144 | 299 | 276 | 345 |
| | | | $r = .33^*$ | |

*Note:* Total percentages may not equal 100 because of rounding.
$^*p < .001$

between civic and political participation across the three national surveys. As can be seen from the data analyzed, the two variables are fairly strongly correlated (between .33 and .41). Probably the clearest evidence of the fact that the two activities are related is obtained by examining those who did not report any civic participation. In both the 1996 NES and the 2000 Saguaro survey, the vast majority of those who reported no civic activity also reported no political activity. In other words, lack of public engagement in the civic domain is strongly associated with lack of public engagement in the political domain. Similarly, the majority of those who exhibit some level of civic engagement also exhibit some level of political participation, and those who tend to be the most engaged civically are also the most likely to be the most engaged politically.

Nevertheless, while related, the two are empirically distinct. In fact, some respondents report very high levels of civic engagement coupled with no political activity, while some others report relatively high levels of political activity coupled with no reported acts of civic participation. Some individuals are more likely to be involved in civic activities than political activities, and the reverse is true as well. Consequently, while some individuals may choose to concentrate their public endeavors primarily within civic life, others may tend to focus their public endeavors largely within political life.

## Religion and Public Engagement

Clearly individuals exhibit varying levels of engagement in public life. Recognizing this, scholars have created a fourfold typology of public engagement based on differences in the levels of engagement in civic and political life (Zukin et al. 2006). "Electoral specialists" focus the bulk of their attention on electoral politics, choosing to engage more heavily in electoral than civic endeavors. "Civic specialists" focus their attention on civic life, engaging more heavily in civic than political activities. "Dual activists" are those who are highly engaged in both civic and political activities, while the "disengaged" report little activity in either domain.

For purposes of the analysis presented here, electoral specialists are classified as those who report at least two political acts but fewer than two civic acts in the past year.[15] The converse is true for civic specialists, those who engage in two or more civic, but fewer than two political, acts. Dual activists are those who report two or more acts of civic engage-

Table 6. The Distribution of the Nature of Engagement in Public Life

| | Nature of engagement in public life | | | | | |
|---|---|---|---|---|---|---|
| | Disengaged (%) | Electoral specialist (%) | Civic specialist (%) | Dual activist (%) | Total (%) | N |
| National Election Study 1996 | 22 | 1 | 64 | 14 | 101 | 1513 |
| Saguaro 2000 | 20 | 4 | 42 | 34 | 100 | 2837 |
| National Election Study 2004 | 35 | 6 | 38 | 20 | 100 | 1064 |

Note: Total percentages may not equal 100 because of rounding.

ment as well as two or more acts of political participation, while the disengaged are those who indicate that they participated in fewer than two civic activities as well as fewer than two political activities over the past year.

Table 6 examines the distribution of these forms of engagement in public life across the three surveys analyzed. It should be noted, however, that one should not compare the specific percentages associated with each pattern over time because the component measures are not identical across the three studies. Rather, the data should be examined in terms of the general patterns of public engagement.

This classification scheme reveals that most Americans are actively engaged in either some civic or political capacity. Indeed, only about one-fifth to one-third of Americans can be classified as disengaged. A majority of Americans (though a plurality of Americans in 2004) can be classified as civic specialists, while very few Americans can be classified as electoral specialists.[16] Finally, an important segment, somewhere roughly between one-seventh and one-third of the American people, might be viewed as dual activists—highly involved in both civic and political life.

Clearly, based on these measures, Americans are far more likely to focus their efforts on civic than political life. Most Americans are civic specialists, and to the extent that people are engaged politically, they tend to couple such political activism with civic activism, as they are far more likely to indicate that they are dual activists than electoral specialists.

To what extent then, if at all, is religion related to such differences in public engagement? Are those who exhibit more diminished and private forms of religious expression less likely to engage in civic and political life than those who exhibit more public and integrated forms of religious expression? Are those who are relatively religious more likely to specialize in civic than political life, and do such levels of engagement in civic and public life vary by the particular ways in which their religiosity is expressed? These questions are addressed in table 7.

There is a relatively strong relationship between one's form of religious expression and the nature of one's engagement in public life. First of all, those who exhibit a highly private form of religious expression are the most likely to be classified as disengaged from both civic and politi-

Table 7. The Nature of Public Engagement by Form of Religious Expression

| Nature of public engagement | Form of religious expression | | | |
| | Diminished (%) | Private (%) | Public (%) | Integrated (%) |
| --- | --- | --- | --- | --- |
| National Election Study 1996 | | | | |
|   Disengaged | 35 | 35 | 14 | 8 |
|   Electoral specialist | 2 | 1 | 1 | 0 |
|   Civic specialist | 53 | 54 | 75 | 72 |
|   Dual activist | 10 | 10 | 10 | 19 |
|   Total | 100 | 100 | 100 | 99 |
| | | $eta = .31^*$ | | |
| Saguaro 2000 | | | | |
|   Disengaged | 25 | 36 | 17 | 14 |
|   Electoral specialist | 4 | 6 | 4 | 3 |
|   Civic specialist | 37 | 40 | 45 | 45 |
|   Dual activist | 33 | 19 | 35 | 39 |
|   Total | 99 | 101 | 101 | 101 |
| | | $eta = .20^*$ | | |
| National Election Study 2004 | | | | |
|   Disengaged | 43 | 46 | 34 | 26 |
|   Electoral specialist | 8 | 4 | 6 | 5 |
|   Civic specialist | 32 | 34 | 40 | 44 |
|   Dual activist | 17 | 16 | 21 | 24 |
|   Total | 100 | 100 | 101 | 99 |
| | | $eta = .18^*$ | | |

Note: Total percentages may not equal 100 because of rounding.
$^*p < .001$

cal life. In fact, nearly a majority of those with a private religious form exhibited a pattern of relative disengagement from public life in 2004, despite that there was a major increase in voter turnout in the presidential election of that year. Nevertheless, a majority of private religionists were civic specialists in 1996, and a plurality were so in 2000, while a little more than one-third were civic specialists in 2004. However, those who exhibit high levels of activism in both civic and public life are the least likely to be found within the ranks of those with a private religious form of expression; only between one-tenth and one-fifth of their ranks can be so classified, depending on the survey.

Those who exhibit a diminished form of religious expression tend to rival the private religionists in the extent to which they are disengaged, but overall a smaller percentage of the disengaged are found among those with a diminished form of religious expression than among those with a private form. And, of the four forms of religious expression, those with a diminished form of religious expression are consistently the least likely to be civic specialists.

Those with a public form of religious expression tend to be more engaged in public life than either those with a diminished or a private form of expression, but less likely to be so engaged than those with an integrated form of religious expression. Still, overall, those with a public form of religious expression tend to be relatively active, as anywhere from six of seven (86 percent in 1996) to two of three (66 percent in 2004) were active in public life in some capacity. The bulk of those who exhibit a public form of religious expression are civic specialists, and substantial numbers tend to be dual activists.

Those who exhibit an integrated form of religious expression are the least likely to exhibit disengagement from public life, and relatively few within their ranks indicate that they are election specialists. As is true with the other forms of religious expression, the bulk of those with an integrated form of religious expression are most likely to be civic specialists, but, of the four categories examined, those with an integrated form of religious expression are the most likely to be dual activists. This pattern holds true across the three surveys examined.

Thus several important conclusions can be drawn from this exploratory analysis. First, the ways in which people express their religiosity are related to different patterns of civic and political engagement. Those for whom their religious faith is highly private are the least likely to exhibit any form of activity in public life, whereas those who are inclined to express their religious faith through attendance at public worship services are the most likely to report engagement in civic and political life as well.

Therefore, in trying to determine what it may be about religion that serves to shape civic and political engagement, an important starting point is to examine whether such religious people engage in public worship activities on a regular basis, as public activity in one sphere of life is linked to public activity in other spheres of life. Religious beliefs may also matter, particularly in terms of theological understandings related to the role of religion in engaging the broader culture. However, such questions are hardly ever asked in surveys and consequently are not examined here. Nevertheless, it is likely that such religious beliefs are more likely to refine than alter the broad relationships revealed here between forms of religiosity and public engagement.

Second, while attendance at religious services is the more important of the two variables used to construct the variable reflecting the form by which the respondent's religiosity is expressed, the prayer variable nevertheless provides important information about the respondent. Clearly, as revealed by the differences evident between those who exhibit a public and those who exhibit an integrated form of religious expression, those high church attenders who report praying on a daily basis exhibit different political characteristics than those high attenders who do not pray daily.

## The Unique Contribution of Religion

The question now becomes whether religion continues to be significantly related to civic and political participation once controls have been introduced for other variables related to such participation. In other words, does the religious character of the respondent add anything to the likelihood of either civic or political participation beyond what one might expect once other factors related to engagement in public life are taken into account?

Table 8 addresses this issue, examining civic and political participation separately as dependent variables while assessing the relative strength of the relationship between various independent variables on each form of participation once the effects of the other independent

Table 8. The Relative Importance of Religion in Fostering Civic and Political
Participation

|  | NES 1996 | Saguaro 2000 | NES 2004 |
|---|---|---|---|
| Civic participation |  |  |  |
| Age | .18* | .03 | .09* |
| Race | .08 | .07 | .03 |
| Sex | .00 | .01 | .06 |
| Education | .25* | .22* | .28* |
| Family income | .17* | .18* | .19* |
| Marital status | .05 | .03 | .06 |
| Form of religious expression | .33* | .22* | .20* |
|  | $r^2 = .30$ | .17 | .23 |
| Political participation |  |  |  |
| Age | .12* | .17* | .15* |
| Race | .06 | .07 | .09 |
| Sex | .05 | .02 | .00 |
| Education | .26* | .23* | .18* |
| Family income | .09 | .13* | .15* |
| Marital status | .13* | .05 | .05 |
| Form of religious expression | .17* | .07 | .11* |
|  | $r^2 = .17$ | .15 | .12 |

*$p < .001$

variables have been taken into account. This analysis was conducted by
means of multiple classification analysis (MCA) to enable the use of categorical variables within a multivariate analysis.[17] The relative effects of
seven variables on civic and political participation are examined, since
previous research has revealed that both civic and political participation
are related to a number of individual characteristics, including gender,
marital status, age, education, and income (e.g., Conway 1991; Burns,
Schlozman, and Verba 2001).

As shown in table 8, a number of variables help to explain the likelihood of participation in public life. Most variables that are significantly
related to civic participation are also significantly related to political

participation. Generally speaking, education, form of religious expression, family income, and age are the primary variables that are related to engagement in public life.

Education and form of religious expression are the primary variables explaining variance in civic participation, with each variable attaining statistical significance across all three surveys even when controlling for the effects of all other variables. Form of religious expression exhibits the largest *beta* (.33) in the 1996 NES, is tied with education in exhibiting the largest *beta* (.22) in the 2000 Saguaro survey, and ranks second behind education in the 2004 NES (*beta* = .20).

With civic participation as the dependent variable, family income ranks as a significant explanatory variable, as it too attains statistical significance across all three studies. Age is also related to civic participation, though its effects fail to attain statistical significance in the 2000 Saguaro survey. None of the remaining variables—race, sex, and marital status—attain statistical significance in any of the three surveys.

When the focus shifts to political participation, one's form of religious expression is generally a significant factor, but its relative importance does not match that of education, family income, or age. The resultant *beta* coefficients for the level of education variable are statistically significant, and they rank highest in relative magnitude across all three surveys analyzed. Age too is related to political participation, as in all three surveys age proves to be statistically significant, ranking second in relative importance in two of the three surveys analyzed. Similarly, family income is statistically significant in two of the three surveys analyzed, ranking third and second in relative importance in the 2000 Saguaro survey and 2004 NES survey, respectively. Whereas the magnitude of the *beta* associated with the form of religious expression ranks second in the 1996 NES, the magnitude of its *beta* ranks only fourth in the remaining two studies (though in the 2004 NES its *beta* is still statistically significant). Of the remaining variables—race, sex, and marital status—only marital status, in the 1996 NES, attains statistical significance in any of the three surveys.

Overall, therefore, the data presented in table 8 demonstrate that the relationship between religion and participation in public life is not spurious and that one's form of religious expression appears to be more strongly related to civic than political participation. Nevertheless, even in terms of political participation, form of religious expression remains

Table 9. The Relative Importance of Religion in Fostering Political Participation

|  | NES 1996 | Saguaro 2000 | NES 2004 |
|---|---|---|---|
| Political participation |  |  |  |
| Age | .09* | .17* | .14* |
| Race | .04 | .05 | .08 |
| Sex | .05 | .01 | .02 |
| Education | .21* | .16* | .10 |
| Family income | .07 | .08* | .10 |
| Marital status | .12* | .04 | .05 |
| Form of religious expression | .11* | .03 | .09 |
| Civic participation | .21* | .31* | .29* |
| $r^2 =$ | .20 | .19 | .18 |

*$p < .001$

a relatively important explanatory factor, attaining statistical significance in two of the three surveys analyzed.

Since the way in which one expresses one's religiosity is so strongly related to civic participation, and since civic participation is related to political participation, the question arises whether one's form of religious expression continues to be related to political participation after taking into account the relationship between civic participation and political participation. As a result, one final MCA was conducted, similar to the previous one examining political participation in table 8, but this time adding the civic participation variable within the mix of independent variables shaping political participation. The results of this analysis are presented in table 9.

Not surprisingly, the variable having the strongest relationship with political participation across the three studies is civic participation. The magnitude of its *beta* coefficient is the highest across all three studies, far exceeding the magnitude of the variable ranking second in the two more recent surveys. However, even with the addition of the civic participation variable, one's form of religious expression continues to be a statistically significant variable related to political participation in the 1996 NES and narrowly misses attaining statistical significance at the .001 level in the 2004 NES. Thus, although one's form of religious expression is more strongly related to civic participation than political participation, even when one takes into account the effects of civic participation (as well as the other independent variables) on political participation, the effects of religion on political participation are fairly substantial (at least in two of the three cases examined).

Several important conclusions can be drawn from this exploratory analysis. First, the ways in which people express their religiosity are related to different patterns of social and political engagement. Those whose religious faith is highly private are the least likely to exhibit any form of activity in public life, whereas those who are inclined to express their religious faith publicly through attendance at public worship services are the most likely to report engagement in civic and political life.

Second, although one might anticipate that religious activity would be more strongly related to civic than political activity, the analysis of this paper does not suggest such. At least in terms of the rough measures employed here, the ways in which respondents exhibit their religious faith is similarly related to involvement in both civic and political life. While other religious variables (e.g., expression of particular religious beliefs or membership in particular religious traditions) might reveal such a differential pattern, the form of religiosity analyzed here is similarly related to public engagement, whether civic or political in nature.

Third, in trying to determine what about religion may shape civic and political engagement, it appears that an important first question is whether religious people engage in public worship activities on a regular basis. In other words, public activity in one sphere of life is, perhaps not surprisingly, linked to public activity in other spheres of life. Religious beliefs may matter as well, particularly in terms of theological understandings related to the role of religion in engaging the broader culture.

Fourth, while attendance at religious services is the more important of the two variables used to construct the form by which the respondent's religiosity is expressed, the prayer variable provides important information about the respondent. Devotional life, absent public worship, is likely to lead to withdrawal from public life. But for those who are already publicly inclined, frequency of prayer may act as a further stimulus to public life. Why might that be the case? Some (e.g., Lam 2002) have suggested that devotional activities such as prayer may serve to reinforce religious values that promote associational life. But most of the little research that has been done on the relationship between private prayer and public life has generally pointed to the social psychological effects of prayer on civic and political engagement.[18] For example, based on their findings, Matthew Loveland and his colleagues (2005, 13) conclude that "prayer fosters a cognitive connection to the needs of others" which then "manifests itself in the civic involvement choices of the prayerful." As a result, it is those respondents whose religious life is integrated (exhibiting high levels of public worship attendance and high levels of private devotional life) that are the most socially and politically engaged. The results of the analyses presented here reinforce other researchers' contentions that both the depth and type of religiosity are tied, in varying degrees, to civic engagement (Wilson and Janoski 1995).

## NOTES

An earlier version of this chapter was presented at the 2006 annual meeting of the American Political Science Association, Philadelphia, August 30–September 3. Portions of this chapter can also be found in *Pews, Prayers, and Participation: The Role of Religion in Fostering Civic Responsibility* (Georgetown University Press, 2008).

1. Civic (and public) life is more than simply the life two or more people share (e.g., sharing a language). Otherwise the term "social life" would serve sufficiently well, and there would be no need conceptually for the term "public life." Public life "adds to social life a reference to power, especially shared power" and "demands active participation" (Cochran 1990, 46). For a discussion of various characteristics of private life, along with some its limitations and negative tendencies, see Cochran 1990, particularly chap. 2 and 3. Of course, this statement reflects more a general quality of associational involvement than some universal causal property, as the statement is partially dependent on the nature of the associations with which individuals are affiliated.

2. Religion has been found to be related to both civic engagement and political participation, further suggesting that civic life and political life are related. However, while public life is generally lauded and met with approval by analysts and practitioners alike, the same cannot necessarily be said about the role of religion in public life. That topic is much more controversial, as the role of religion in public life has both potentially beneficial and potentially detrimental effects.

3. Turnout in presidential elections declined by nearly a quarter between 1960 (62.8 percent) and 1996 (48.9 percent), with turnout in off-year and local elections declining by approximately the same proportion (Putnam 2000,

32). Turnout in the 2000 presidential election was roughly similar to that of the 1996 election. Of course, the exception to this general pattern was the upswing in voter turnout in the 2004 presidential election, when the turnout rate was once again at the 60 percent mark.

4. For example, some observers contend that by examining the historical trends in membership in longstanding organizations, one fails to discern the rise of membership in newly forged organizations, a rise that may well offset the decline of memberships in longer-standing organizations. Other analysts sometimes point to the explosive growth evident in interest groups represented in Washington DC; they note the establishment of, and the rise of membership within, what might be labeled "mailing list" organizations (e.g., the AARP and the Sierra Club) as counterevidence to the contention that there has been a decline in civic engagement within American public life over the past several decades.

5. Again, perhaps the strongest piece of counterevidence is the strong up-turn in voter turnout in the 2004 presidential election.

6. One other counterargument against the thesis of decline is the argu-ment that what has changed is not so much the total level of activity as the particular mix of activities in which people are publicly engaged. Accordingly, engagement in public life has not so much declined "as it has spread to [a] wide variety of channels," with the mix of public activities in which citizens are participating being different today from that in the past (Zukin et al. 2006, 3)—with the totality of such engagement having become more civic and less political in nature.

7. Secularization theory is plagued by a number of both conceptual and empirical problems. At a minimum, scholars need to clarify the particular di-mension and level of analysis to which they are applying the theory. For ex-ample, secularization can be assessed along three dimensions: as a decline in religiosity, as the adaptation of religion to modernization, and as the restriction of religion's range of influence. Likewise, these dimensions can operate at three different levels of analysis: the individual, the organizational or institutional, and the societal. For a discussion of the analytical issues related to the theory of secularization, see Penning and Smidt 2002, chap. 2.

8. For example, reported levels of church membership and attendance at religious services have remained relatively stable since the 1950s (Smidt et al. 2003, 34). Still, while the tendency to report church membership has not changed, there has been some increase in the proportion of the electorate that reports no church affiliation, with affiliation being a less formal relation with religious bodies than membership. See, for example, Hout and Fischer 2002.

9. Questions related to church attendance apparently were not asked in all surveys.

10. The number of respondents for each of the years for the Roper data ranges from a low of 1,969 (in 1989) to a high of 4,000 (in 1979).

11. A number of more recent surveys ask questions related to civic and political behavior but inquire about such civic behavior only among those respondents who first report that they are a member of some voluntary association.

12. The GSS of 2004 contains questions tapping civic and political participation. However, one major component measure of civic participation, namely, membership in voluntary associations, was asked of one-half of the respondents, while the other civic participation questions were asked of the other half of the respondents. As a result, it is not possible to create a measure of civic participation that is roughly equivalent to the measures of civic engagement utilized in the three studies employed for this analysis.

13. For the component measures of civic and political participation in each survey, see the notes to table 4.

14. While the focus of the specific activity remained the same, the NES 1996 and NES 2004 differed in the specific manner in which the relevant question was posed.

15. The procedure employed in classifying respondents into the various categories of public engagement follows that employed in Zukin et al. 2006. While the component measures are, for the most part, similar, they are not totally identical. Moreover, whereas the analysis here uses four component variables each for civic and political participation, the Zukin et al. 2006 measure of political engagement employed five activities.

16. Because Zukin et al. 2006 included a fifth component measure for political engagement, it was potentially easier for respondents to report a minimum of two political activities. As a result, they report a higher level of electoral specialists than that reported here (Zukin et al. 2006, 64).

17. MCA provides the mean score on the dependent variable for each category of the independent variable. This procedure yields a bivariate measure of association (*eta*) between the independent and dependent variables. In addition, MCA provides deviations from the mean score on the dependent variable for each category of the independent variables after controls for each of the other independent variables have been entered in the analysis, with the statistic *beta* being the multivariate equivalent of *eta*—revealing the relative strength of the relationship once the effects of the other variables in the analysis have been taken into account. Thus a distinct advantage of using MCA is that it can provide one single, summary *beta* value for a categorical variable as a whole, rather than a score for each of the various categories of that variable. Only the *beta* values for the independent variables are presented in the tables, along with the resulting $r^2$ value, which represents the total amount of variance in reported organizational memberships explained by the independent variables contained in the tables.

18. For example, Harris 1999 (82) argues that prayer may "empower individuals with a sense of competence and resilience, inspiring them to believe in their own ability, with the assistance of an acknowledged sacred force, to influence or affect governmental affairs, thus—in some instances—to act politically." Likewise, Poloma and Gallup 1991 (178) contend that prayer heightens an "awareness that lessens the separation between the private religious side and the public political side of life."

## References

Allport, Gordon, and J. M. Ross. 1967. "Personal Religious Orientation and Prejudice." *Journal of Personality and Social Psychology* 5:432–43.

Ammerman, Nancy. 1997. "Organized Religion in a Voluntaristic Society." *Sociology of Religion* 58 (3): 203–15.

Becker, Penny Edgell, and Pawan Dhingra. 2001. "Religious Involvement and Volunteering: Implications for Civil Society." *Sociology of Religion* 62 (3): 315–35.

Burns, Nancy, Kay Lehman Schlozman, and Sidney Verba. 2001. *The Private Roots of Public Action: Gender, Equality, and Political Participation.* Cambridge, MA: Harvard University Press.

Campbell, David. 2004. "Community Heterogeneity and Participation." Paper presented at the annual meeting of the American Political Science Association, Chicago, September 2–5.

Cochran, Clarke. 1990. *Religion in Public and Private Life.* New York: Routledge.

Conway, M. Margaret. 1991. *Political Participation in the United States.* 2nd ed. Washington, DC: Congressional Quarterly Press.

Davie, Grace. 1994. *Religion in Britain since 1945: Believing without Belonging.* Oxford: Blackwell.

Edgell, Penny. 2006. *Religion and Family in a Changing Society.* Princeton, NJ: Princeton University Press.

Elshtain, Jean Bethke. 2002. "Religion and American Democracy." In *Religion, Politics, and the American Experience: Reflections on Religion and American Public Life,* edited by Edith Blumhofer, 16–26. Tuscaloosa: University of Alabama Press.

Hadden, Jeffrey. 1989. "Desacralizing Secularization Theory." In *Secularization and Fundamentalism Reconsidered: Religion and the Political Order,* vol. 3, edited by Jeffrey Hadden and Anson Shupe, chap. 1. New York: Paragon House.

Harris, Fred. 1999. *Something Within: Religion in African-American Political Activism.* New York: Oxford University Press.

Hout, M., and C. S. Fischer. 2002. "Why Americans Have No Religious Preference: Politics and Generations." *American Sociological Review* 76 (April): 165–90.

Jenkins, Krista, Molly Andolina, Scott Keeter, and Cliff Zukin. 2003. "Is Civic Behavior Political? Exploring the Multidimensional Nature of Political Participation." Paper presented at the annual meeting of the Midwest Political Science Association, Chicago, April 3–6.

Ladd, Everett C. 1996. "The Data Just Don't Show Erosion of America's Social Capital." *Public Perspective* 7 (4): 7–16.

Lam, Pui-Yan. 2002. "As the Flocks Gather: How Religion Affects Voluntary Association Participation." *Journal for the Scientific Study of Religion* 41 (3): 405–22.

Loveland, Matthew, David Sikkink, Daniel Myers, and Benjamin Radcliff. 2005. "Private Prayer and Civic Involvement." *Journal for the Scientific Study of Religion* 44 (1): 1–14.

Macedo, Stephen, et al. 2005. *Democracy at Risk: How Political Choices Undermine Citizen Participation, and What We Can Do about It.* Washington, DC: Brookings Institution Press.

Miller, Melissa K. 2003. *The Joiners: Voluntary Organizations and Political Participation in the United States.* PhD diss., Northwestern University.

Penning, James M., and Corwin E. Smidt. 2002. *Evangelicalism: The Next Generation.* Grand Rapids, MI: Baker Academic.

Poloma, Margaret, and George C. Gallup. 1991. *Varieties of Prayer.* Philadelphia: Trinity International Press.

Putnam, Robert. 1995. "Bowling Alone: America's Declining Social Capital." *Journal of Democracy* 6 (January): 65–79.

———. 2000. *Bowling Alone: The Collapse and Revival of American Community.* New York: Simon and Schuster.

Roof, Wade Clark, and William McKinney. 1987. *American Mainline Religion: Its Changing Shape and Future.* New Brunswick, NJ: Rutgers University Press.

Schlesinger, Arthur. 1944. "Biography of a Nation of Joiners." *American Historical Review* 50 (1): 1–25.

Skocpol, Theda, and Morris Fiorina. 1999. *Civic Engagement in American Democracy.* Washington, DC: Brookings Institution Press.

Smidt, Corwin E., Lyman Kellstedt, John Green, and James Guth. 2003. "Religion and Politics in the United States." In *The Secular and the Sacred: Nation, Religion and Politics,* edited by William Safran, 32–53. Portland, OR: Frank Cass.

Theiss-Morse, Elizabeth, and John Hibbing. 2005. "Citizenship and Civic Engagement." *Annual Review of Political Science* 8:227–49.

Tocqueville, Alexis de. 1969. *Democracy in America.* Garden City, NY: Doubleday.

Verba, Sidney, Kay Lehman Schlozman, and Henry E. Brady. 1995. *Voice and Equality: Civic Voluntarism in American Politics.* Cambridge, MA: Harvard University Press.

Wilson, John, and Thomas Janoski. 1995. "The Contribution of Religion to Volunteer Work." *Sociology of Religion* 56 (2): 137–52.

Wuthnow, Robert. 1996. *Christianity and Civil Society: The Contemporary Debate.* Valley Forge, PA: Trinity Press.

Zukin, Cliff, Scott Keeter, Molly Anderson, Krista Jenkins, and Michael Delli Carpini. 2006. *A New Engagement? Political Participation, Civic Life, and the Changing American Citizen.* New York: Oxford University Press.

# FAITH-BASED POLITICS IN AMERICAN PRESIDENTIAL ELECTIONS

## Trends and Possibilities

## John C. Green

Many journalists and pundits rediscovered the political impact of religion in the 2004 presidential election. Their reporting and commentary focused largely on traditionally religious white Christians, variously described as the "religious Right" or "fundamentalists." These voters were credited—and blamed—for President Bush's close reelection (Green 2007). To many such observers, it appeared that a "traditionalist alliance" had taken control of the Republican Party, introducing a new era of faith-based politics (Rozell and Das Gupta 2006).

Although such conclusions were often overstated, they contained an element of truth: traditionally religious white Christians did play an important role in Bush's reelection, and moreover, they were a good example of a relatively new kind of faith-based politics in the United States. However, this structure of faith-based politics developed over time and may change in the future. The purpose of this essay is to describe the structure of faith-based politics in the Bush era, show how it differed from faith-based politics in the past, chart the trends over time, and sketch out future possibilities. A good place to begin is with a brief review of the literature on the subject.

### RELIGION AND THE PRESIDENTIAL VOTE

The impact of religion in the 2004 election may have surprised journalists and pundits, but the underlying patterns have been well documented by social scientists. Indeed, scholars experienced their own "rediscovery" of the political impact of religion nearly three decades before, in the 1976 and 1980 presidential elections (Leege and Kellstedt 1993). Since then the literature has recorded a significant change in the nature of faith-based politics in presidential elections (Kellstedt, Green, et al. 2007).

Historically, religious affiliation was the prime means by which religion influenced the vote in the United States. This pattern was common in the nineteenth century and through the middle of the twentieth century (McCormick 1974). So, for example, in the 1940s members of northern, white mainline Protestant denominations tended to vote Republican, while northern, white Roman Catholics tended to vote Democratic. Religious affiliation was often closely linked to race and ethnicity, so that the major political parties were in large part coalitions of ethnoreligious groups (Kleppner 1979). Such coalitions differed somewhat from place to place and changed over time, but religious affiliation remained the central feature of the religious elements of voter alignments. Franklin Roosevelt's New Deal coalition and its Republican counterpart are perhaps the best-known examples. This "old politics of belonging" has been usefully captured by denomination affiliation, aggregated into religious traditions (Green 2007, chap. 2).

By the late 1980s, scholars noticed new political differences based on traditional religious practices and beliefs. For example, voters who claimed to attend worship services once a week or more tended to vote more Republican, while the less observant tended to vote more Democratic (Kohut et al. 2000). These divisions appeared within the largest religious traditions in the United States, so that the Republican and Democratic voter coalitions acquired new components, with the GOP gaining support from the traditionally religious in various religious communities and the Democrats picking up support from the less traditionally religious from these same communities, as well as increased support from the religiously unaffiliated population (Layman 2001). Scholars labeled these changes the "restructuring of religion" (Wuthnow 1988, 1996) and "culture wars" (Hunter 1991, 1994).

This "new politics of behaving and believing" has been usefully captured by the extent of religious traditionalism (Green 2007, chap. 3). Different terms have been used for these new religious divisions, including "conservatives" or "fundamentalists" versus "liberals" and "orthodox" versus "progressive." Unfortunately, many of these terms also have political meanings and thus risk confusing the religious underpinning of politics with politics itself. Although no labels are perfect, the terms "traditionalist" and "modernist" are useful in describing these new religious differences (Layman and Green 2005).

What caused religious traditionalism to be politicized? One common explanation is the appearance of new cultural issues on the national political agenda, including the nationalization of topics such as abortion and gay rights, including, eventually, same-sex marriage (Lowi 1995). There has been a steady stream of such controversy since the 1960s. Another common explanation is that efforts were undertaken to mobilize religious traditionalists on the basis of cultural issues. One example was the development of the Christian Right, a social movement dedicated to returning traditional moral values to public policy, and another was the pursuit of such voters by Republican candidates and party officials (Wilcox and Larson 2006).

## A Look at the Recent Past: Religion and the 2000 Election

Table 1 reports the two-party presidential vote of sixteen religious categories defined by both religious tradition and traditionalism in the 2000 election. This contest was one of the closest—and most controversial—presidential elections on record, with Republican George W. Bush prevailing in the Electoral College but losing the popular vote to Democrat Al Gore. This contest is thus a good place to assess the nature of faith-based politics in presidential elections (and it closely resembles the results of the 2004 election, when George W. Bush was reelected).

The basic building block for the religious categories listed in table 1 is denominational affiliation (see the appendix for details). Specific affiliations are aggregated into religious traditions, defined in part by race and ethnicity, including white evangelical and mainline Protestants, black and Latino Protestants, non-Latino and Latino Catholics, Jews, and respondents unaffiliated with organized religion. The two remaining categories, other Christians (Mormons, Eastern Orthodox) and other faiths (Muslims, Hindus, Unitarians), are composite categories of smaller religious groups (see Green 2007, chap. 2, for a fuller discussion of such religious groups).

Within the three largest religious traditions (evangelical Protestants,

Table 1. Religion and the 2000 Presidential Vote

| Religious category | % of electorate | Preference (%) | | Coalition (%) | |
|---|---|---|---|---|---|
| | | Bush | Gore | Bush | Gore |
| Evangelical Protestant | | | | | |
|    Traditionalist | 11.5 | 87.3 | 12.7 | 24.9 | 3.5 |
|    Centrist | 8.3 | 63.2 | 36.8 | 9.5 | 5.4 |
|    Modernist | 4.8 | 43.1 | 56.9 | 3.2 | 4.2 |
| Black Protestant | 9.0 | 3.5 | 96.5 | 0.6 | 17.6 |
| Latino Protestant | 2.6 | 28.6 | 71.4 | 1.0 | 2.5 |
| Mainline Protestant | | | | | |
|    Traditionalist | 4.8 | 75.9 | 24.1 | 8.5 | 2.7 |
|    Centrist | 6.5 | 51.5 | 48.5 | 6.4 | 5.9 |
|    Modernist | 6.2 | 53.8 | 46.2 | 7.2 | 6.1 |
| Roman Catholic | | | | | |
|    Traditionalist | 5.8 | 60.7 | 39.3 | 8.4 | 5.3 |
|    Centrist | 6.9 | 49.6 | 50.4 | 7.6 | 7.6 |
|    Modernist | 6.5 | 39.4 | 60.6 | 4.8 | 7.2 |
| Latino Catholic | 4.5 | 28.6 | 71.4 | 1.8 | 4.4 |
| Other Christians | 2.5 | 70.6 | 29.4 | 3.1 | 1.3 |
| Jews | 2.1 | 23.3 | 76.7 | 1.3 | 4.2 |
| Other Faiths | 2.5 | 26.0 | 74.0 | 1.7 | 4.7 |
| Unaffiliated | 15.6 | 36.0 | 64.0 | 9.9 | 17.3 |
| Total | 100.0 | 49.6 | 50.4 | 100.0 | 100.0 |

Source: National Survey of Religion and Politics, 2000.

mainline Protestants, and Catholics), three subdivisions are defined by the extent of traditional religious behaviors and beliefs: "traditionalists" (with the most traditional practices and beliefs), "centrists" (with moderate levels of traditional practices and beliefs), and "modernists" (with the least traditional practices and beliefs). Some religious traditions where such divisions exist are too small to be subdivided in this fashion, such as Jews. For other religious traditions, such as black Protestants, such divisions are present but are not reported because they had little effect on the vote (see Green, Kellstedt, et al. 2007 for evidence on this point and more on the voting behavior of these groups in 2004).

The second and third columns in table 1 report the 2000 presidential preferences of the religious categories. Several patterns are immediately apparent. First, traditionalists within the major religious traditions tended to vote for Bush, while the modernists tended to voted for Gore, with the centrists falling in between. A good example is Catholics: 60.7 percent of the traditionalists supported the Republican, 60.6 percent of the modernists backed the Democrat, and the centrists divided their votes almost evenly. This is prime evidence for the "new politics of behaving and believing" in presidential elections.

However, religious tradition also mattered. Note, for example, how the level of Bush support declined from traditionalist evangelicals (87.3 percent) to traditionalist mainline Protestants (75.9 percent) to traditionalist Catholics (60.7 percent). And affiliation was the dominant influence among the religious minorities, who tended to vote Democratic, including black Protestants, Jews, members of other faiths, Latino Protestants, and Catholics. Here the other Christians were an exception, voting strongly Republican. Finally, the unaffiliated voted solidly for Gore over Bush. This is prime evidence for the "old politics of belonging" in presidential elections.

The fourth and fifth columns in table 1 report the relative importance of these religious groups in the Republican and Democratic voter coalitions in 2000. Bush's single largest constituency was traditionalist evangelical Protestants, who provided nearly one-quarter of all his ballots (24.9 percent). When the mainline Protestant and Catholic traditionalists are added in, the total comes to just over two-fifths of the Republican vote (41.8 percent). All three centrist groups plus the other Christians provided another one-quarter of the GOP vote (26.6 percent), and when combined with the traditionalists, the sum accounted for about two-thirds of the 2000 Bush vote.

Gore's coalition was more diverse and of a different cast in religious terms. The single largest group was black Protestants, providing about one-sixth of all Gore's ballots (17.6 percent). About the same level of Democratic support came from three other groupings: all the other religious minorities combined (15.8 percent), all modernist categories combined (17.5 percent), and the unaffiliated (17.3 percent). Taken together, these groupings accounted for about two-thirds of the 2000 Gore vote.

These patterns are striking: the Republicans were substantially a party of traditionalists, evangelical Protestants, and other white Christians, while the Democrats were a party of religious minorities, modernists, and the unaffiliated. However, these tendencies should not be overstated: more than one-third of the Bush and Gore votes came from religious groups that voted on balance for the other party. For example, about one-tenth of the Bush vote came from the unaffiliated, and nearly one-sixth from modernists. And Gore received almost one-eighth of his ballots from traditionalists and more than one-sixth from centrists. So the religious components of the presidential vote were embedded within broader voter coalitions.

How are these patterns of religion related to other demographic factors, such as gender and income? Although a full analysis of these relationships is beyond the scope of this essay, the conclusion of such an analysis can be stated succinctly (Olson and Green 2006). First, religion had an independent impact on the vote when other demographic factors were controlled in statistical models. Indeed, the only categories that became insignificant were the closely divided ones, such as centrist Catholics. Gender and income were important to the vote, but their influence was independent of religion. In fact, there were gender and income gaps within most of these religious categories, with female and lower-income respondents voting more Democratic, and male and upper-income respondents voting more Republican (Green 2007, chap. 5).

What created these connections between religious groups and the vote? Political attitudes were an important part of the answer to this question. For example, party identification was a powerful linkage, with the religious groups that strongly backed Bush in 2000 tending to be Republicans and the strong Gore backers tending to be Democrats. Issues mattered as well. Cultural issues, such as abortion and same-sex marriage, were closely associated with traditionalism, with traditionalists holding conservative views on these matters and modernists taking liberal positions. In 2000, foreign policy was especially important, but since then it has become more so, and it is also linked to traditionalism. Social welfare issues are also a factor in voting behavior, but in 2000 traditionalism was less of a factor and religious tradition more of one, especially among minority faiths.

When partisanship and issue positions are taken into account in statistical analyses, many of the religious groups in table 1 lose their independent impact on the vote. But some groups still make significant contributions, including traditionalist and centrist evangelicals, black Protestants, and Latino Catholics. It could be that other factors explain these results, such as campaign contact and views of the candidates.

## A Look into the Distant Past: Religion and the 1960 Election

Table 2 reports the two-party presidential vote of fourteen religious categories defined by both religious tradition and traditionalism in the 1960 election. This contest was also one of the closest on record, with Republican Richard M. Nixon losing to Democrat John F. Kennedy. This election was also significant in terms of religion and politics because Kennedy was the first (and so far only) Roman Catholic elected to the presidency. Thus the 1960 election provides a good comparison to 2000 and a chance to assess changes in faith-based politics over a forty-year period.

Comparing surveys over such a long period is problematic, given the large changes in the nation's religious and political life as well as differences in the way religious questions have been asked in surveys. Fortunately, a survey conducted in 1964 contained extensive religion items that allow for a comparison to 2000 (see the appendix for details).

Table 2. Religion and the 1960 Presidential Vote

| Religious category | % of electorate | Preference (%) Nixon | Kennedy | Coalition (%) Nixon | Kennedy |
|---|---|---|---|---|---|
| Evangelical Protestant | | | | | |
| Traditionalist | 10.4 | 71.9 | 28.1 | 15.0 | 5.9 |
| Centrist | 6.2 | 55.8 | 44.2 | 6.9 | 5.4 |
| Modernist | 3.6 | 60.0 | 40.0 | 4.3 | 2.9 |
| Black Protestant | 8.1 | 16.8 | 83.2 | 2.7 | 13.5 |
| Mainline Protestant | | | | | |
| Traditionalist | 13.5 | 67.6 | 32.4 | 18.2 | 8.7 |
| Centrist | 15.8 | 68.6 | 31.4 | 21.6 | 9.9 |
| Modernist | 6.7 | 77.4 | 22.6 | 10.3 | 3.0 |
| Roman Catholic | | | | | |
| Traditionalist | 11.2 | 21.8 | 78.2 | 4.9 | 17.5 |
| Centrist | 7.8 | 30.9 | 69.1 | 4.9 | 10.9 |
| Modernist | 4.7 | 18.2 | 81.8 | 1.7 | 7.7 |
| Other Christians | 2.4 | 57.6 | 42.4 | 2.7 | 2.0 |
| Jews | 2.3 | 9.1 | 90.9 | 0.4 | 4.3 |
| Other Faiths | 1.2 | 56.3 | 43.8 | 1.3 | 1.0 |
| Unaffiliated | 6.2 | 40.7 | 59.3 | 5.0 | 7.3 |
| Total | 100.0 | 50.0 | 50.0 | 100.0 | 100.0 |

Source: Anti-Semitism in the United States, 1964.

The fourteen categories in table 2 are analogous to those in table 1, and the exception is the absence of Latino Protestants and Catholics as separate groups in 1960. Latino respondents were not numerous enough at that time to form a separate category. Indeed, the growth in the Latino population is a good symbol of the increased diversity of American religion in the second half of the twentieth century. Other important changes are the growth in the unaffiliated population and the proportion of modernists. At the same time, there was sharp decline in the number of mainline Protestants. (A comparison of the first columns in tables 1 and 2 provides a rough sense of these changes and how they impacted the electorate.)

As in table 1, the second and third columns in table 2 report the presidential preferences of the religious categories. Here the most striking pattern is by religious tradition: large majorities of all three Catholic categories voted for Kennedy, and all the mainline Protestants voted for Nixon by large margins. Evangelical Protestants of all sorts also voted Republican. Indeed, the prospect of a Catholic president may have moved many evangelical Democrats to vote Republican in 1960—but not quite enough to cost Kennedy the election. This sharp division by religious tradition is an excellent example of ethnoreligious voter alignments.

The 1960 vote of the religious minorities closely resembled the 2000 vote, with black Protestants and Jews voting Democratic by large margins. An exception was the composite category of other faiths, which joined the other Christians in the Republican camp. The change in the voting preference of members of other faiths may well reflect changes within that category between 1964 and 2000, such as the increased number of non-Christians. The unaffiliated also voted Democratic in 1960.

Religious traditionalism was not nearly as important in the 1960 vote as in 2000. Note that the modernist mainline Protestants voted the most Republican (77.4 percent) and their traditionalist coreligionists the least (67.6 percent). Similarly, it was the modernist Catholics who were the most Democratic, slightly ahead of the Catholic traditionalists (78.2 percent), with the centrists backing Kennedy the least (69.1 percent). Only among evangelical Protestant categories did the 1960 vote resemble 2000. Here the traditionalists were the most Republican (71.9 percent), ahead of the modernists (60.0 percent), but it was the centrists who were the least Republican (55.8 percent).

These patterns are reinforced by the pattern in the fourth and fifth columns in table 2, which look at the role of religious groups in the 1960 vote coalitions. The mainline Protestants provided one-half of all Nixon's ballots, and adding in the traditionalist evangelicals accounts for nearly two-thirds of the Republican vote. Once again, the Democrats had a more diverse coalition: all the Catholic categories provided more than one-third of Kennedy's ballots, and the combination of black Protestants, the other religious minorities, and the unaffiliated provided more than one-quarter (28.1 percent), with the sum of these two groupings approaching two-thirds of the Democratic vote.

Thus the 1960 patterns are as striking in their own way as those in 2000: the Republicans were substantially the party of white Protestants, especially mainline Protestants, while the Democrats were the party of non-Protestants and minority faiths. Both of these coalitions are recognizable as versions of the New Deal coalition—which is hardly surprising, since this election occurred just sixteen years after FDR's fourth election in 1944. And as in 2000, both of the major party candidates drew crucial votes from religious groups that on balance backed the other party. For instance, more than one-third of Kennedy's ballots came from mainline and evangelical Protestants, while about the same proportion of Nixon's support came from Catholics, the unaffiliated, and religious minorities. So here, too, the religious element of the presidential vote coalitions was embedded in broader voter coalitions.

As in 2000, statistical controls from other demographic factors did not eliminate the influence of religion. The diverse Democratic constituencies continued to be significant, including all the Catholic groups, black Protestants, Jews, and the unaffiliated. Interestingly, so did traditionalist evangelical Protestants. But all of the other white Protestant groups dropped out once demography was controlled statistically. Partisanship and issues mattered in 1960 as well, but these did not completely eliminate the distinctiveness of the Democratic religious constituencies either.

## A LOOK AT THE TRENDS: RELIGION AND THE PRESIDENTIAL VOTE, 1960–2004

How did faith-based politics change between 1960 and 2004? This question is difficult to answer with precision, given the absence of consistent measures of religion over the period in question. However, a crude measure of religious traditionalists and modernists can be developed from a variety of sources, and the results are displayed in figures 1–3 (see appendix for details).

As a point of reference, the Republican presidential vote is included in each of the figures. The series begins with Nixon receiving nearly one-half of the two-party vote in 1960 and ends with Bush obtaining a little more than one-half of the two-party vote in 2004. Low points for the GOP occurred in 1964 (Johnson landslide) and in 1992 and 1996 (Clinton's election and reelection); high points occurred in 1972 and 1984 (Nixon and Reagan landslides).

Figure 1 plots the estimate for traditionalist evangelical Protestants, mainline Protestants, and Catholics from 1960 to 2004. Each group has its own pattern. Overall, traditionalist evangelical Protestants moved in the Republican direction over the period. In 1960, they voted Republican, with their GOP support declining in 1964 but then rising again in 1972—only to drop a bit in 1976, when fellow evangelical Jimmy Carter won a close election. Beginning with Ronald Reagan in the 1980s, traditionalist evangelical Protestants continued in a GOP direction through 2004, becoming the most Republican of these groups in the 1990s.

Traditionalist mainline Protestants remained Republican over the period. Until 1984, they tended to be the most Republican of these groups, and after 1984, their GOP support waned a bit until 1996, when it began to wax again. By the end of the series, traditionalist mainline Protestants were still in the GOP camp, but less Republican than their evangelical counterparts. Meanwhile, traditionalist Catholics showed a fairly steady movement toward Republicans over the period. Starting solidly in the Democratic camp, this group took halting steps toward

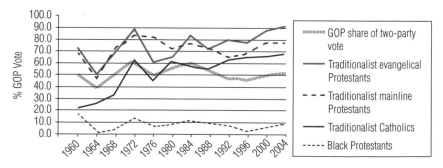

Figure 1. Religious Traditionalists and the Republican Vote

the GOP in 1972, 1980, and 1992. However, after 1992, traditionalist Catholics became steadily more Republican, paralleling the track of traditionalist mainline Protestants. (As a reminder that not all religious groups were affected by these changes, black Protestants are also plotted in figure 1; they showed only modest variation in the Republican vote over this period.)

Figure 2 looks at the other side of these developments, plotting the estimate for modernist evangelical Protestants, mainline Protestants, and Catholics. Here the trends were more complex. Modernist mainline Protestants were solidly Republican in 1960 and remained so until 1984, after which the modernist mainline shifted sharply away from the GOP. Modernist evangelical Protestants followed the same basic trajectory as their mainline counterparts until 1988, when they also took a sharp turn away from the GOP—but then returned to support Bush in 2000 and 2004.

In partial contrast, modernist Catholics started out voting Democratic in 1960, then moved toward the GOP in the 1980s, only to follow the other modernists away from the Republicans through 2004. The unaffiliated are also plotted in figure 2; their pattern closely tracked the overall Republican vote but remained on the Democratic side of the ledger throughout the series.

Thus the "traditionalist alliance" noted by journalists in 2004 was substantially in place within the Republican presidential coalition by 1992. In contrast, a "modernist-secular" alliance was much slower to develop and was not as evident even in 2004. However, since 2004 there has been something of a revival of the "religious Left," and if it proves to

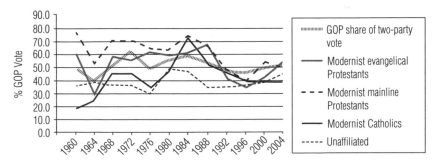

Figure 2. Religious Modernists and the Republican Vote

be successful, there may be a fuller polarization of faith-based politics (Kellstedt, Smidt, et al. 2007).

Figure 3 summarizes these trends by plotting a "traditionalism gap" over time, the difference in the Republican presidential vote between all traditionalists combined and all modernists and unaffiliated combined. This traditionalism gap peaked in 1960, 1972, and 1992–1996. Around these peaks, the GOP did relatively better among modernists and the unaffiliated, reducing the relevance of the traditionalist alliance, sometimes because of defeat (1964) and sometimes because of victory (1984 and 2004), as measured by the Republican share of the two-party vote.

Figure 3 also provides some modest evidence regarding the most common explanations for these trends: the rise of cultural conflict and political mobilization of religious traditionalists. On the first count, the percentage of all traditionalists who listed cultural issues as the most important problem facing the country paralleled the fluctuations in the traditionalism gap fairly closely. Note that there was a surge in the percentage of traditionalists who gave priority to cultural issues during the 1990s, when the traditionalist alliance appeared. On the second count, the percentage of the combined traditionalists who reported being contacted by the Republican Party during the election campaigns followed the traditionalism gap fairly closely until 1984. There was an upsurge in GOP contacting of traditionalist voters in the 1990s that continued through 2004. Interestingly, there was no similar pattern for modernists and unaffiliated voters on either cultural issue salience or Democratic Party contacting.

Another interesting pattern shown in figure 3 occurred in the late 1970s and the 1980s, when there was a trough in the traditionalism gap and also a decline in both the salience of cultural issues for tradition-

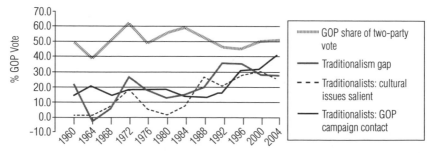

Figure 3. Traditionalism Gap, Cultural Issue Salience, and GOP Campaign Contact

alists and the GOP's contacting of traditionalists. This much-studied period saw the emergence of the Christian Right and Ronald Reagan's two successful presidential campaigns. However, the presumed effects of these events on the traditionalist vote did not appear until the 1990s (Wilcox 1992). These patterns reveal something about the gestation period for faith-based political change in the electorate.

## A Look at the Future

What about the future? Although forecasting presidential politics is hazardous, at this writing the faith-based alignment of 2000 (and 2004) is likely to be present in the 2008 election. This means that both religious traditions and traditionalism will be a central part of the structure of presidential voter coalitions. But this pattern does not necessarily mean that the Republicans will prevail in 2008. After all, the GOP lost the popular vote in 2000 despite the prominence of this structure of faith-based politics. And in this regard, a fuller development of a religious Left could benefit the Democrats. Put another way, the outcome of the 2008 election will likely depend on the actual performance of the religious groups, but this performance will occur within the structure of contemporary faith-based politics.

But what about the longer-term character of faith-based politics in presidential elections? The trends described here developed over a forty-year period, and it is worth briefly speculating about what faith-based politics may look like forty or so years from now. Here three possibilities suggest themselves: a continuation of these trends, a pause and reversal of them, and the development of an entirely new religious cleavage (see Green 2007, chap. 8).

The first possibility is that the development of the "new politics of behaving and believing" will continue to expand, so that ultimately religious traditionalism is the dominant aspect of faith-based politics and the impact of religious tradition largely disappears. If this possibility were to obtain, then the faith-based vote in 2040 would have an opposite pattern to 1960 (and 2000 would be about halfway between 1960 and 2040), and the traditionalism gap would continue to grow. This prospect has been suggested by James Davison Hunter, the chief advocate of the "culture wars" thesis (Hunter 1991). Such an eventuality would probably require that cultural conflict become a cornerstone of presidential politics and that foreign policy and economic issues be reinterpreted in cultural terms.

The results of the 2006 midterm elections revealed some evidence of this possibility. One reason the Democrats took control of the House of Representatives was a surge in support among their strong religious constituencies, especially the unaffiliated and the less traditionally religious. As a result, the gap in the vote between the most frequent and least frequent worship service attenders widened (Pew Forum on Religion and Public Life 2006). These changes represented an increased impact of traditionalism at the ballot box.

The second possibility is that the "new politics of behaving and belonging" will pause and then reverse itself, so that such political differences are subsumed by the religious traditions. If this possibility were to obtain, then the faith-based vote in 2040 would have the same kind of pattern as 1960 (through perhaps with different religious groups and group alignments), and the traditionalism gap would contract. It is likely that this scenario would require the decline of cultural conflict, perhaps in some form of widely accepted compromise on issues like abortion and homosexuality. However, the current impact of such cultural conflict would be preserved in the partisan identification of religious groups. Such an eventuality is not unlike the effects the Great Depression exerted on political alignments into the 1950s and 1960s (Miller and Shanks 1996).

The results of the 2006 congressional elections also revealed evidence relevant to this possibility. Overall the Democrats made some gains among Republican religious constituencies, including Catholic voters and those who reported attending worship services once a week (Pew Forum on Religion and Public Life 2006). Some Democratic candidates made even larger gains of this sort in particular races. These changes represented a decline in the impact of traditionalism at the ballot box.

The third possibility is the most speculative: another dimension of religion will become important politically, cutting across existing religious groups. The rise of religious traditionalism between 1960 and 2004 was largely unanticipated by observers at the time, and novel developments in faith-based politics may appear in the next several decades. If this possibility were to occur, then the faith-based vote in 2040 would follow a completely different pattern than in 2000 or 1960, and the traditionalism gap would be much less significant politically.

One candidate for such a transformation might be spirituality, and a key issue might be environmentalism. Like religious traditionalism, spirituality extends across religious traditions, potentially uniting—and dividing—religious people in new ways. Thus the extent of spirituality could have a political impact analogous to that of religious traditionalism. Environmental concern has been tied to spirituality, the topic has been gaining public attention, and there is every reason to expect it to be more salient in the future. In fact, something like this possibility was suggested by Michael Lerner (2006) in his call for "spiritual Progressives," who list environmental protection among their political priorities. Lerner clearly believes that such "spiritual politics" will benefit the Democrats, but that need not be the case. Recently, leaders of Republican religious constituencies such as the National Association of Evangelicals have embraced the cause of climate change. Whether such a pattern will develop remains to be seen, of course, but the past suggests that observers should be prepared for the unexpected when considering faith-based politics in the United States.

Thus the rediscovery of the impact of religion by pundits and journalists after the 2004 presidential election contains important elements of truth: religious traditionalists did have an impact at the polls, and they do represent a relatively new kind of faith-based politics. This structure of faith-based politics developed over time from another kind of structure, and it may change to another structure in the future. There may be no necessary or permanent relationship between religion and American presidential politics—except that faith is likely to matter one way or another.

## APPENDIX: SURVEYS AND RELIGIOUS CATEGORIES

*The 2000 survey.* This analysis uses the Third National Survey of Religion and Politics, conducted by the Bliss Institute at the University of Akron. This survey was a national random sample of adult Americans (eighteen years or older) conducted in the spring and fall of 2000 ($N = 6,000$).

The National Survey of Religion and Politics contains an extensive series of questions to determine the specific religious affiliation of respondents as accurately as possible. This standard classification is based on the formal beliefs, behaviors, and histories of the denominations and churches involved, with the most detail dedicated to sorting out the many kinds of Protestants in the United States (see Kellstedt and Green 1993; Green, Guth, et al. 1996; Layman 2001; and Layman and Green 2005). Black Protestants and Latinos were separated on the basis of race and ethnicity.

The National Survey of Religion and Politics also contains extensive measures of religious belief and behavior. Five belief items appear in all four surveys (view of the Bible, belief in God, belief in the afterlife, view of the devil, and view of evolution), and so were five behavior items (frequency of worship service attendance, frequency of prayer, frequency of Bible reading, frequency of participation in small groups, and level of financial contribution to a congregation). These belief and behavior items were subjected to separate factor analyses in each of the surveys. The factor loadings were quite similar on all these analyses. Belief and behavior factor scores were then generated, and the two scores were subjected to a second factor analysis to extract the underlying traditionalism. This final factor analysis also generated a factor score, which was adjusted to the mean score for each survey by each religious tradition. This adjustment was very modest but corrected for the peculiarities of each survey. (For a similar approach, see Layman and Green 2005, where the belief and behavior items were used independently.)

In the final step, the adjusted traditionalism scale was divided into four categories within the three largest religious traditions. The cut points were the mean traditionalism scores of four levels of religious salience. These were chosen because they were specific to the religious traditions, unambiguous, and consistent across surveys. Also, traditional religiosity stresses the importance of religion over other aspects of life (Guth and Green 1993). The unaffiliated believers were defined as scoring in the top two-thirds of the belief factor score in each survey.

Although this categorization process is complex, it was remarkably robust, with a wide range of alternative measures, methods, and cut points producing essentially the same results. (See Green, Kellstedt, et al. 2007 for more details; for other versions of these categories, see Guth et al. 2006; Green and Waldman 2006; and Green 2004.)

*The 1964 survey.* This analysis uses the Anti-Semitism in the United States survey conducted in 1964 ($N = 1,975$; Glock et al. 1979). This survey contained measures of the 1960 vote, which were weighted to reflect the actual election outcomes.

The religious categories were calculated in the same way as in the 2000–2004 surveys. First, religious traditions were based on denominational affiliations using the same coding scheme, and second, a traditionalism scale was calculated by factor analyzing five items: worship service attendance, belief in God, belief in life after death, belief in the devil, and belief that Jesus is the only way to salvation. The factor score was then adjusted to match the 2000–2004 scores by religious tradition to correct for differences in the measures used. The cut points for the traditionalist-modernist categories were the mean scores for four levels of religious salience. Nominal and Latino respondents were not numerous enough to create separate categories.

*The 1960–2004 time series.* The 1960 to 2004 time series data are based on the National Election Survey Cumulative File (American National Election Studies [ANES] 2005). The ANES data have the virtue of consistent political variables over this four-decade period; the election results were weighted to reflect the actual election results.

Unfortunately, the ANES series lacks consistent and detailed religion measures. Thus the traditionalists and modernists were estimated from the available data. Traditionalists were defined as weekly worship service attenders who had a literal view of the Bible; when a Bible item was not available, a proxy for it was estimated using cultural issue positions and ideology. Whenever possible, these estimates were compared to other contemporary surveys with more complete religion measures, and in a few instances, where the number of cases was small and the results out of line with a survey that had more detailed religion variables, the figures were adjusted to match the better surveys. To be consistent, the data from the anti-Semitism study were substituted for the ANES data in 1960.

The perceived salience of social issues presented in figure 3 was calculated by aggregating an open-ended question on the most important problem facing the nation (see Green 2007, chap. 4); the ANES party contact variable was used directly.

### References

American National Election Studies. 2005. The 1948–2004 ANES Cumulative Data File [dataset]. Produced and distributed by Stanford University and the University of Michigan. http://www.electionstudies.org/.

Campbell, David E., ed. 2007. *A Matter of Faith: Religion in the 2004 Presidential Election*. Washington, DC: Brookings Institution Press.

Glock, Charles, Gertrude Selznick, Rodney Stark, and Stephen Steinberg. 1979. Anti-Semitism in the United States, 1964 [computer file]. Conducted by National Opinion Research Center, University of Chicago. ICPSR ed. Produced and Distributed by Inter-university Consortium for Political and Social Research, Ann Arbor, MI.

Green, John C. 2004. "Religion and the 2004 Election: A Pre-election Analysis." Pew Forum on Religion and Public Life, September 9, 2004. http://pewforum.org/docs/index.php?DocID=55.

—————. 2007. *The Faith Factor: How Religion Influences the Vote*. Westport, CT: Praeger.

Green, John C., James L. Guth, Corwin E. Smidt, and Lyman A. Kellstedt. 1996. *Religion and the Culture Wars: Dispatches from the Front*. Lanham, MD: Rowman and Littlefield.

Green, John C., Lyman A. Kellstedt, Corwin E. Smidt, and James L. Guth. 2007. "How the Faithful Voted: Religious Communities and the Presidential Vote." In Campbell 2007, 15–36.

Green, John C., and Steve Waldman. 2006. "Tribal Politics." *Atlantic*, January–February, 10–14.

Guth, James L., and John C. Green. 1993. "Religious Salience: The Core Concept?" In Leege and Kellstedt 1993, 157–74.

Guth, James L., Lyman A. Kellstedt, Corwin E. Smidt, and John C. Green. 2006. "Religious Influences in the 2004 Presidential Election." *Presidential Studies Quarterly* 36 (June): 223–42.

Hunter, James Davison. 1991. *Culture Wars: The Struggle to Define America*. New York: Basic Books.

—————. 1994. *Before the Shooting Begins: Searching for Democracy in America's Culture War*. New York: Macmillan.

Kellstedt, Lyman A., and John C. Green. 1993. "Knowing God's Many People: Denominational Preference and Political Behavior." In Leege and Kellstedt 1993, 53–71.

Kellstedt, Lyman A., John C. Green, James L. Guth, and Corwin E. Smidt. 2007. "Faith Transformed: Religion and American Politics from FDR to George W. Bush." In *Religion and American Politics: From the Colonial Period to the Present*, edited by Mark A. Noll and Luke E. Harlow, 269–95. 2nd ed. Oxford: Oxford University Press.

Kellstedt, Lyman A., Corwin E. Smidt, John C. Green, and James L. Guth. 2007. "A Gentle Stream or a 'River Glorious'? The Religious Left in the 2004 Election." In Campbell 2007, 232–56.

Kleppner, Paul. 1979. *The Third Electoral System: Parties, Voters and Political Cultures.* Chapel Hill: University of North Carolina Press.

Kohut, Andrew, John C. Green, Scott Keeter, and Robert Toth. 2000. *The Diminishing Divide: Religion's Changing Role in American Politics.* Washington, DC: Brookings Institution Press.

Layman, Geoffrey C. 2001. *The Great Divide: Religious and Cultural Conflict in American Party Politics.* New York: Columbia University Press.

Layman, Geoffrey C., and John C. Green. 2005. "Wars and Rumors of Wars: The Contexts of Cultural Conflict in American Political Behavior." *British Journal of Political Science* 36 (1): 61–89.

Leege, David C., and Lyman A. Kellstedt, eds. 1993. *Rediscovering the Religious Factor in American Politics.* Armonk, NY: M.E. Sharpe.

Lerner, Michael. 2006. *The Left Hand of God.* New York: HarperCollins.

Lowi, Theodore J. 1995. *The End of the Republican Era.* Norman: University of Oklahoma Press.

McCormick, Richard L. 1974. "Ethno-cultural Interpretations of Nineteenth-Century American Voting Behavior." *Political Science Quarterly* 89:351–77.

Miller, Warren E., and J. Merrill Shanks. 1996. *The New American Voter.* Cambridge, MA: Harvard University Press.

Olson, Laura R., and John C. Green. 2006. "Symposium: Voting Gaps in the 2004 Presidential Election." *PS: Political Science and Politics* 39:443–72.

Pew Forum on Religion and Public Life. 2006. "Understanding Religion's Role in the 2006 Election." http://pewforum.org/events/?EventID=135.

Rozell, Mark J., and Debasree Das Gupta. 2006. "The 'Values Vote'? Moral Issues and the 2004 Election." In *The Values Campaign? The Christian Right and the 2004 Elections,* edited by John C. Green, Mark J. Rozell, and Clyde Wilcox, 11–21. Washington, DC: Georgetown University Press.

Wilcox, Clyde. 1992. *God's Warriors: The Christian Right in Twentieth-Century America.* Baltimore: Johns Hopkins University Press.

Wilcox, Clyde, and Carin Larson. 2006. *Onward Christian Soldiers? The Religious Right in American Politics.* Boulder, CO: Westview.

Wuthnow, Robert. 1988. *The Restructuring of American Religion.* Princeton, NJ: Princeton University Press.

———. 1996. "Restructuring of American Religion: Further Evidence." *Sociological Inquiry* 66:303–29.

# EMERGING TRENDS IN RELIGION, SOCIETY, AND POLITICS

## Allen D. Hertzke

A consultancy for the Pew Charitable Trusts in the winter of 2005–2006 involved an effort on my part to chart the current status of and emerging trends in religion, society, and politics. This effort entailed wide-ranging interviews with a number of the nation's prominent scholars, journalists, religious leaders, and policy makers, along with an extensive review of academic literature. In the interviews I asked respondents to reflect on key trends—both globally and domestically—and what they portend for the future of religion and civic life in America. Pew has graciously granted permission for me to draw on this work for independent publication. What follows is the fruit of that research endeavor.

If a clash of ideologies—communism, fascism, imperialism, nationalism, and democratic liberalism—marked the twentieth century, the new millennium ushered in powerful religious forces. Contrary to expectations of the West's great scholars, modernization and science did not produce an inexorable decline in religious adherence.[1] Instead, religion has shown remarkable resilience and endures as a pervasive life dimension of the overwhelming majority of people on earth. Moreover, not only is religion resurgent in the daily lives of many people, but it is increasingly assertive and political.[2] Islamist movements are only the most visible and extreme expressions of this assertiveness. Thus religion, whether overtly political or not, looks to play a huge role in societal developments, national politics, and global affairs in the coming decades. It is not a subject relegated to the religion section of the newspaper; it is front-page news.

This is not to say that counterforces are not also afoot. Powerful economic transformations, scientific wonders, instantaneous communication, commercialization, mass culture, the allure of hedonic fulfillment, elite secularization, and the looming biogenetic revolution can challenge religious worldviews or sever religious ties between generations. But the very forces of the global marketplace and technological change that uproot people from their villages and expose them to mass-mediated images can also produce spiritual vacuums that religious movements fill.[3]

Central to modern religion, therefore, is its dynamism. Some religions grow while others decline.[4] New faiths sprout, small sects expand rapidly into global ministries, conversions and migrations alter the composition of societies, and religiously infused movements shape national politics and international relations in ways unimaginable a few years ago.

Religion, of course, is a protean force. It can inspire the highest acts of human benevolence or spark fanatical violence. It can be a source of division or solidarity. It can be an engine of democracy or a bulwark of despotism. Comprehending such a dynamically changing force, and harnessing its better angels for public good, demands that the best academic minds, the most dedicated religious leaders, and the most enlightened statesmen work in concert.

As the world's dominant power, America bears a special burden to act with responsible leadership in the midst of such complex religious forces. The United States is also exceptional among developed countries for the high level of religious adherence among its citizens and its close link between faith and society. And because of its nondiscriminatory immigration policies since 1965, diverse world religions and movements are increasingly woven into American cultural and political life.

Immigration, for example, has made the already polyglot United States into "the world's most religiously diverse nation," with Buddhists, Hindus, Muslims, Sikhs and others transforming the kaleidoscope of American religious life and linking it to communities abroad.[5] Simultaneously, many immigrants from Africa, Asia, and Latin America also bring with them vibrant forms of Christianity blossoming in the third world, strengthening the vitality of Christianity here in a kind of reverse missionary movement.[6]

Thus it is less and less tenable to draw sharp distinctions between domestic and global realms, between U.S. religious life at home and the nation's global role. Not only does American foreign policy profoundly shape the global scene, but our cultural, educational, and democratic institutions operate in a fishbowl of intense international scrutiny.

This scrutiny raises a number of weighty questions. Does U.S. constitutional protection of religious pluralism provide a global model for peaceful coexistence of religions? What role do free religious institutions play in democratic civic life? Is that role weakening in the United States? What are the implications of loosening ties to organized denominations in American civic life? Given concerns about weakening community life, fractured family integrity, and lagging educational attainment in America, is the nation's cultural and religious heritage worthy of emulation or not? Can our institutions of higher education provide insight and leadership to strengthen that heritage? In a shrinking world, these questions about the health, civility, justice, and vibrancy of American society loom large as emerging societies evaluate their posture toward U.S. global influence.

Globalization thus dominates the horizon and serves as the grand theme for this prospective analysis. In a sense, not to comprehend these globalizing forces is not to understand ourselves.

## GLOBALIZATION AS THE CRUCIAL CONTEXT

The "globalization of everyone," as one person I spoke with put it, characterizes twenty-first-century reality. Yet a consistent theme in interviews was the enormous gulf between the importance of globalization for religion and our grasp of it.

Globalization is a term with multiple connotations. In economics it represents powerful market forces that, while capable of producing enormous wealth, can exaggerate disparities between rich and poor, undermine local economies, disrupt village cultures, and subvert transmission of faith-based moral norms. Millions of people are drawn into teeming cities in the developing world, often living bereft of the barest of necessities. With capital moving at the speed of light around the globe and multinational corporations diversifying operations, people enjoy less job security and rootedness, which can translate into a transience that undermines community ties and involvement.

Globalism also means a shrinking world in which people of diverse religious backgrounds come into intense contact with one another—"cheek to jowl," as one person put it—requiring religionists to negotiate their exclusivist beliefs with seemingly alien or competing faiths. While this contact need not result in what Samuel Huntington describes as a "clash of civilizations," it can produce suspicion, strife, and fundamentalist impulses.[7] Or, with enlightened religious and political leadership, it can lead to enhanced understanding and mutual respect—seeing the common humanity in each other. Genuine dialogue between those at the center of their faiths appears a must to facilitate this vision.

The shrinking globe also drives a momentous trend in religion: the emergence of greater marketplace competition among faiths. This competition can increase the vitality of religion, as the American historical experience demonstrates.[8] Previously monopolistic and often lax religious traditions, such as Catholicism in Latin America, now must revitalize themselves in the face of intense competition from rapidly spreading Pentecostal churches. We see similar reactions from Buddhists in Asia who respond to the growth of Christianity by developing actual, though atypical, congregations to meet the spiritual needs of people. This phenomenon of competition will to varying degrees increase religious pluralism in formerly monistic societies. Under the right conditions, this competition can nurture civil society and expand democratization; on the other hand, it could lead religious communities to demonize each other and fracture societies. A great question, as one commentator mused, "is where competition is fruitful and where it is not." Another issue concerns the outer limits of tolerance: "How much diversity can people tolerate?" Or, put another way, how can people maintain the particularity of their evangelizing faiths while getting along with other particularities?

This emerging open marketplace for religion, combined with population migrations, global travel, and the Internet, creates conditions for truly transnational religion, not only for the large proselytizing faiths, such as mainstream Christianity and Islam, but for smaller and less orthodox groups, such as Mormons, Sufi Muslims, and Pentecostals, whose networks reach widely. Vivid examples illustrate this yeasty environment of cross-fertilization. A Turkish Sufi movement builds schools in the United States. A huge Nigerian evangelical church plants a branch in Plano, Texas. A Chinese Christian sect establishes a thriving congregation in London. Korean Protestant missionaries set up churches in Mexico. Brazilian Pentecostals seed churches in Africa. And the Word of

Life Ministry in Sweden founds a large church in Armenia, which then plants churches in Russia.

Transnational religious movements, not surprisingly, can provoke repression and harassment of newcomers—and not only in autocratic nations. Restrictions on a wide array of groups deemed "cults" in western Europe have chipped away at genuine religious freedom.

Transnational religion also poses profound implications for the future of the state. Since the treaty of Westphalia in 1648, which ended the religious wars in Europe, states in the West have agreed not to intervene in the religious affairs of other states or foment sectarian movements that might undermine them. With transnational religious movements, we may be entering a post-Westphalian era in some parts of the world, such as Africa and Arabia, where religious loyalties transcend or even violently threaten national boundaries. On the global stage, we see this most dramatically with militant Islamist movements, which seek to destroy what they view as artificial state boundaries and restore the unity of an Islamic empire under a caliphate.

With this global context in mind, I now turn to more specific trends on the religious horizon.

## RESURGENCE AND CRISIS IN THE ISLAMIC WORLD

It may seem paradoxical, but the Islamic world is experiencing a massive resurgence at the same time it faces crisis and inner turmoil. This produces the combustible mixture from which Islamist terror networks have sprung. Thus a momentous question of our time is "what to do about 1.2 billion people roiling on issues of identity, development, and civic questions."

Muslim resurgence is reflected in both in dramatic demographic growth, with high birth rates in Islamic countries (and corresponding youth bulges), and a reassertion of Islamic religious practice and identity. Societies that once were nominally Islamic have experienced massive revivals; Islam also rushed into the vacuum created by the collapse of the Soviet Union. Where fewer than two hundred mosques operated in all of central Asia during the Soviet era, today some ten thousand exist.[9] Muslims have grown from 12 percent of the world's population in 1900 to 20 percent today, and rising. This puts Islam second to Christianity's one-third of the world's population.[10] The re-

234 • Allen D. Hertzke

lationship between these two great faiths looms large on the international stage.

But if Islam is resurgent, it also is afflicted with a sense of crisis. This crisis has been described as (1) a sense of siege in the face of global forces that threaten the Muslim faith and traditional moral codes; (2) the humiliation of Islamic countries seeing their lagging economies and political weakness compared to Western and Asian countries, or even compared to their own great civilizations of the past; and (3) a virtual civil war within Islam—a struggle for the soul of the faith between militant Islamists who seek to construct theocracies and moderates who in varying ways seek to reclaim the best of their heritage and join the mainstream of economic and political life on the global stage.[11]

The United States can ameliorate or aggravate the crisis within the Islamic world, and American Muslims may play a key role in that process. But our learning curve has not kept pace with events. Certainly the war on terror takes us into uncharted terrain, requiring the keenest of analyses and sensitivity to religious sensibilities. And the stakes could not be higher, because the relationship between the Islamic world and the West, led by the United States, will remain a dominant feature of international relations in the coming decades.

A crucial question in the coming years is the prospect for democracy in the Islamic world. While it is true that many Muslims live in democracies, such as India, Malaysia, and Indonesia, the majority of Muslim countries (especially Arabic ones) are not democracies. Regrettably, vast Saudi oil money spreads the fundamentalist Wahhabi vision of Islam around the globe—a vision hostile to democracy, pluralism, and the legacy of much Islamic scholarship and civilization. Publicity about this phenomenon may inhibit such influence, but Saudi actions in the future deserve continued scrutiny.

What we do know is that militant movements present a barrier to democratization, not only in Islamist regimes such as Iran and Sudan, but also in countries ruled by autocrats who buy legitimacy with concessions to extremists, and even in democracies where local interpretations of sharia intimidate religious minorities, including many Muslims viewed as unorthodox. This environment has allowed a virulent anti-Semitism to metastasize, undermining peacemaking efforts in the Middle East. And "since women's rights are critical to democratic consolidation,"[12] narrow Islamist interpretations of Islamic law that repress women stall the democratization process.

Because of the youth bulge in the Islamic world, failure to provide adequate education and employment will inevitably fuel fundamentalist religious movements that promise meaning, pride, solidarity, and even networks for employment. Islamic economic development, especially in Arabic lands, is thus closely tied to America's national interest.

A hopeful trend is a growing scholarship and soul searching in Islamic circles about how to draw on Islamic teachings and traditions to nurture democratic governance. Intellectual ferment in the Islamic world, plus the thriving civic experience of American Muslims, will contribute to this process, but intimidation by extremists remains a barrier to positive evolution. Providing sanctuary for often besieged moderates, and a megaphone for their voices, might help tip the balance.

## THE RISE OF GLOBAL CHRISTIANITY

As Phillip Jenkins documents vividly, a demographic revolution has occurred in the past century, a tectonic shift of the Christian population to the developing world of the "global south." Whereas the vast majority of Christians in 1900 lived in greater Europe and North America, today some two-thirds of all believers hail from Asia, Africa, and Latin America, and that proportion—fueled by indigenous mission activity and population growth—is rising.[13] Thus American churches will increasingly become branches of assertive global ministries, which often blend orthodox theology, missionary zeal, and traditional morality with commitment to fighting poverty and exploitation. While we can expect theological tensions between North and South, American churches will also become more internationally conscious and internationally focused.

A key reason for this shift, as scholars of missions note, is that Christianity historically tends to wither at the center (where it becomes established and comfortable) and grow at the periphery.[14] The gospel message of good news to the poor and afflicted obviously resonates with those so characterized. Over half of sub-Saharan Africa, for example, is now Christian, while Christianity is rapidly growing in parts of Asia and becoming more vital in Latin America with the introduction of true marketplace competition for the faithful. Many Christian congregations, therefore, are nested amid poverty, violence, exploitation, persecution, and war.

Unfortunately, Christian growth often occurs in places where it collides with militant Islamic communities or regimes, causing strife and sometimes massive violence. In Africa, exploding Pentecostalism and Islam vie for influence, raising the specter of cross-border clashes. Throughout parts of the Islamic world, especially under pressure by extremist movements, Christians and other religious minorities have been victims of mob attacks and persecution.

Believers also suffer persecution because churches threaten autocratic control of society. Expansion of Christianity in Asia planted the seeds of nascent civil society in predemocratic South Korea and Taiwan (where Christian leaders played a crucial role in democratic evolution). In eastern Europe, Christian congregations provided sanctuary for dissent, solidarity, and mobilization against Communist regimes. That appears to be what Communist authorities in China and Vietnam fear, resulting in efforts to regulate or repress believers, often harshly.

As a result of these and other developments, numerous Christian minorities around the world suffer for their beliefs. According to Paul Marshall, an estimated 250 million Christians live in conditions of serious persecution, while another 400 million experience nontrivial restrictions on the practice of their faith. Martyrdom itself is not a thing of the past but a daily global phenomenon.[15]

Through global communications, travel, and international development networks, American Christians increasingly learn about persecuted fellow believers. And because of the exceptionally high level of religious adherence in the United States, Americans are more likely than their counterparts in western Europe to identify with the "suffering church" abroad. This reality fuels a new ecumenical movement for global religious freedom. Evangelicals, Catholics, Anglicans, and other Christian advocates have forged alliances with Jews, Tibetan Buddhists, Baha'is, Sufi Muslims, and others persecuted for their faith. In 1998 the movement gained enactment of the landmark International Religious Freedom Act, making the promotion of religious freedom "a basic aim" of American foreign policy. Propelled by this campaign, the movement of unlikely allies subsequently passed a succession of human rights initiatives on human trafficking, genocide in Sudan, and gulags in North Korea—filling a void in human rights advocacy.

Providing the grassroots muscle for this movement are American evangelicals, often associated with isolationism but now increasingly engaged in international affairs. This new engagement has enabled evangelicals to build relationships with liberal church leaders they often oppose on many domestic issues, but also with such diverse groups as secular human rights organizations (on North Korea), the Congressional Black Caucus (on Sudan), and feminists (on human trafficking). Not only is this an important movement in its own right, but it may play a role in breaking down stereotypes and forging healthy relationships across cultural divides.[16]

Through international church networks, American religionists are awakening more generally to the afflictions visited on the world's vulnerable. Not only do international relief and development programs continue to grow in size and sophistication, but Christian groups have backed efforts for debt relief, AIDS funding for Africa, and an end to modern slavery and other injustices. Thus the globalization of Christianity provides an influential constituency of advocacy for the world's destitute. But we don't know how deep in the pews that advocacy reaches, or how it will evolve if nurtured. We do know that in certain parts of Africa, clergy may form a crucial leadership cadre in addressing AIDS, government corruption, and educational needs, and their stories may move their Western counterparts to support such efforts.

One phenomenon noted by a number of commentators is the astonishing global growth of Pentecostal forms of Christianity (including some Catholic ones). Along with ecstatic worship, these congregations stress strict moral codes, thrift, sobriety, and fidelity in marriage, which can provide a tangible economic uplift in impoverished areas. One researcher found that these traits enabled communities to take advantage of microcredit to build businesses and prepare for participation in the global economy. Given the strong linkage between economic advancement and democratization,[17] this uplift can also play a role in nurturing democratic culture.

### DEMOGRAPHIC AND CIVILIZATIONAL CHALLENGES

Related to the above trends are contrasting demographic challenges: the aging and shrinking of advanced societies and the rapid growth and youth bulges of developing nations. The average age in Uganda is fourteen; in Italy, forty. For the developed world this means sustaining an expensive older population with a shriveling base of existing workers, straining welfare states and increasing the burden on religious charities.

This is especially true in western Europe. Because secular people tend to marry less and have fewer children than the religious, these secular nations are now experiencing birthrates below replacement levels, resulting in inexorable population shrinkage over the coming decades. The countertrend in Europe is rapid growth of the Muslim population, both by immigration and birth, which will transform the cultural landscape of the continent in the future. The implications of such a transformation are both extraordinary and murky, and the United States has an obvious stake in the outcome.

When these demographic trends are linked with the global growth of Christianity and Islam, concerns emerge about potential civilizational conflicts around the world. Though many take issue with the oversimplification of Huntington's "clash of civilizations" thesis, violent skirmishes are occurring on the fault lines of different cultures and civilizations—most of which are infused with religious-based identities. We see civilizational clashes today not only along many of Islam's borders (with Orthodox in Russia, Hindus in Kashmir, tribal religionists and Christians in Africa), but in such movements as a fierce Hindu nationalism that sparks mob violence against religious minorities in India, hyper-Zionists in Israel who resist abandoning settlements for peace with Palestine, and Christian fundamentalists who cast Islam as the new enemy (replacing communism). Containing and diffusing these tensions remains a major challenge for the world community, especially for its religious and political leaders.

## Religious Freedom and Democracy

The link between religion and democracy gains even greater significance in light of the developments mentioned above. Though some scholars stress economic thresholds as key factors driving democratization, religious freedom is a linchpin of expanding democracy because it is a potent right, involving as it does the right of people to act on their consciences, to speak freely, assemble, organize, and own property. The last great wave of democratization, starting in 1975 and continuing through the collapse of communism in eastern Europe, was largely a Catholic wave, driven by changes in the Catholic Church after Vatican II that placed its powerful imprimatur and institutional structures behind human rights, religious freedom, and democracy.[18]

Some scholars believe that the continued indigenous growth of Christianity in certain regions can lead to another wave of democratization. This flows from the fact that, at least in current Protestant and Catholic forms, congregations are voluntary societies and thus seedbeds of the kind of civil society and social capital necessary for free cooperative endeavors.

This apparently salutary role of churches as voluntary organizations dovetails with a renewed intellectual interest in the doctrine of sphere sovereignty as articulated by nineteenth-century Reformed leader Abraham Kuyper. Scholars from the Reformed and Catholic traditions have been exploring the similarities between the Catholic doctrine of subsidiarity and sphere sovereignty, both of which stress the importance of autonomy and cooperation between different levels of society. This discussion bears more than academic interest, as we saw how the "velvet revolution" against Communist dictatorships in eastern Europe depended on churches that carved out some independence from state control. In America a rich public discourse suggests the importance of churches as mediating institutions that should not be supplanted by the state or subsumed in the marketplace. There is every reason to believe that such understandings transcend Christianity and may apply to emergent democracies in other religious cultures.

As we would expect from this analysis, those faiths still closely tied to state sponsorship remain less conducive to democratization. This includes, for example, Orthodoxy in Russia and Islam especially in Arab nations. But we need to know a lot more about the complex relationship between different religious traditions and democracy, what elements are conducive or resistant to democratic evolution, and how religious traditions can reinterpret their roots in ways more accepting of pluralism. As the Catholic example shows, a tradition once hostile to democracy and religious freedom can be transformed.

The fate of religious freedom, enshrined in the Universal Declaration of Human Rights promulgated by the United Nations in 1948, will also shape the extent to which clashes occur across the borders of civilizations. Again, the American experience shows that religious communities that once did not believe in or practice religious toleration can be transformed. Religious freedom thus not only is an aim of American foreign policy but must be appreciated and promoted as a universal right, inherent in the dignity of human persons.

## THE RISE OF RELIGIOUS NONGOVERNMENTAL ORGANIZATIONS

The dramatic growth of the number, size, and type of international religious nongovernmental organizations (NGOs) is an important countertrend to the picture of religious conflict we see so often, as they play an important role in global economic development, advancement of human rights, promotion of justice, and peacemaking. Moreover, with foreign nationals increasingly leading regional and global programs, NGOs have become truly transnational, not American, institutions.[19] Yet we know little in a systematic way about how they operate, their accountability structures, or their relationships across different religions (say the Islamic-based Red Crescent, Catholic Relief Services, and the evangelical World Vision). And we don't know the extent to which these groups learn from and coordinate or compete with each other. Some local studies tease us with counterintuitive findings: World Vision working together with local party officials in Chinese villages to provide health care and microcredit, cooperative ventures between Muslim and Christian groups on agricultural development projects in Tanzania, unusual partnerships in the struggle against AIDS. But such fragmentary studies only scratch the surface of current knowledge.

A very promising development that needs nurturing and support is the emergence of a cadre of individuals and organizations that practice faith-based diplomacy aimed at mediating conflicts and reconciling post–civil war societies. As Doug Johnston and others have shown, there are a number of remarkable examples of religious actors playing vital roles in such peacemaking, and they are not utilized enough by traditional diplomats.[20] But the field is in its infancy. What measures make mediation successful? How does one balance justice versus reconciliation? What teachings and resources do different religious traditions bring to peacemaking? Enormous potential exists for codifying best practices and principles of such work and convincing conventional diplomats to draw on this resource.

ISSUES OF SCIENCE AND RELIGION

Science is a truly global enterprise, with advances rapidly ramifying around the world. Inevitably these developments impinge on religious communities in complex ways, and they will do so increasingly.

Throughout Western history scientists such as Isaac Newton did their work embedded in religious understandings. Probing the secrets of the natural world and the universe was a way to understand the creation of God. The emergence of evolutionary biology in the nineteenth century, however, posed a unique challenge to religious worldviews because it seemed to many to eliminate the need for a creator. Darwin himself wrestled with the theological implications of his work, sometimes seeing the wastefulness and violence of natural selection as antithetical to a created order.[21] Moreover, some scientists and rationalists hailed natural selection because they saw it as undermining religious "superstition," along with ideas of divine intervention, miracles, and "outdated" moral codes. Religious thinkers who embraced this new science went on to apply its presuppositions to investigations of the Bible, casting doubt on basic Christian teachings, such as the virgin birth, Jesus' miracles, and bodily resurrection. Not surprisingly, this was profoundly disquieting to the devout and remains a source of tension within religious communities.

Controversies over the teaching of evolution in public schools and debates over whether "intelligent design" is a genuine science thus mask deeper tensions between science and religion that will continue to spark controversy and provoke religious responses. On the one hand, the scientific community remains deeply disturbed by public misunderstanding of the nature of scientific theories and tests, along with broad American public support for the teaching of both evolution and intelligent design in public schools. Proposals to teach the idea of intelligence in creation alongside evolutionary biology thus meet vociferous scientific opposition. On the other hand, many in the religious community are disturbed by what they see as metaphysical claims by some scientists that life, not just its evolution over time—or even the existence of the universe—must be explained by purely blind naturalistic forces. Notably, several Templeton Award winners (for contributions to science and religion) have been world-renowned physicists who challenge this latter view as not testable science but rather ideological "scientism" or philosophical materialism, which they believe contributes to the clash of faith and science.[22] How to teach science while respecting religious faith remains a unique challenge in the United States because of its greater levels of religious adherence and orthodoxy compared to other modern societies.

But if the evolution controversy plays a larger role in the United States than elsewhere, the looming biogenetic revolution presents a stunning global challenge to basic theological understandings of the unique giftedness of persons made in the image and likeness of God. Though hardly on the radar of religious communities, revolutionary developments in biogenetic engineering pose profound questions about the dignity of human life, even about the definition of human life itself. Cloning, fetal farming, patenting life forms, designer babies engineered with specific traits, even the chimera of human-animal hybrids used to harvest organs mark the horizon. If the abortion controversy hinged on when human life begins, the genetic revolution thrusts forward such questions as, What is a human being? Who decides? What about new creations? This new technology may also widen the gap between the poor and the affluent, who are most likely to engineer advantageous traits in their offspring. This prospect raises the further question of how society will perceive the imperfect. With only a bit of hyperbole, some commentators suggest that these fundamental issues in the genetic revolution will make the abortion controversy seem trivial by comparison.[23]

Faith communities seem unprepared theologically to provide ethical leadership as societies grapple with these developments. And "not to act will be to act," as others will take the initiative in either pushing the envelope or providing medically narrow ethical guidance that avoids the profound spiritual dimensions of this new technology. Moreover, even if certain societies take the initiative in banning the most egregious practices, others in the global village with fewer scruples or less spiritual ballast will push forward. Conversations among the leaders of the great faiths around the world, along with ethicists and philosophers, need to occur at the highest levels. Otherwise, potentially fruitful deliberation will be short-circuited into a "science versus religion" debate. With the proper catalyst, however, we may well see broad religious alliances emerge to challenge the use of certain biogenetic techniques deemed offensive to the dignity of human persons.

A hopeful scenario in the relation between science and religion exists in the realm of the religious response to the degradation of the natural world. New alliances are emerging in concern for the environment, particularly as a growing number of religious leaders link the concept of stewardship of creation with an acceptance of scientific evidence for major global impacts of human activity. The major mainline Protestant, Catholic, and Jewish public bodies all maintain strong official statements on the environment and lobby for new environmental initiatives and robust enforcement of existing laws. Notably, in 2005 the National Association of Evangelicals joined them by promulgating "An Evangelical Call to Civic Responsibility," which contained a clear declaration on "care of creation," which some prominent leaders bolstered with subsequent statements on the importance of addressing global warming.

## Religion and Civic Health

From its beginnings, religion has been closely tethered to civic life in the United States. As Alexis de Tocqueville observed a century and a half ago, churches, because they generate mores and cooperative enterprise, can be viewed as "the first of the American political institutions."[24] Moreover, now that troubling questions are being raised about the health of the world's oldest democracy—with its anemic and unequal political participation, weakening civil society, public cynicism, and cultural anomie—American houses of worship cannot be ignored in the effort to strengthen U.S. civic life.

Church vitality is tied to civic health for several reasons. As Robert Putnam documents, half of all the nation's social capital—the norms and networks of reciprocity and trust necessary for cooperative endeavors—is generated in American churches, synagogues, temples, and mosques (for brevity the term "churches" will denote all of these). Churchgoers are more likely to volunteer in their communities, vote, and participate in civic affairs.[25] In addition, many laypeople learn civic skills and confidence through their churches, which translates into community participation and even political leadership.[26]

Religious adherence also correlates with cultural health. Churches play a key role in transmitting the moral codes and obligations that underpin civic life, providing compelling narratives that link past, present, and future generations. Young people rooted in religious institutions, for example, are less likely than their peers to engage in risky behavior and more likely to succeed in school and participate in their communities. In our fragile inner cities, religious institutions are among the most important centers of neighborhood stability, while religious schools are often a haven from unhealthy environments.

Again, a grand question is the extent to which religious communities can play similar roles elsewhere around the world. Recent research is suggestive that, under the right conditions, this may be the case.[27] This inquiry, however, is in its infancy.

But here we must confront the Tocquevillian paradox: people do not join churches to become better citizens, though churches can make them so. The renewal of civic life through religious initiatives, consequently, must engage the faithful in more robust and healthy citizenship in ways that simultaneously address their aspirations for spiritual meaning and human solidarity. Put another way, initiatives aimed at helping faith communities deepen civic practices must flow out of transcendent missions; otherwise they treat religion instrumentally, potentially undermining its core purpose.

Unfortunately, other societal pressures and diversions, such as the pull of popular culture, commercialism, and mass media, may undermine the capacity of churches to bear the weight of increasing demands and needs. We see a weakening of institutional loyalty to denominations, greater transience of commitment, and less success in passing religious traditions to the next generation. The fluidity of American religion also translates into individualist spiritualism among American youth, producing a thinner, less deeply engaged religious life. Many young people know little of the particularities of their faith traditions and seek therapeutic comfort in a vaguer and more syncretic religious belief.

Since women historically have formed the backbone of lay participation in many congregations, their changing status in society may also have broad ramifications for the nature of religious life. On the one hand, women are playing larger leadership roles in religious communities; on the other hand, many face demands of work and parenthood that can cut into their voluntary participation.

Of course, religious communities across the world face challenges in passing along their teachings to the next generation. But in the United States there may be unique factors, such as the elimination of literary treatments of sacred scriptures in public schools and many universities, coupled with inadequate treatment of religion's role in the nation's history. One result is a striking "biblical illiteracy" compared to past generations. Thus many Americans cannot recognize biblical allusions in great literature or in the speeches of Abraham Lincoln, Franklin Roosevelt, or even Bill Clinton and George W. Bush. Not only is American culture impoverished by this ignorance, but respect for our heritage abroad is undermined. Attempts to reintroduce the reading of scriptures as classic literature of Western civilization, unfortunately, produce controversies about which versions to use and how to treat them. The fact is that our teachers are neither aware of what is constitutionally permissible nor prepared to handle the delicate task of respecting students' different beliefs while treating sacred writings in an objective fashion.

This issue will intensify as efforts are introduced in schools to help students understand the Islamic faith, perhaps even with assignments of Koranic passages, which will inevitably result in calls for equal treatment of Christianity, Judaism, Hinduism, and so forth. Again, the infusion of global religions into the fabric of the United States requires new thinking and capacities.

The evolving picture of religion and civic health carries global ramifications, as others cast a critical eye on the freewheeling freedom (or license) of American society. Indeed, Muslim skepticism about the influence of the United States is often not focused on its predominant Christian heritage but on its perceived secularism, materialism, radical individualism, and hedonism.

In America, religious communities will experience challenges in the years ahead that will bear significantly on their contribution to civic health. Some of these challenges are unique to specific groups; others are shared across traditions. Among Jews, assimilation through intermarriage—and the related shrinkage of Judaism's proportion of the U.S. population—is of deep concern and contributes to strained ecumenical relations, such as those emerging with liberal Protestant churches over their criticism of Israel. For mainline Protestant denominations, continuing membership declines call into question the "mainline" appellation and undermine Protestant national prominence. At the same time, many specific congregations continue to play important roles in their local communities, and liberal Protestant theology offers alternative intellectual resources for grounding public discourse in moral traditions. For the Catholic Church, struggling to recover lost vitality, the priest shortage poses an enormous challenge and will likely usher in new patterns of lay leadership. Immigration will also transform the makeup of the church and its role in American religious life. For evangelicalism, the vitality that flows from its plethora of entrepreneurial leaders also presents a dilemma: certain high-profile figures who speak solely on their own authority issue intemperate public statements, thus polarizing civic life and reinforcing stereotypes of the evangelical community. In the black community, the African American church remains a central institution, but it confronts a decline in male participation and competition for the attention of the young. Hispanic congregations, on the other hand, will continue to sprout and grow, but cultivating talented new leaders will be vital for the community to achieve greater integration into mainstream life. Finally, Muslims in America present a fascinating and dynamic picture: they enjoy higher socioeconomic status than Muslims in Europe and engage in civic activities. Thus they may provide models for integrating religious commitment and citizenship for Muslim democrats abroad. All these groups will struggle to elicit strong commitments from adherents whose attention is also claimed by a vast menu of competing cultural influences. All will also have to navigate complex political dynamics, as partisan organizations increasingly reach out to religious communities for their support.

One of the most crucial trends to emerge is the growing number of independent congregations unconnected to larger institutional bodies. Many of these are megachurches that represent a striking trend in religious life whose meaning and impact we barely understand. These institutions, on the one hand, adapt and even contribute to trends in popular culture. They employ high-tech worship and broadcast entertaining services. On the other hand, they serve the changing lifestyles of their members by creating comprehensive communities, complete with child care, adult education, groups for people of different ages and stations in life, coffee shops for socializing, even banking services. One question is whether these institutions produce mostly what Putnam describes as bonding social capital—relationships among the members—as opposed to bridging social capital, which involves reaching out to the wider community. There are indications that at least some of the leaders of this movement, such as Rick Warren, see the need to reach out on issues of poverty, and in his case on a massive scale with work against AIDS in Africa. Though Warren's ability to influence the evangelical subculture is formidable (with thousands of followers globally), we just don't know enough about what these cutting-edge churches represent in the evolving religious landscape—in black churches and white, both here and around the world. Megachurch networks could remain disparate strands of entrepreneurial efforts or become like denominations in new forms.

Related to the megachurch phenomenon is the emergence of a cadre of devoutly committed people, mostly of college age and into their twenties, who branch out beyond their churches to form their own fellowship groups complete with intense scripture study, service, and mutual accountability. On a number of college campuses we see thriving religious life compared to a generation ago, partly as students seek refuge from what they experience as campus environments hostile to their beliefs. Thus at places like Princeton, a huge evangelical community floods the chapel while Catholics have built an aggressive set of ministries—and they collaborate and share worship experiences. But again, we don't know much about how these independent believers will shape church institutions or American society in the future.

## The Culture Wars

A trend that continues to shape American religion and civic health is the rancorous battle over the shape of our culture.[28] The heated rhetoric of the "culture war" exaggerates the extent to which average Americans feel engaged in a struggle for the soul of America and understates the pluralism within the evangelical community.[29] Nonetheless, cultural issues continue to roil the body politic. Clashes over abortion, gay marriage, the nature of sex education in public schools, church-state issues, and the teaching of naturalistic evolution show no sign of going away, and they intensely engage America's religious communities—often on both sides of these issues.

Because the cultural divide often runs right through denominations, we see a kind of restructuring of religion in which modernists in various denominations feel more aligned with each other than with traditionalists in their own churches. For example, liberal religionists, whether Protestant, Catholic, or Jewish, articulate theological grounds for defending gay rights and choice on abortion, placing them at odds with their conservative counterparts. In turn, a new ecumenism of orthodox religionists is emerging, in which evangelicals, conservative Catholics, and Orthodox Jews find common cause. On some college campuses such groups are teaming up to challenge coed dorms and a libertine atmosphere they believe is antithetical to faithful modesty and fidelity.

Some see the roots of this clash stemming from the counterculture era of the 1960s, combined with Supreme Court decisions that removed certain moral questions from public deliberation and decision. Often overlooked, however, are deeper cultural forces that flow from modernity and advanced capitalism, which cannot contain the hedonistic excesses of entertainment media, youth marketing, and the like.

The potency of cultural issues has produced an unprecedented partisan division on the basis of religious commitment. Religious fissures in the past tended to break on denominational lines—Protestants were Republicans, Catholics were Democrats, and so forth. Now church attendance divides the parties and outstrips other traditional factors, such as income, union membership, and denominational affiliation. Simply put, the more frequently people attend church, the more likely they are to vote Republican. Why? The religiously observant tend more than others to "decry what they see as the morally decadent influence of movies, songs, music videos, television programs, video games and the like."[30] The GOP has embraced, at least rhetorically, this moral concern while Democrats have come to be associated with secularism, Hollywood, and nonjudgmental responses to the degradation of the moral ecology. Unfortunately for the Democratic Party, a majority of the public sees Republicans as "friendly" to religion while only a minority view Democrats likewise.

As several commentators noted, political progressives are showing signs of awakening to this problem and addressing it. The dilemma is that liberal elites—especially in the universities, the mass media, and entertainment—are largely detached from religious life in America, making it difficult for them to connect with enough religious moderates to forge the kind of progressive alliance that could address such issues as the growing economic gulf between rich and poor and the continuing racial divide in the nation. Lacking in politics today, it would seem, is an alternative that blends respect for moral traditions with progressive economic policies, which was characteristic of American populists in the past and of European Christian democrats in their heyday.

Cultural clashes have clearly made churches more politicized than at any time in recent history. In 2004 we witnessed a presidential campaign in which some Catholic bishops threatened to withhold communion from John Kerry, evangelicals were mobilized on an unprecedented scale by the Bush reelection team, and black churches served in many cases as precincts for Democratic Party organization. This trend would horrify Tocqueville, who feared that if churches became too closely tied with a particular political party or regime they would suffer loss of legitimacy and consequently fail to play their vital role in shaping the mores of the culture.

Serious cultural issues in fact have become political footballs in partisan warfare. Mutual stereotyping and demonizing by a "secular Left" coalition versus a "religious Right" alliance foster a polarized partisan environment not healthy for policy making in a pluralistic society—which requires compromise and accommodation. People in the muddled middle (and that includes moderate evangelicals and Catholics) often find themselves frustrated and unrepresented, and American politics as a result offers a rather unsavory picture abroad.

Efforts have been undertaken to bridge the cultural divides. Democrats are exploring ways to speak to orthodox religionists in moral language that resonates, while some evangelical leaders have sought to broaden their agenda beyond the divisive hot-button issues. These forays deserve watching because they promise a more civil politics in which religious leaders find more common ground, as they have on international human rights initiatives. But with the prominence of the courts as arbiters of cultural conflicts, litigation will remain an arena of intense contestation in which democratic deliberation and consensus building give way to the adversarial mode of legal battles. Finding common ground to solve societal problems will thus remain a worthy challenge of forward-thinking initiatives.

A key trend that bears on this search for common ground is the growing effort to address what Mark Noll called the "scandal of the evangelical mind," by which he meant the anti-intellectual, emotive, and reactive tendencies within the born-again community.[31] In part because of Pew efforts, a cadre of evangelical intellectuals have been developing a much more sophisticated understanding of the link between orthodox Christian theology and civic engagement, often borrowing from Reform and Catholic scholastic traditions. Remarkably, as one prominent mainline Protestant historian noted, many of the top historians of religion in America today are evangelicals, as are a growing number of sociologists and political scientists. Still lagging, however, is the close transmission of the insights of these scholars to evangelical political activists.

### FAITH-BASED PARTNERSHIPS AND THE FATE OF AMERICAN CITIES

Though international religious NGOs receive U.S. government dollars without controversy (because they have on-the-ground networks the government needs for famine relief and the like), the expansion of domestic faith-based partnerships involves greater complications. Church-state concerns, fears of discrimination on the basis of religion, and the potential loss of independent prophetic voices by churches dependent on government money are looming issues.

Missed in this debate is a larger trend in the push for government contracting with faith-based groups. The devolution of power to state and local governments, often with less money from the federal government, means that local services will be stretched. This trend will continue as entitlement programs for the aging population squeeze out national discretionary spending. So not only is the push for faith-based partnerships governed by a genuine sense that these groups may do certain things better and shouldn't be penalized in competition for grants, but it is driven by dwindling resources. Government officials hope that faith-based groups can be more efficient or effective—which research has yet to show definitively—meaning that fewer federal dollars can go farther. But can faith-based groups bear the weight of this expectation in an era of cutbacks and public scarcity?

This issue takes on a keener edge when placed in the context of our devastated inner cities. Over the past decades we have seen a loss of inner-city jobs and the abandonment by middle-class residents. In the midst of this crisis, the "lights of the inner city," as one person put it, are the churches, gospel choirs for young people, faith-based groups, and parochial schools, which remain among the few institutions operating in vulnerable neighborhoods. Sadly, a number of these lights are going out as a retrenching Catholic Church closes parishes and schools and even black churches that once anchored community life move to the suburbs.

Bolstering the religious fabric of inner cities is a pressing need, and it is natural for the government to funnel resources into faith-based programs to combat blight and pathologies. But government grants may turn independent pastors into supplicants competing with each other. A further issue is whether the inner-city churches can add new responsibilities as they prepare for enormous burdens on the horizon—

from reintegrating thousands of ex-prisoners to dealing with parentless children to handling the fallout of failing schools. Another question is whether national faith-based programs can do a better job of working with city officials on the ground, rather than circumventing them. These pressing questions cry out for determined, long-term initiatives.

## RELIGION AND EDUCATION

The issue of religion and education traces far back through American history. Not only was education largely faith infused in the colonial and early republican years, but the "common school" movement in the early nineteenth century ushered in a kind of Protestant hegemony in the public schools. This led American Catholics to do something unheard of in the Old World: create their own schools supported by voluntary contributions. Today it is hard to appreciate how intensely battles were fought between Protestants and Catholics over education in America from the mid-nineteenth century onward, and how state constitutional provisions prohibiting state aid for parochial schools stemmed from Protestant opposition to Catholic education.

Today we can discern two trends likely to dominate the debate in the coming years. The first trend is a challenge to what some see as a kind of hypersecular environment in many schools. From the 1960s onward, public education has been cut off from its generalized Protestant moorings and become more overtly secular. These trends have resulted both from Supreme Court rulings and, more often, from misinterpretations of court rulings that led school officials to cleanse their curriculum of any hint of religion, even in its historical, literary, and political impact. The complaint is that by ignoring religion, the schools send a powerful message that religion is, to use Stephen Carter's word, "trivial" to modern life.[32] Thus schools unwittingly compete with parents and ministers trying to pass along the faith to their youth. Moreover, battles continue to be fought to maintain the right of religious-based student clubs to operate on equal footing with other organizations.

The secular atmosphere of public education is linked with a common concern that many schools are not generally doing a very good job at character development, preparing students for ethical lives and responsible citizenship. This assessment has led evangelicals, Jews, and others to follow the lead of Catholics to establish their own private schools, or home school, which will intensify the call for more forms of state aid to private schools or tax credits for parents schooling their own kids. One argument they advance for such support is religious freedom. If wealthy parents can send their kids to schools that reinforce their faith and values, why should poorer parents be denied that opportunity?

A second trend dovetails with concern about secularization and the moral environment of public education. That is the decaying of public schools in inner cities, and the vast disparities between lavishly funded schools in wealthy suburbs and crumbling infrastructures in impoverished areas. Various reform initiatives over the past decades have not fundamentally altered such structural problems, which are less and less tenable as we attempt to prepare our youth for competition in the global economy. So it is likely that fundamental rethinking about education will emerge, including voucher schemes that would have seemed radical a few years ago but now enjoy greater support, especially among inner-city parents. Tentative indications suggest court approval of such schemes under certain circumstances, indicating a vastly altered educational landscape. Though such a landscape may involve more flexible approaches to education, it presents profound issues on the religious scene. If parents themselves take vouchers to religious schools, will government regulations follow? Will such regulations alter the religious character of parochial schools? Can a religious community establish any sort of school it wishes and receive such indirect aid—including, say, overtly Islamist schools that teach theocracy or Wiccan schools that promote witchcraft? What will be the response of others to such developments? Attempting to solve one crisis—the abject failure of some schools—will inevitably create new issues and challenges. Our colleges of education sadly seem ill equipped to prepare future teachers for the challenging new environment they will face.

This leads to the issue of the academy. Despite expansion of religious studies programs and centers at select universities, the American academy remains strongly secular, often giving short shrift to the force of religion in the past and present. And as several major studies have shown, this tendency extends to religiously founded and affiliated institutions.[33] Professional norms, disciplinary control of curricula, and aspirations for top research status have led such previously religious schools to become highly secularized over time, with only a patina of the religious legacy. The question of whether a university can attain top-tier status and retain strong religious roots is much debated today.

There are two problems with this situation. First, academic studies, especially at our major state universities, have not caught up with the enduring salience of religion and thus are not adequately preparing their students for the world they will inhabit. One former student, currently a vice president at Goldman Sachs, relayed to me that, ironically, it is the religion course he took years ago that helps him the most in his current position because he works with people of different faiths and does global business in religiously diverse cultures. Second, without the kind of theologically sophisticated training provided at religious universities, religious leaders of tomorrow will not be equipped to negotiate the kinds of challenges described in this essay. This "leaves religion," as one commentator despaired, "without a place to engage the big issues" of the future. The president of an evangelical college lamented that the public voices of his own community often lack anchoring in the best scholarship in theology and social science and thus make ill-informed or rash statements that undermine the credibility of the faith while failing to influence solutions to legitimate problems. Another person remarked that "the world is inflamed with faith" and we have only superficial knowledge of its historical roots.

In sum, universities must not be bystanders amid the whirlwind of religious forces on the move today.

## NOTES

1. José Casanova, *Public Religions in the Modern World* (Chicago: University of Chicago Press, 1994).

2. Gilles Kepel, *The Revenge of God: The Resurgence of Islam, Christianity, and Judaism in the Modern World*, trans. Alan Braley (University Park: Pennsylvania State University Press, 1994).

3. Samuel P. Huntington, *The Clash of Civilizations and the Remaking of World Order* (New York: Simon and Schuster, 1996).

4. Roger Finke and Rodney Stark, *The Churching of America, 1776–1990: Winners and Losers in Our Religious Economy* (New Brunswick, NJ: Rutgers University Press, 1992).

5. Diana L. Eck, *A New Religious America: How a "Christian Country" Has Now Become the World's Most Religiously Diverse Nation* (San Francisco: HarperSanFrancisco, 2001).

6. Phillip Jenkins, *The Next Christendom: The Coming of Global Christianity* (Oxford: Oxford University Press, 2002).

7. Huntington quoted in *Fundamentalisms Comprehended*, ed. Martin E. Marty and R. Scott Appleby (Chicago: University of Chicago Press, 1995). This is one of several volumes from the Fundamentalism Project at the University of Chicago.

8. Finke and Stark, *Churching of America*.

9. Huntington, *Clash of Civilizations*.

10. *World Christian Encyclopedia*, ed. David Barrett, George T. Kurian, and Todd Johnson (New York: Oxford University Press, 2001).

11. Akbar S. Ahmed, *Islam under Siege* (Cambridge, UK: Polity, 2003); Bassam Tibi, *The Challenge of Fundamentalism: Political Islam and the New World Disorder* (Berkeley: University of California Press, 1998); Bernard Lewis, *The Crisis of Islam: Holy War and Unholy Terror* (New York: Random House, 2003).

12. Isobel Coleman, "Women, Islam, and the New Iraq," *Foreign Affairs*, January–February 2006, 25.

13. Jenkins, *Next Christendom*.

14. Andrew Walls, "On the Road with Christianity: A Conversation with Missiologist Andrew Walls," interview by Donald A. Yerxa, *Books and Culture*, May–June 2001, 9.

15. Paul Marshall, *Their Blood Cries Out* (Dallas: Word, 1997).

16. Allen D. Hertzke, *Freeing God's Children: The Unlikely Alliance for Global Human Rights* (Lanham, NJ: Rowman and Littlefield, 2005).

17. Adam Przeworski, *Democracy and Development* (Cambridge: Cambridge University Press, 2000).

18. Samuel P. Huntington, *The Third Wave: Democratization in the Late Twentieth Century* (Norman: University of Oklahoma Press, 1991).

19. Andrew Natsios, former head of the U.S. Agency for International Development, described the transformation of NGOs as decolonialization.

20. Douglas Johnston and Cynthia Sampson, eds., *Religion, the Missing Dimension of Statecraft* (New York: Oxford University Press, 1994); Douglas Johnston, ed., *Faith-Based Diplomacy: Trumping Realpolitik* (New York: Oxford University Press, 2003).

21. Cornelius Hunter, *Darwin's God: Evolution and the Problem of Evil* (Grand Rapids, MI: Brazos Press, 2001).

22. These include George Ellis and Charles Townes.

23. Nigel Cameron made this statement in a presentation of his research. See also Nigel M. Cameron, "Evangelicals and Bioethics: An Extraordinary Failure," in *A Public Faith: Evangelicals and Civic Engagement*, ed. Michael Cromartie (Lanham, MD: Rowman and Littlefield, 2003).

24. Alexis de Tocqueville, *Democracy in America*, trans. Harvey C. Mansfield and Delba Winthrop (Chicago: University of Chicago Press, 2000).

25. Robert D. Putnam, *Bowling Alone: The Collapse and Revival of American Community* (New York: Simon and Schuster, 2000).

26. Sidney Verba, Kay Lehman Schlozman, and Henry E. Brady, *Voice and Equality: Civic Voluntarism in American Politics* (Cambridge, MA: Harvard University Press, 1995).

27. Questions added to the World Values Survey by Roger Stark found that belief in a personal God was correlated with upholding the social order, not cheating, and not leaving the scene of an accident.

28. James Davison Hunter, *Culture Wars: The Struggle to Define America* (New York: Basic Books, 1991).

29. Morris P. Fiorina, *Culture War? The Myth of a Polarized America* (New York: Pearson Longman, 2005).

30. Pew Forum on Religion and Public Life, "Religion and Public Life: A Faith-Based Partisan Divide," http://pewforum.org/docs/?DocID=61.

31. Mark A. Noll, *The Scandal of the Evangelical Mind* (Grand Rapids, MI: Eerdmans, 1994).

32. Stephen Carter, *The Culture of Disbelief: How Law and Politics Trivialize Religious Devotion* (New York: Basic Books, 1993).

33. George M. Marsden, *The Soul of the American University: From Protestant Establishment to Established Unbelief* (New York: Oxford University Press, 1994); James Tunstead Burtchaell, *The Dying of the Light: The Disengagement of Colleges and Universities from Their Christian Churches* (Grand Rapids, MI: Eerdmans, 1998).

# CONTRIBUTORS

HADLEY ARKES serves as a senior fellow of the Ethics and Public Policy Center in Washington DC. The Princeton University Press has published all of his books, including *Natural Rights and the Right to Choose*, *First Things*, *Beyond the Constitution*, and *The Philosopher in the City*. His writings have appeared in the *Wall Street Journal*, *Washington Post*, *Weekly Standard*, and *National Review*. He has also held academic appointments at Princeton University. His BA is from the University of Illinois, and his PhD is from the University of Chicago.

MICHAEL BARONE, a senior writer for *U.S. News and World Report*, graduated from Harvard College and Yale Law School, where he served as editor of the *Harvard Crimson* and the *Yale Law Journal*. His books include *The Almanac of American Politics* (16th ed.), *The New Americans: How the Melting Pot Can Work Again*, and *Our Country: The Shaping of America from Roosevelt to Reagan*. His travels have taken him to all fifty states, to all 435 congressional districts, and to thirty-seven foreign countries. He regularly appears on *The McLaughlin Group* and the Fox News Channel.

MICHAEL CROMARTIE, vice president of the Ethics and Public Policy Center, directs programs on evangelicals in civic life and on religion and the media. Besides hosting Radio America's *Faith and Life* program, he serves as an adjunct professor at the Reformed Theological Seminary and as an advisory editor for *Christianity Today*. His writings have appeared in many popular publications, such as *World*, *Washington Times*, and *First Things*. His fourteen edited books include the award-winning *Piety and Politics: Evangelicals and Fundamentalists Confront the World*, coedited with Michael Novak. He has also appeared on NPR's *Morning Edition* and *All Things Considered* and NBC Evening News. He earned a BA from Covenant College and an MA from American University.

**DANIEL L. DREISBACH** is the William E. Simon Fellow at Princeton University and a Rhodes Scholar at Oxford University, where he earned a PhD. He also holds a JD from the University of Virginia and a BA from the University of South Carolina–Spartanburg. He served as a clerk on the U.S. Fourth Circuit Court of Appeals. His scholarly articles have appeared in such journals as the *American Journal of Legal History* and *Constitutional Commentary*. Among his books are *The Founders on God and Government, Thomas Jefferson and the Wall of Separation, Religion and Politics in the Early Republic*, and *Real Threat and Mere Shadow: Religious Liberty and the First Amendment*. He serves as a professor in the School of Public Affairs at American University.

**CHARLES W. DUNN,** dean of the School of Government at Regent University, has taught at Clemson University, Grove City College, the University of Illinois–Urbana, and Florida State University. His fifteen books include *The Seven Laws of Presidential Leadership* and *The Future of Conservatism: Conflict and Consensus in the Post-Reagan Era*, which the *New York Times* favorably reviewed. He has appeared on NBC's *Today Show*, ABC's *World News Tonight*, NPR's *All Things Considered*, CNN's *The Situation Room*, Fox's *The O'Reilly Factor*, and others. He served as a member and chair of the U.S. J. William Fulbright Foreign Scholarship Board under Presidents Reagan, George H. W. Bush, and Clinton.

**JEAN BETHKE ELSHTAIN,** the Laura Spelman Rockefeller Professor at the University of Chicago, has authored four hundred scholarly articles and essays and sixteen books, including *Just War against Terror, Augustine and the Limits of Politics, Democracy on Trial, New Wine in Old Bottles*, and *Women at War*. Her faculty appointments include positions at Vanderbilt, Harvard, and Yale. The American Academy of Arts and Sciences elected her as a fellow, and the Rockefeller and Guggenheim foundations granted her research awards. She earned a PhD and an MA from Brandeis University and an AB from Colorado State University, and she holds nine honorary doctorates.

**JOHN C. GREEN** is Distinguished Professor of Political Science and director of the Ray C. Bliss Institute of Applied Politics at the University of Akron as well as a senior fellow at the Pew Forum on Religion and Public Life in Washington DC. He has done extensive research on religion and American politics; his most recent book is *The Faith Factor: How Religion Influences American Elections.*

**D. G. HART** is the director of honors programs and faculty development at the Intercollegiate Studies Institute. His books include *Secular Faith: Why Christianity Favors the Separation of Church and State, Deconstructing Evangelicalism, The Lost Soul of American Protestantism,* and *The University Gets Religion.* His degrees include a PhD, an MTS, and an MA from Harvard University; an MAR from Westminster Theological Seminary; and a BA from Temple University. He has held academic positions at Westminster Seminary and Wheaton College. He serves as a member of the Orthodox Presbyterian Church's Committee on Christian Education.

**HUGH HECLO** is formerly a professor of government at Harvard University and is a recognized expert on American democratic institutions as well as the international development of modern welfare states. He has received national awards for his books, including *Comparative Public Policy, A Government of Strangers: Executive Politics in Washington,* and *Modern Social Politics in Britain and Sweden.* He is an elected member of the American Academy of Arts and Sciences and the recipient of a Guggenheim Fellowship, and he has served in the White House and as a senior fellow at the Brookings Institution. He is senior editor and a contributor to the 2003 volume *Religion Returns to the Public Square: Faith and Policy in America* and a member of the Council of Scholars advising the Librarian of Congress.

**ALLEN D. HERTZKE,** an internationally recognized expert on religion and politics, is a professor of political science and the director of religious studies at the University of Oklahoma. He is the author of several books, including *Representing God in Washington,* an award-winning analysis of religious lobbies, which has been issued in Chinese language translation, and *Echoes of Discontent,* an account of church-rooted populist movements, and is the coauthor of *Religion and Politics in America,* a comprehensive text on faith and politics, now in its third edition. His most recent book is *Freeing God's Children: The Unlikely Alliance for Global Human Rights.*

MICHAEL NOVAK, the George Frederick Jewett Scholar at the American Enterprise Institute, has written twenty-five books—all translated into all major languages—including *Washington's God, The Universal Hunger for Liberty, The Spirit of Democratic Capitalism,* and *On Two Wings: Humble Faith and Common Sense at the American Founding.* He has held faculty positions at Harvard, Stanford, Syracuse, and Notre Dame. Three times presidents have named him an American ambassador, two times to the UN Human Rights Commission, and once to the Conference on Security and Cooperation in Europe. His education includes a BA from Stonehill College, an STB from Gregorian University in Rome, and an MA from Harvard University.

MARVIN OLASKY edits the nation's fourth most widely read weekly news magazine, *World,* and serves as a professor of journalism at the University of Texas. He has written fifteen novels and books of history and cultural analysis, including *Scimitar's Edge, Compassionate Conservatism, The Politics of Disaster, Abortion Rites, Standing for Christ in Modern Babylon, The American Leadership Tradition,* and *The Religions Next Door.* He received an AB from Yale University and a PhD in American culture from the University of Michigan.

CORWIN E. SMIDT serves as a professor of political science and the executive director of the Henry Institute for the Study of Christianity and Politics at Calvin College. He is the author, editor, or coauthor of twelve books, including *Religion as Social Capital: Producing the Common Good, Evangelicalism: The Next Generation, Pulpit and Politics,* and *The Bully Pulpit: The Politics of Protestant Clergy.* He has recently completed *Pews, Prayers, and Participation: The Role of Religion in Fostering Civic Responsibility* and is currently coediting the *Oxford Handbook on Religion and American Politics.*

# INDEX

abolitionist movement, 17, 19–20, 84, 144. *See also* slavery
abortion, 2, 45, 128, 141, 211
  African American conservatism and, 32
  Catholicism and, 31
  controversy over beginning of human life, 242
  culture wars and, 247
  declining magnitude as cultural issue, 156–57
  as "first freedom," 49
  legalization of, 30
  political parties and, 155
  Supreme Court ruling on, 133
  weakening of conservative Protestantism and, 29
Adams, John, 6, 7, 40, 80, 105
Africa, 232, 233, 235, 238
  AIDS crisis in, 237, 246
  Pentecostalism in, 236
African Americans, 28, 155
  church as community institution, 246, 250
  elections and, 211, 213, 216, 219, 224
  identification with Democratic Party, 32, 249
*Agenda for a Biblical People* (Wallis), 136
agnosticism, 92n11, 183
AIDS crisis, 141, 237, 240, 246
alcohol consumption, 30
Allen, Woody, 58
Alley, Robert, 23
*Amazing Grace* (film), 124
American Assembly, 41

American Civil Liberties Union, 30
American National Election Studies (ANES), 225
American Revolution, 40, 82, 85, 106, 121
Ames, Fisher, 6
Amos (biblical prophet), 44
Anabaptists, 135, 136
Anglicans/Anglicanism, 12, 115, 236. *See also* Church of England; Episcopal Church
animal liberation, 53
anti-Semitism, 234
Anti-Semitism in the United States survey (1964), 224, 225
antisodomy laws, 83
Aristotle, 53, 57
Arts and Religion Survey, 184, *185,* 186
Asia, 233, 235
Assemblies of God, 31
atheism, 85, 92n11, 103, 183
Augustine, St., 87, 89, 149

Baha'i faith, 236
Balmer, Randall, 137
Baptists, 12, 15, 31, 115, 116
Barone, Michael, 160, 165
*Believers: A Journey into Evangelical America* (Sheler), 141
Bellah, Robert, 4, 7, 12–13, 18, 33
Belmonte, Kevin, 125
benevolence, rule of, 84
Berger, Peter, 166
*Better Hour, The* (documentary broadcast), 124
Bible, 24, 68, 90, 145–49

Bible *(cont.)*
  belief in Christian doctrines and,
    72–73
  Bible clubs, 2
  "biblical illiteracy," 244–45
  founders of United States and, 5–6,
    7, 9
  ideals of justice based on, 142
  moral guidance and, 69
  partisan politics and, 130, 131
  readership of, 75, 224
  in schools, 30, 133
  science and, 241
  as "word of God," 24
Bill of Rights, 8, 9, 40, 47, 80
  natural rights and, 51
  role of Virginia Baptists in, 115, 116
  *See also* First Amendment
biology, evolutionary, 241
Black, Amy, 2
blacks. *See* African Americans
Blackstone, William, 6, 10–11, 50, 51
blasphemy, 78, 82
Bliss Institute at University of Akron,
    223–24
Bob Jones University, 131
Boice, Montgomery, 76
Bolce, Louis, 162, 163, 164
Bonaparte, Napoleon, 123, 128
Bork, Robert, 49
born-again Christians, 68–69, 75–76,
    93n33, 132
  Democratic Party and, 131
  religious Right and, 130
  *See also* evangelical Christians
Boswell, James, 125–26
Boyd, Gregory, 137
Brewer, Justice David J., 64, 65, 68
Brodsky, Chuck, 165
Brooks, David, 165–66
Brown, John, 44
Brownback, Sam, 157
Bruce, Steve, 146–47
Bryan, William Jennings, 142–44, 154
Buddhism, 116, 230, 232, 236

Bush, George W., 1, 122, 131, 137, 156,
    164
  biblical allusions in speeches of, 245
  evangelicals and, 248–49
  God gap and, 160
  ideal of compassionate conservatism,
    138
  influence over public policy, 3
  reelection of, 209
  2000 presidential election, 211, *212,*
    213–14
Byron, Lord, 126

Calvinism, 154
capitalism, 2, 144, 248
capital punishment, 45
Carpenter, Joel, 135
Carroll, Charles, 106
Carter, Jimmy, 136, 143, 155, 218
Carter, Stephen, 43, 251
Casey, Shaun, 159
Catholic Charities, 1
Catholicism, Roman, 3, 47, 68, 155
  conservative, 31, 32, 167
  culture wars and, 247, 248, 249
  decline of Protestant dominance
    and, 30
  dual vision of cult and culture, 149
  ecumenical movements and, 236
  elections and, 211–19, 218–19
  environmental issues and, 243
  in founding era, 12, 13
  in history of England, 153, 154
  immigrants and, 22, 82
  inner cities of America and, 250
  in Latin America, 232
  liberal, 167
  New Deal and, 28, 29
  parochial schools, 251
  priest shortage, 245
  state funding of Catholic institutions,
    138
  subsidiarity doctrine, 239
  Vatican II and, 31, 239
Catholic Relief Services, 240

Chambers, Whittaker, 131
charismatic movement, 31
checks and balances, 22
Chesterton, G. K., 47, 50, 54, 56
Chicago Declaration of Evangelical
    Concern, 135, 141, 145
China, People's Republic of, 85, 236
Chinese immigrant workers, 63
"Christendom," of medieval Europe, 79
Christian Broadcasting Network, 31
*Christian Century* magazine, 159
Christian Coalition, 3, 16, 31
Christianity, 4, 13–14, 127
    American nationhood and, 64–65
    Americans' political ethos and, 81–87
    in Asia, 232
    belief in doctrines of, 70–74
    as civic religion, 44
    demographic challenges and, 238
    denominations, 70
    "establishment Christianity," 136
    expression in Americans' behavior,
        74–78
    founders of United States and, 8, 9
    global, 235–37
    noncreedal, 73–74
    percentage of world's population,
        68, 233
    in political institutions, 78–81
    as proselytizing faith, 232
    republican government and, 119
    self-identification of Americans and,
        67–68
    as source of moral guidance, 68–70
    spread of, 64
    in third world, 230
    *See also specific denominations*
*Christianity Today* magazine, 77, 131
church attendance, 173, 178, 182, 187,
    204n8
    in colonial era, 12
    culture wars and, 248
    overreporting of, 75
    spiritual growth and, 188
    two-decade survey of, 179, *180*

Churchill, Winston, 1
church membership, 12, 173, 204n8
Church of England, 79, 82, 153. *See also*
    Anglicans/Anglicanism; Episcopal
    Church
Church of God, 31
church-state separation, 1, 9, 83, 87,
    178
    "church-state debate," 40–41
    culture wars and, 247
    evangelicals and, 134
    logic of engagement and, 41–42
    National Association of Evangelicals
        and, 138
    in state constitutions, 82
citizenship, 45
*City of God, The* (Augustine), 149
civic engagement, 173, 175–76
    frequency of participation, 191–93
    politics in relation to, 193–94, 203n2
    religion and, 194–203
civilization, Western, 4, 7, 245
civilizations, clash of, 232, 239
civil religion, 13, 83
civil rights, 30, 42, 121, 133
Civil Rights Act (1964), 32
civil society, 41, 42, 46, 95n45, 174
    Madison's view of, 50, 118
    religious liberty and, 108, 239
    rights under, 51
    state of nature and, 52
    Washington's views on, 97, 103–4,
        105
Cizik, Richard, 139–40, 141
Clapham Fellowship, 127
class, socioeconomic, 136, 248
climate change, 139–40
Clinton, Bill, 129, 138, 156, 158, 218
    administration officials under, 159
    anti-fundamentalist voters and, 164
    biblical allusions in speeches of, 245
Clinton, Hillary Rodham, 1, 156, 160
cloning, 2, 45, 242
Cobbett, William, 126
colonies, American, 12

Colson, Chuck, 124, 139
*Commentaries on the Laws of England* (Blackstone), 6
commercialism, 244
communism, 131, 132, 144, 229, 236, 238
  atheism and, 85
  "velvet revolution" against, 239
Congregationalism, 12, 64, 154
Congress, U.S., 8–9, 15, 21, 63, 65, 157
Connecticut, 12, 82, 155
conservatives/conservatism, 2, 5, 134, 136
  in Civil War era, 18, 19
  defining political convictions of, 140
  founders of United States, 6, 7, 8–9
  Jews and, 3
  rise after World War II, 142
*Conservative Soul, The* (Sullivan), 134
Constitution, U.S., 6, 9, 24, 40, 112–13n24
  Bill of Rights and, 47–48, 59n8, 94n45
  Constitutional Convention, 7, 15
  First Amendment, 81
  Madison and, 23
  moral law and, 51
  New Deal liberalism and, 26
  secular heritage of, 7
consumer protection movement, 86
contextual engagement, 45–46
Continental Congress, 106
contraceptives, 133
Cooper, James Fenimore, 123
Cooper, Rev. Samuel, 105–6
Cromwell, Oliver, 153
culture wars, 62, 66, 81, 162–66, 221, 247–49
*Culture Wars* (Hunter), 166–67

Darwin, Charles, 241
Dean, Howard, 161
Declaration of Independence, 6, 7, 14–15, 21, 106, 115
Declaration of Rights, 116–17

deism, 9, 12–13, 15, 39, 80–81
Delaware, 12, 82
DeMaio, Gerald, 162, 163, 164
democracy, 1, 3, 54, 90, 132, 243
  Christianity and, 236
  Emerson's vision, 18–19
  "forgotten foundations" of, 7
  in Islamic world, 234–35, 239
  natural law and, 39
  religion as engine of, 230
  religious freedom and, 238–40
  spiritual heritage and, 34
  Tocqueville on "republican religion," 8
  Wilsonian, 24
*Democracy in America* (Tocqueville), 40
Democratic Party, 1, 61, 122, 129
  abortion issue and, 155
  African Americans and, 22, 32, 249
  Catholics and, 22, 31, 210
  cultural issues and, 157
  culture wars and, 162–65, 168–69, 248
  economic issues and, 157–58
  evangelical Christians and, 21, 32, 131, 140, 142, 143
  God gap and, 159–66
  Jews and, 32
  post-1960 elections and, 218–20, 222
  religious outreach advisors and, 128
  secularists in, 163, 164–65, 166, 169
  southern Protestants and, 27
  2000 election and, 213, 214
Dewey, John, 9
Dickinson, John, 6
Dionne, E. J., 32
*Dissent of the Governed, The* (Carter), 43
divorce, 62
Dobson, James, 1, 139, 140, 145, 166
Dole, Robert, 164
Dostoyevsky, Fyodor, 53
Douglass, Frederick, 124
Dred Scott case, 54
Dreisbach, Daniel L., 6

dual activists, 195, *196*, 197
Dulce, Berton, 24
Dunphy, John, 4
Durkheim, Émile, 4
Dwight, Timothy, 16

Eagle Forum, 31
economic issues, 5, 157–58, 222
ecumenism, 236, 247
educational institutions, 5, 11, 251–53.
    *See also* schools
Edwards, Jonathan, 16
Elazar, Daniel, 10
elections, 130, 159, 161, 191, 192
    1960 presidential election, 215–17
    religion and, 209–11
    2000 presidential election, 211–14
    voter turnout, 197, 203–4n3
Elementary and Secondary Education
    Act (1965), 30
Elshtain, Jean Bethke, 178
Emergent Church, 140
Emerson, Joseph, 15
Emerson, Ralph Waldo, 18–19
England, 153–54
Enlightenment, 80
environmental movement, 86, 138, 141,
    223
Episcopal Church, 20, 23, 33. *See also*
    Anglicans/Anglicanism; Church of
    England
equality, 16, 17, 19, 21
Equal Rights Amendment, 143
ethnicity, 210, 224
Europe, 72, 79, 246
euthanasia, 45
evangelical Christians, 21, 31, 129–31
    Bush supporters, 122
    conduct of, 75–76
    culture wars and, 247, 248–49
    elections and, 211, *212, 215*, 216, 218,
        219
    Greatest Generation of, 130, 131
    moving beyond biblical politics,
        145–49

private schools and, 251–52
Republican Party and, 32
return of evangelical biblicism,
    141–45
*See also* born-again Christians
Evangelical Climate Initiative, 139, 140
evolution, 2, 224, 241, 242, 247

Fair Deal, 28
faith-based partnerships, 250–51
Falwell, Jerry, 3, 133, 134, 141, 145
family values, 133, 137, 141, 147, 231
    biblical politics and, 145
    civil society and, 118
    cold war conservatism and, 134
    culture wars and, 167
    Democratic Party and, 161, 163
    National Association of Evangelicals
        and, 139
    prayer and, 128
    priority given to, 69
*Farmer Refuted, The* (Hamilton), 52
fascism, 229
Federal Council of Churches, 139
federalism, 10, 130, 134
Federalist papers, 5, 6, 25, 52
Federalists, 49, 52
feminism, 133, 237
"Fenimore Cooper's Literary Offenses"
    (Twain), 123
Finney, Charles, 17, 19, 20, 22
First Amendment, 9, 15, 48, 49, 80, 85.
    *See also* Bill of Rights
Focus on the Family, 3, 16, 139
"For the Health of the Nation:
    An Evangelical Call to Civic
    Responsibility" (NAE policy
    statement), 137, 139
foul language, 76
founding fathers, 44, 106–8, 110, 153
Fourteenth Amendment, 21, 38n51, 85
Fowler, Robert Booth, 131
France, 41, 85
Frank, Thomas, 158
Frankfurter, Justice Felix, 26

Franklin, Benjamin, 6, 9, 12, 16
French Revolution, 41
fundamentalists, 31, 69, 76, 209, 210
Fundamental Orders of Connecticut, 11
Furneaux, Robert, 127

gambling, 30, 76–77
Garrison, William Lloyd, 17, 19
gay rights, 155, 157, 211, 247. *See also*
	marriage, same-sex
General Social Survey (GSS), 181, *189,*
	189–90, 205
genetic revolution, 242
George, Robert, 55
George III, King, 153
Georgia, 12
Germany, 22
Gerry, Elbridge, 6
Giamatti, A. Bartlett, 34
Gingrich, Newt, 158
Giuliani, Rudy, 156, 157
Glazer, Nathan, 164
globalization, 231–33
global warming, 140, 243
Glorious Revolution, 153–54
God and Society in North America
	(survey), 184, *185*
*God's Politics* (Wallis), 137
Goldwater, Barry, 31
Gore, Al, 163, 164, 211, *212,* 213–14
government, 21, 23, 126
grace of God, 25, 39, 73, 93n33
Graham, Billy, 132–33, 134, 135, 136
*Grassroots* (McGovern), 28
Great Awakening, 14, 15, 128
Great Depression, 2, 27, 222
Great Respecting, 127–28
Great Society, 29
Greeley, Andrew, 62, 167
Green, Ashbel, 103
Greenberg, Stanley, 162
Gurney, Joseph, 126

Hamilton, Alexander, 8, 48, 52–53, 109
Hancock, John, 6

Harvard College/University, 4, 11
hate speech, 58
Hatfield, Mark, 143
Hayek, Friedrich, 131
Hazlitt, Henry, 126
health care, 138
Hegel, G.W.F., 28
Henry, Carl, 132, 134, 135, 136
Henry, Patrick, 81, 115, 117
Himmelfarb, Gertrude, 165, 166,
	167–68
Hinduism, 116, 245
Hindus, 68, 117, 211, 230, 238
Hispanics. *See* Latinos/Hispanics
Hobbes, Thomas, 52–53
Hofstadter, Richard, 7–8
Holmes, Justice Oliver Wendell, 26
Holocaust, 54
homosexuality, 2, 29, 30, 31, 32
Hout, Michael, 62
Huckabee, Mike, 1
humanism, 4
human rights, 10, 83, 138, 236, 237
Hunter, James Davison, 165, 166–67, 221
Huntington, Samuel, 232
Hybels, Bill, 140

immigrants/immigration, 2, 63, 84,
	138, 230, 245–46
India, 166, 234, 238
individualism, 10, 76, 177, 186, 245
	expressive, 2, 3
	laissez-faire, 2
	spiritualism and, 244
Indonesia, 234
industrialization, 27, 84
"intelligent design," 241
interest-group activism, 23
International Religious Freedom Act,
	236
Internet, 77–78, 167
Iraq war, 156, 157
Islam and Muslims, 2, 32, 116, 117, 211,
	238
	in Africa, 236

American pluralism and, 33, 230
democratization and, 239
Islamic fascists, 157
Koran, 146, 245
Muslim powers of Tripoli, 80
Muslims as percentage of world
    population, 68
Muslims in America, 246
as proselytizing faith, 232
Red Crescent organization, 240
resurgence and crisis of, 233–35
Sufi Muslims, 232, 236
Islamism, 229, 233–35, 252
Israel, biblical, 13
Israel, state of, 3, 32, 238

Jackson, Jesse, 1, 32
Jaffa, Harry, 54
James II, King, 153
Jay, John, 6
Jefferson, Thomas, 5–6, 16, 54
    Christian faith and, 119
    Declaration of Independence and,
        6–7, 14–15
    as deist, 9, 12, 13, 15, 111n18
    Notes on the State of Virginia, 103
    on "pursuit of happiness," 126
    Washington's criticism of, 108, 109,
        114n36
Jenkins, Jerry, 166
Jenkins, Phillip, 235
Jesuits, 31
Jesus Christ, 71, 72, 73, 88–89, 127, 225
    forgiveness of sins and, 148
    miracles of, 241
    personal commitment to, 76
    return of, 149
    sinless life of, 93n33
Jews, 3, 154, 155, 236
    assimilation through intermarriage,
        245
    civil rights movement and, 32
    culture wars and, 247
    decline of Protestant dominance
        and, 30

elections and, 126, 211, *212, 215*
environmental issues and, 243
in founding era, 12, 13
in history of England, 153, 154
immigrants from Germany, 22
loyalty to Democratic Party, 32
New Deal and, 28, 29
Orthodox, 167, 247
private schools and, 251–52
John Paul II, Pope, 31
Johnson, Lyndon, 133, 218
Johnston, Doug, 240
Judaism, 32, 71, 116, 119, 245

Kant, Immanuel, 55–56
Kazin, Michael, 143–44
Keller, Wes, 127
Kennan, George, 23
Kennedy, John F., 154, 215, 216–17
Kennedy, Ted, 3
Kerry, John, 160, 165, 248
King, Martin Luther, Jr., 30, 44, 45
King, Rufus, 6
Kirk, Russell, 131
Knox, Ronald, 57
Korea, North, 236, 237
Korea, South, 236
Kuyper, Abraham, 239

labor unions, 22, 132
LaHaye, Tim, 166
Land, Richard, 139, 140
Langdon, Samuel, 14
Lasch, Christopher, 166, 168
Latin America, 232, 235
Latinos/Hispanics, 211–16, 224, 246
law, American, 10, 18, 50, 78
League of Nations, 22, 29
League of Women Voters, 175
Lears, Jackson, 144
Lee, Richard Henry, 6
Left, religious, 2, 130, 142
Left, secular, 90, 137, 249
Legionnaires of Christ, 31
Leland, John, 15

Lerner, Michael, 223
*Leviathan* (Hobbes), 52
"Liberal Moment, The" (Dionne), 32
liberals/liberalism, 2, 5
   in Civil War era, 18, 20
   clash of ideologies and, 229
   evangelicals and, 32
   Jews and, 3
   liberal theology, 22, 23–25
   moral truth and, 56
   National Association of Evangelicals
      (NAE) and, 138–39
   in New Deal era, 25–26
libertarians, 144
liberty, 16, 17, 21, 132, 147
Liberty University, 31
Lieberman, Joseph, 155
Lincoln, Abraham, 32, 52, 54, 58
   biblical allusions in speeches of, 245
   Civil War and, 85
   emancipation of slaves and, 22, 142
   on equality, 56
   religious language used by, 154
   on Wilberforce, 124
Lippmann, Walter, 7
Litfin, A. Duane, 140
Livingston, William, 6
Locke, John, 10, 81, 112n24
Loveland, Matthew, 203
Lovin, Robin, 46
Lustiger, Cardinal Jean-Marie, 56
Lutheran Church, 149, 154

MacCulloch, Diarmaid, 153–54
Machen, J. Gresham, 147–48
Mackintosh, James, 127
Madison, James, 5–6, 8
   Declaration of Rights and, 116
   First Amendment and, 15
   on limited government, 25
   "Memorial and Remonstrance
      against Religious Assessments," 50
   Virginia remonstrance and, 81,
      94–95n45, 115–16, 117–18
Malaysia, 234

Mann, Horace, 9
Mansfield, Harvey, 21
marriage, same-sex, 83, 141, 155, 157,
   211, 247. *See also* gay rights
marriage, traditional, 82, 122
Marsden, George, 142
Marshall, John, 48
Marshall, Paul, 236
Marx, Karl, 28
Maryland, 12, 82, 106
Mason, George, 6, 116
Massachusetts, 12, 14, 82, 157
materialism, 76, 132, 245
Mayflower Compact, 9–10
McCain, John, 156
McClay, Wilfred, 163
McCurry, Michael, 159
McDonald, Heather, 169
McGovern, George, 28, 163
McGuffey Readers, 9
McLaren, Brian, 140
McLean, Justice John, 54
media, mass, 27, 30, 34, 77, 244
megachurch networks, 31, 247
"Memorial and Remonstrance against
   Religious Assessments" (Madison),
   50
Mennonites, 12
mercy, deeds of, 136
Messiah College, 135
Methodism, 12, 20, 23
Middle East, war in, 137
military, gays in the, 157
Mill, John Stuart, 56
modernism, 211, 212, 213, 225, 247
Mohler, Al, 141
moral crusades, 84
moral freedom, 70
morality, 29, 73, 90
   absolutist, 34
   biblical standards of, 145, 146
   primacy of moral law, 51–53
   Washington's views on, 98, 103–9
Moral Majority, 16, 31
moral philosophy, 56–57

Moravian Church, 12
Morison, Samuel Eliot, 11, 18
Mormons, 31, 146, 155, 211, 232
Morris, Gouverneur, 6
Mouw, Richard, 141
MoveOn.org, 3
multiple classification analysis (MCA), 199, 201, 205n17
Muslims. *See* Islam and Muslims

National Association of Evangelicals (NAE), 137–40, 155, 223, 243
National Council of Churches, 3, 16, 20, 27, 31
National Election Studies (NES), 189–90, 191, *192–93*
    distribution of forms of religion over time, *189*
    on importance of religion, *199,* 200, *201*
National Election Survey Cumulative File, 225
nationalism, 229
nativity scenes, 2, 30
natural (divine) law, 6, 10, 18, 39–40, 56
natural rights, 50, 53–56, 59n8
*Natural Rights and the Right to Choose* (Arkes), 53
natural selection, 241
"Neo-orthodox" theology, 29
Neuhaus, Richard John, 146
New Age movement, 33
New Frontier, 29
New Hampshire, 12, 82
New Jersey, 12, 82, 157
New Testament, 12, 13, 28, 71
Newton, Isaac, 241
Newton, John, 124, 125
New York, 12, 82
Niebuhr, Reinhold, 23, 29, 46, 89
Nietzsche, Friedrich, 53
Nixon, Richard M., 154, 215, 217, 218
Noll, Mark, 142, 143, 145, 147, 249
nongovernmental organizations (NGOs), 240, 250

North Carolina, 12, 82
Northwest Ordinance (1787), 106
*Notes on the State of Virginia* (Jefferson), 103
Novak, Michael, 11, 160, 169

oaths, religion and, 103, 112n24
Obama, Barack, 1, 32, 156, 160–61
O'Connor, Justice Sandra, 157
Old Testament, 12, 13, 130
*One Nation, Two Cultures* (Himmelfarb), 167
orphanage reform, 84
Orthodox Christians, 70–71, 211, 238, 239

Paine, Thomas, 5, 7
Parker, Theodore, 19
Parliament, English, 14, 15
parties, political
    "antiparty" bias of Americans, 191
    culture wars and, 162–66
    God gap and, 159–66
    party platforms, 21
    third parties, 21, 158
    *See also* Democratic Party; Republican Party (GOP)
Paul, St., 71, 92n21, 127, 137
Pennsylvania, 12, 155
Pentecostalism, 31, 166, 232, 236, 237
perfectionism, 17, 19
Perot, Ross, 158
Pew Charitable Trust, 229
Pew Forum on Religion and Public Life, 160, 164, 169
Pinckney, C. C., 6
Plato, 51
pluralism, religious, 33, 43–45
Ponnuru, Ramesh, 169
Pontius Pilate, 88
populism, 84, 143, 145, 248
Populist Party, 231
pornography, mass consumption of, 76, 77–78
Powell, Colin, 158

prayer, 9, 68
  civic/political engagement and, 203
  frequency of, 178, 181–82, 198, 202,
    224
  private, 183
  at public events, 2
  in schools, 30
Presbyterianism, 12, 23, 103, 106, 143
  as established church in Scotland,
    153
  modernism and, 147
  Prohibition supported by, 148
prison reform, 84
Progressive Party, 21
Prohibition, 29, 30, 148
Protestant ethic, 2–3
Protestantism, 11, 78
  "common school" movement, 251
  Dissenters, 79–80, 81, 83, 153
  ethnicity and, 211, 212, 213
  mainline, 210, 211, 213, 218, 243, 245
  pluralism of, 12
Protestantism, conservative
  Catholics in common cause with, 31
  decline in dominance of, 23, 29, 30
  fundamentalist controversy and, 134,
    143
  political polarization and, 61
  pride in America and, 90
  Republican Party and, 32
  resurgence of, 33
Protestantism, liberal, 28, 30, 33, 147
  Christian Century magazine, 159
  culture wars and, 167, 247
  fundamentalist controversy and,
    134
  social gospel of, 135, 139
public policy, 3, 5, 21, 22, 170, 211
  Christianity and, 13
  conservative influence over, 3
  indirect influence on, 20
  liberal churches and, 27
  in New Deal era, 23, 25–26, 27
Puritanism, 11–12, 79
"Puritans, traditional," 2

Purpose Driven Life (Warren), 140
Putnam, Robert, 243

Quakers, 12, 117

race and racism, 134, 135, 248
  elections and, 224
  mixing of races, 84
  race relations, 133
  voting patterns and, 210
Racketeer Influenced and Corrupt
    Organizations Act (RICO), 43
Ramsay, David, 106
Reagan, Ronald, 1, 3, 29, 131, 218
  Democratic votes for, 121
  election of, 31
  National Association of Evangelicals
    and, 138, 155
  traditionalist vote and, 221
Reaganomics, 143
Reasonableness of Christianity, The
    (Locke), 10
Reformation, 153
Regent University, 31
relativism, 2, 67, 76, 187
religion/religious organizations
  challenges to, 230
  changing patterns of, 190–203
  civic health and, 243–47
  civic/political participation and,
    198–203
  declining political role of, 156–58
  democracy and religious freedom,
    238–40
  education and, 251–53
  election of 2000 and, 211–14
  as "first freedom," 50
  free exercise of, 44, 45, 80
  globalization and, 231–33
  government financial aid and, 1
  impact on American politics, 121–23
  moral philosophy and, 56–57
  in post-1960 politics, 154–56, 217–21
  private and public behavior, 177,
    178–90

public life and, 58, 173–78
realistic and utopian, 124–27
resilience in modern world, 229
science and, 241–43
standards for employees, 2
theoretical role in society, 4–5
republicanism, 83, 84, 86
Republican Party (GOP), 1, 61, 125, 129
abortion issue and, 155
African Americans and, 22, 32
anti-Communism of, 138
born-again Protestants and, 131
conservative Catholics in, 31
culture wars and, 162, 168–69, 248
economic issues and, 157–58
evangelical Christians and, 140, 142, 150n2, 166
God gap and, 159–66
mainline Protestants and, 210
post-1960 elections and, 218–21
"traditionalist alliance" in control of, 209, 218–21
2000 election and, 213–14
Republicans, Jeffersonian, 15
Reston, James, 7
Revolt of the Elites and the Betrayal of Democracy, The (Lasch), 168
Revolutionary War, 14, 15
Rhode Island, 12, 82
Rich Christians in an Age of Hunger (Sider), 135–36
Richter, Edward, 24
Right, religious/Christian, 2, 34, 65, 85, 137
ascendancy of, 146
culture wars and, 81, 249
elections and, 209
emergence of, 133, 221
evangelical turn away from, 136
faltering hold on born-again Protestants, 130
irony of faith-based politics and, 145
leaders of, 134
rights, inalienable, 118–19
rights of man, 10

Robertson, Pat, 3, 133, 134, 145
Roe v. Wade, 156
Roosevelt, Franklin D., 22, 23, 27, 210, 217
African Americans and, 32
biblical allusions in speeches of, 245
Thanksgiving Day proclamation, 24, 25
United Nations and, 29
Rothman, Stanley, 2
Rousseau, Jean-Jacques, 43–44
Rumsfeld, Donald, 130
Rush, Benjamin, 6, 59n8, 105, 106
Russia, 238, 239
Rutledge, John, 6

Saguaro Social Capital Community Benchmark Survey
on importance of religion, 199, 200, 201
on relationship of civic and political participation, 190–96, 192, 193, 195, 196
Salvation Army, 1
Scalia, Antonin, 3
Schiavo, Terry, 157
schools, private/religious, 1, 30, 244, 250, 251, 252
schools, public, 2, 142
in founding era, 9
prayer and Bible reading in, 133
Protestant "common school" movement, 251
secularizing influences of, 30–31
sex education in, 247
science, 27, 160, 229, 241–43
Scopes trial, 143
Scott, Thomas, 124–25
Second Awakening, 121
secular humanism, 3, 113n35
secularism, 66, 132, 245
in Democratic Party, 163, 164–65, 166, 169
in education, 251–52
most secular country, 166

secularization theory, 176, 204n7
Sedgwick, Theodore, 49
September 11, 2001, attacks, 55, 156
sex education, 247
sexuality, 78, 145
sexual revolution, 133
Sheler, Jeffery, 141
Sider, Ron, 135–36, 137, 138, 139, 140, 145
Sikhs, 230
"Sinners in the Hands of an Angry God" (Edwards sermon), 16
slavery, 17, 19, 22, 54, 124, 125
    abolition of, 126
    British slave trade, 123
    new international slave trade, 127
    *See also* abolitionist movement
Smith, Al, 154
social capital, 246
*Social Contract* (Rousseau), 43–44
social gospel movement, 23, 24, 28, 84, 132, 139
social justice, 42, 136, 141
social reform, 17, 20
*Sojourners* magazine, 136, 137
Solzhenitsyn, Aleksandr, 4, 34
South Carolina, 12, 82, 131
South Dakota, 156
Southern Baptist Convention, 139
Southern Christian Leadership Conference, 121
Soviet Union, former, 85, 144, 233
speech, freedom of, 49
spiritual growth, 188
spiritualism, 244
state church, establishment of, 107
state constitutions, 12
state governments, 82, 85
stem cells, embryonic, 45, 155, 157
Strickland, Ted, 161
Sudan, 236, 237
Sullivan, Amy, 162
Sullivan, Andrew, 134
Sunday Sabbath, 30, 78, 82
Sunday schools, 75

superintending principle, 47–49
Supreme Court, 37–38n51, 63, 80, 128, 134
    abortion rulings, 157
    on contraception and abortion, 133
    culture wars and, 248
    education rulings, 251
    Fourteenth Amendment and, 85
    *Holy Trinity Church* decision, 63–65
    on United States as Christian nation, 63–64
Sweden, 166, 233

Taiwan, 236
taxation without representation, 14, 15, 85
technology, 77, 230
Templeton Award, 241
Ten Commandments, 2
terrorism, 85
theocracy, 40, 42, 57, 61, 252
theology, 72, 84, 87
Third National Survey of Religion and Politics, 223
Thomas, John, 17
Thomas Aquinas, 52, 116
Thompson, Kenneth W., 7
Thoreau, Henry David, 18
Tillich, Paul, 23
tithing, 75
Tocqueville, Alexis de, 8, 13–14, 18, 20, 83
    on churches as political institutions, 243
    on contrast between France and America, 40–41
    on politics and religion, 249
    on Puritan principles, 79
traditionalism, 209, 210–11, 213, 222, 224, 247
transcendentalism, 17, 19
Trinity Evangelical Divinity School, 136
Trinity Forum, 124
Tugwell, Rexford Guy, 25–26

Twain, Mark, 123
*Two Treatises on Government* (Locke), 10

"un-Americanism," 84
Unitarianism, 9, 17, 19, 211
United Nations, 22, 29, 239
United States
  American exceptionalism, 74
  Christianity as self-identification, 67–68, 90
  civic health of, 243–47
  Civil War era, 5, 16–23, 29, 85
  demographic identification with Christianity, 68, 89
  evolution controversy in, 242
  fate of American cities, 250–51
  founding era, 5–16, 29, 39–40
  global religions infused into life of, 245
  immigrants in, 230, 245–46
  Islamic world and, 234, 235
  modern era, 5, 30–35
  New Deal era, 5, 16, 22, 23–30, 210
  Protestant hegemony in, 138
  religious pluralism in, 230–31
  treaty with Muslim powers of Tripoli, 80
Universal Declaration of Human Rights, 239
urbanization, 27

values voters, 62
Vanderslice, Mara, 162
Vermont, 82
Vietnam, 236
Vietnam War, 155
Viguerie, Richard, 145
Virginia, 12, 15, 50, 153
  Anglicans versus Baptists in, 115–16
  colonial charter of, 82
  memorial remonstrance (1785), 117–18
Volstead Act, 148
voluntarism, 126, 177

voter turnout, 197, 203–4n3
Voting Rights Act (1965), 32

Wallis, Jim, 21, 136–37, 139, 140, 141, 145
  Bryan legacy and, 144
  culture wars gap and, 162
War on Poverty, 133
Warren, Rev. E. Walpole, 63
Warren, Rick, 140–41, 145, 246
Washington, George, 6, 40, 97, 98–99, 112n24
  circular letter to the states, 99–102
  farewell address, 102–10
  four themes of, 97–98
  reputation of, 110
Weaver, Richard, 131
Webster, Daniel, 116
welfare state, 131
Wesley, John, 20, 128
Weyrich, Paul, 145
White, Theodore, 34
Whitefield, George, 128
*Who Speaks for God? An Alternative to the Religious Right* (Wallis), 136
Wicca, 252
Wilberforce, William, 123–27, 128
William of Ockham, 116
William of Orange, 153
Williams, Roger, 81
Williams, Archbishop Rowan, 124
Wilson, James, 6, 48, 50, 52
Wilson, Woodrow, 29, 142
Witherspoon, John, 6, 13, 106, 110, 112n24
Wolfe, Alan, 70, 72, 74
women, religious life and, 244
women's movement/rights, 84, 234–35
Word of Life Ministry, 232–33
World Vision, 240
Wuthnow, Robert, 167, 186

Yale College/University, 11, 16